MW00605684

THINK THIS, NOT THAT

THINK THIS, NOT THAT

12 Mindshifts to Break Through
Limiting Beliefs and Become
Who You Were Born to Be

JOSH AXE

W PUBLISHING GROUP

AN IMPRINT OF THOMAS NELSON

Think This, Not That

© 2024 Josh Axe

Published in Nashville, Tennessee, by W Publishing, an imprint of Thomas Nelson.

Thomas Nelson titles may be purchased in bulk for educational, business, fundraising, or sales promotional use. For information, please email SpecialMarkets@ThomasNelson.com.

Unless otherwise noted, Scripture quotations are taken from the Contemporary English Version. Copyright © 1991, 1992, 1995 by American Bible Society. Used by permission.

Scripture quotations marked KJV are taken from the King James Version. Public domain.

Scripture quotations marked YLT are taken from the Young's Literal Translation. Public domain.

Any internet addresses, phone numbers, or company or product information printed in this book are offered as a resource and are not intended in any way to be or to imply an endorsement by Thomas Nelson, nor does Thomas Nelson vouch for the existence, content, or services of these sites, phone numbers, companies, or products beyond the life of this book.

Illustrations by Marcus Meazzo | Meazzo Design Co.

ISBN 978-1-4003-3788-0 (audiobook)
ISBN 978-1-4003-3787-3 (eBook)
ISBN 978-1-4003-3784-2 (HC)

Library of Congress Control Number: 2023946237

Printed in the United States of America
24 25 26 27 28 LBC 5 4 3 2 1

CONTENTS

INTRODUCTION

When I was ten years old, I started spending summers with my grand-parents. They owned a sixty-acre recreational campground in Lima, Ohio, that my grandfather Howard operated. It was an outdoor adventurer's paradise. An assortment of waterslides, diving boards, and rafts accessorized a big lake. The property also boasted an outdoor basketball court, tennis courts, putter golf, and almost fifty RV and tent campsites. While my grandfather Howard helped coordinate guests on family trips or retreats or reunions, I disappeared to catch frogs in the woods, cruise the property on a golf cart, and refine my cannonball technique in the lake.

My first summer at Winona Lake Water Park and Campground, my grandparents allowed me to run wild—and boy, did I. But after a couple of weeks, my grandfather wanted to see me grow and take on some responsibility. So he sat me down one day, put his sun-weathered hand on my shoulder, and said, "Josh, I love you so much, and I love that you're having so much fun. I also wanted you to know that I could really use your help around here. It takes a lot of work to run a place like this." That day, he taught me how to mow the grass and clean up at the campsites. Over time, he gave me additional responsibilities, and I really felt like I was contributing to the success of this magical place he'd created.

As I think about this impactful season today, I realize that my grandfather Howard was the first person who taught me how to *think this, not that*. Through his loving and challenging words, I learned the importance of not just having fun and being happy but also serving others and work-ing hard to build and maintain something meaningful.

Our mindset is the ultimate catalyst for change; it's what propels us forward. It's also what can hold us back. I carried this lesson with me when I became a physician. As a functional medicine practitioner, I observed the incredible power of mindset in my patients' lives. While I firmly believe in the healing potential of food as medicine, I discovered that nothing could match the transformative impact of mindset medi-cine. Not only did I teach my patients to "eat this, not that," but I also helped them understand the transforming power of the mind in how to "think this, not that." The results were outstanding. The patients who were committed to my plan of care and exhibited an all-in, positive, and hopeful mindset reversed disease, lost weight, had more energy, and slept better than they ever had. The patients who were stuck in limiting beliefs remained stuck.

When I transitioned into the entrepreneurial space and built multiple multimillion-dollar businesses, I noticed that when team members pur-sued their goals while anchored in the right mindset, they became more effective and experienced significant growth. As my employees' mindsets strengthened, so did the business. The relationship between mindset and a "masterpiece life" is clear: right thinking is a path to purpose and awak-ening your potential.

The genesis of becoming the person you were born to be is in your mind because wrong thinking will keep you from becoming that per-son. The reason people don't enjoy meaningful relationships, apply for their dream jobs, try something again after they've failed, or execute their five-year plan is not because they don't have the skills or the potential to succeed; it's because limiting beliefs have thwarted their momentum. These roadblocks are nothing more than lies they've been told or have told themselves.

Have you ever wanted something very badly—to build a great mar-riage, start your own business, write a book, be part of a meaningful community—but you eventually gave up on it? Your initial drive was strong, but over time, it dwindled. Maybe now all you can think is how it's not going to work, you're too young or old, you're in it alone, or it's never going to be as good as you want it to be. A mindset of false narratives will keep you stuck, locked in a prison of unpursued dreams and unreached goals. Life may be bearable on this level, but it's also stale and unfulfilling.

The good news is, it doesn't have to stay this way.

I've spent the past decade studying mindset, including time as a student earning my Master of Science in Leadership at Johns Hopkins, as a physician helping patients overcome physical and psychological challenges, and as an entrepreneur leading and mentoring teams to grow. I've collected here what I've learned and experienced—as I continue to do both—to help you begin to think, and live, at a higher level.

In this book, I have curated twelve mental barriers that obstruct personal growth and hinder success. Each chapter explores one of these barriers, peeling back the layers of false narratives that hold us captive, and introduces a transformative mindset shift—a *mindshift*—that can liberate us. By replacing limiting beliefs with empowering truths, we can break free from the chains of self-doubt, optimize our potential, and embark on a journey of personal transformation.

If you're plagued with uncertainty and feel stuck, these mindshifts will help you break through your limiting beliefs, grow beyond your preconceived boundaries, and unlock the greatest version of yourself. Through science, stories, and strategies, each chapter will provide you with the tools it takes to create lasting change and live a life beyond your wildest dreams.

Are you ready to upgrade your thinking, embrace new possibilities, and become the person you were born to be? The journey starts now.

Welcome to *Think This, Not That*.

CREATE A BREAKTHROUGH BY UNLIMITING YOUR BELIEFS

Right before the bell rang, my freshman English teacher peered over her desk, looked straight at me, and asked, "Josh, would you stay after class for a minute?"

"Sure," I said, nervous and unsure.

Once all the other students had scrambled to their next class, it was just Mrs. Nobel and me.

"Josh," my teacher began, "what do you want to do when you're older? Do you want to go to college?"

My shoulders straightened. "Actually, I want to become a doctor or physical therapist. I want to do something that helps get people healthy." I was confident of this answer because of my mother's breast cancer diagnosis the year before. Watching her fight this devastating disease had ignited in me a deep interest in health and wellness.

Without missing a beat, my teacher laughed out loud.

Let me reiterate—*Mrs. Nobel laughed out loud*. Looking back, while the response was unsettling, I can understand her cynicism. Mrs. Nobel had just handed back midterm papers, and I'd gotten an F, making my overall grade in the class a D-. My grades in all my classes were mediocre at best.

After her laughter subsided, Mrs. Nobel leaned in. "Look, Josh, you'll never be able to get into med school, let alone any school, with these grades. My daughter has her doctorate in physical therapy, and she had to have a 3.8 GPA to get into school. With your GPA, no school is going to let you in."

I don't remember much of the conversation after that. I do remember standing there feeling utterly incapable. I felt foolish for sharing my hopes and dreams only to have them cut down. *Why even try?* I wondered. *What's the point?*

My confidence had been spiraling for a while. I'd always had a hard time in school. Paying attention was my biggest challenge. A few months after this chat with Mrs. Nobel, a doctor diagnosed me with ADHD, which reinforced my insecurities. I remember thinking, *Oh no! Mrs. Nobel was right. I'm actually* medically *not smart.* At that point, my main goal was just to get by. I did manage to bump my D average to a C average—only because I didn't want to infuriate my dad, and it was required to play sports. I graduated high school with a dismal 2.3 GPA, and the fire I'd had to pursue a career in health and wellness had been completely extinguished.

How many times over the years has someone doubted you or said you weren't capable? How many times did you believe them? It's shocking to think how much power we've given to other people's views of us as we've internalized their feedback.

What is something you've believed about yourself that has kept you from pursuing your dreams or becoming the person you were born to be? When someone you love and trust, like a parent, coach, or teacher, says something that dismisses your potential or overthrows your confidence, it can be discouraging, even crushing. It's not uncommon to give strangers this power as well. One negative comment on social media directed at you from a random person can prompt you to question your value and create a belief that sticks in your psyche.

Maybe you are your own worst critic, constantly doubting yourself. Are you afraid to move toward a goal because you failed at something a few years back, and your own words echo in your mind?

Regardless of where they originally came from, negative beliefs can become the soundtrack of your life and then start capping your potential and restricting your growth. They leave no room for transformation. When left unchallenged, they will keep you from becoming the person you were born to be.

When you *believe* you are capable of very little, you *become* capable of very little. As Henry Ford once said (and as my dad often told me when I was growing up), "Whether you think you can or you can't, you're right."

> **THINK THIS:** I can because . . .
> **NOT THAT:** I can't because . . .

What Are Beliefs, and Where Do They Come From?

Beliefs are more powerful than most of us can imagine. They may be the single greatest determining factor of what your future will look like. They play a role in whether you become healthy or unhealthy, enjoy loving relationships or remain stuck in a pattern of loneliness, live with significance or wander without purpose. Good or bad, our beliefs influence every part of our lives.

What is a belief? A belief is a mental certainty that something is true.[1] Beliefs can be positive or negative and generally pertain to three areas: (1) self, (2) other people, and (3) the world. Here are some examples.

Self

- I'm not smart.
- I don't deserve to fall in love.
- I'm doing the best I can.
- I'm honest and trustworthy.

Other People

- People are out to get me.
- People don't change.
- People are good for the most part.
- Every human being has value.

World

- The world is not safe.
- The system is rigged against me.
- What goes around comes around.
- Good always wins.

A belief, whether true or false, can change the outcome of your life. Say you have a belief that people are untrustworthy. As a result, you put your guard up and keep people at a distance to avoid rejection and pain. This behavior will perpetuate anxiety and stress around interaction with others and build a barrier between you and any significant relationships. Ultimately, this one belief will prevent you from leading a fulfilling life with meaningful connection.

Beliefs come from many places—upbringing, education, experience, relationships, society, the media. You can connect them to sources that reinforce them, just as a tabletop is connected to its legs. The tabletop represents your belief. The legs propping up the tabletop represent the events, circumstances, and interactions that support your belief. The more legs you have, the stronger your belief.

A mindshift we'll discuss in the next chapter is that who you become—not what you accomplish—is what matters most. Consider for a moment the belief "I am successful" and all the reinforcing factors that, in your mind, might validate that belief.

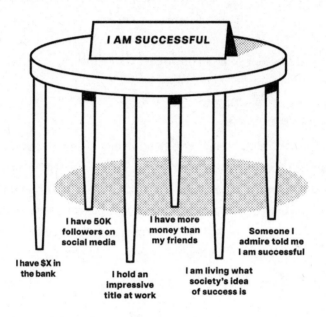

The supporting legs in this graphic show what many of us consider supports for a belief about one's success. Why do we connect these factors to this belief?

Frequently, we believe things because everyone else does (or seems to) or because a so-called expert said so. "Social proof" is a psychological phenomenon that depicts our reliance on the opinions of others to inform our own.[2] If it seems everyone else is buying into a product or an idea, that's a solid enough reason to follow suit. The same is true of a well-known influencer or expert who publishes their opinion. Most people will take their word as gold simply because they admire the person or because of their credentials. Social proof is not always reliable, however, just as following the crowd—without thinking for yourself and forming your own beliefs based on facts—can end up hurting you and limiting your potential.

For example, we now know that smoking is detrimental to health, but it only started attracting negative attention in the early 1920s. As the public became aware of the harmful long-term consequences of smoking, tobacco companies sensed a threat to their bottom line. Knowing that the public trusted physicians, the companies created cigarette ads featuring actors dressed up as doctors who neutralized the negativity. Tobacco companies fooled consumers into thinking cigarettes weren't bad—or *that* bad—for your health. That's the thing about beliefs: they can be biased, misleading, or outright untrue, which is why they demand scrutiny.

There was a time in my life when I believed people couldn't change. I thought they were set in their ways, mostly in negative patterns. If someone was selfish, I believed they would stay that way. If they were constantly late to meetings, I was sure I could never count on them to be on time. I began to realize that this belief wasn't true, and it was getting in the way of my development as a leader and my ability to positively influence others.

To deal with it, I first had to ask, Where did this belief come from? After much reflection, I began to recognize the legs that supported it. One had developed when a respected colleague told me, "People are hard to change." Another had appeared and fortified my belief after an experience with a person who refused to change their toxic behavior. Regardless of my experience with particular people who didn't change, my belief about *all people* wasn't serving me well at all.

Next, I needed to replace my *false belief* with a *true belief.* I reminded myself that people *do* change. I sought out and read stories of people from all walks of life—from entrepreneurs to athletes to scientists—who experienced personal growth and transformation. This evidence reinforced my new belief. Eventually, I replaced that false belief with the truth that people can and do change. With this new, unlimited belief, I was more motivated to lead and influence others, knowing that my actions could have a meaningful impact.

You've heard stories about people who have proved the critics wrong.

(Maybe that someone was you!) At some point those people had to think seriously about the messages they received from others instead of simply absorbing them, and they had to determine for themselves whether those messages were true.

As you pay more attention to beliefs, you'll notice the power they have. Unlimited beliefs ultimately improve your life and others'. They inspire a more positive mood and strengthen your approach to your relationships, career, and life overall. Limiting beliefs, of course, do the opposite.

If you're convinced that you'll never change, you'll never get ahead, or you'll never break that habit, I need to warn you—it's time to challenge that belief or you might get exactly what you believe.

The Power of Beliefs

According to an article published by the University of Pennsylvania's Wharton School of Business, the average person may produce fifty thousand thoughts a day, and 95 percent of those thoughts are on repeat.[3] What if some of those thoughts are untrue? What if you are lying to yourself about something day after day?

In the classic book *The Brothers Karamazov*, Fyodor Dostoevsky wrote, "Above all, do not lie to yourself. A man who lies to himself and listens to his own lie comes to a point where he does not discern any truth either in himself or anywhere around him, and thus falls into disrespect towards himself and others."[4]

As the brilliant Dostoevsky emphasized, when we accept a lie, we begin to lose the ability to discern truth. In the process of self-deception, we weaken our character and diminish the quality of our lives.

Many of us are led to believe that our present situation or our destiny is directly shaped by an event that happened to us, but that's not true. It's not *what happened* to us that dictates our identity or our lot in life; it's *what we believe* about that event and about ourselves that determines our destiny. Our belief about what has occurred is even more important than the event itself. The event may lie in our past, but our perception of that event can impact our entire future.

I'm sure you've heard of the *placebo effect*, the phenomenon that happens when a person's physical health seems to improve after taking a treatment that appears to be real but in truth has zero therapeutic quality, like a sugar pill.

The placebo effect was quantified by a professor of anesthesiology at Harvard Medical School named Dr. Henry Beecher. While Dr. Beecher was tending to wounded soldiers overseas during World War II, morphine began to run low. The doctor started injecting men with saline solution instead of the powerful painkiller, out of necessity, then noticed something fascinating. Some of the men who received the saline solution had the same amount of pain relief as the men who had received the morphine. When he came back to the States, Dr. Beecher studied this phenomenon and published his findings in a landmark paper that revealed how one-third of patients in these studies showed a significant response to placebo. This paper set the foundation for the modern clinical trial, which helps us determine if a drug really works.[5]

Dr. John Kelley, deputy director of Harvard Medical School's program studying placebos, noted, "Just *imagining* something is happening is enough to activate those portions of the brain associated with that thought, or worry, or pain."[6] This is true of placebo as well as *nocebo*, placebo's evil twin. Chances are you're not as familiar with this term. The nocebo effect happens when a person experiences negative or unpleasant effects from being told they may receive a negative outcome from a medical intervention. Negative side effects appear because of negative expectations.

A patient who had been diagnosed with multiple sclerosis and was in a wheelchair once visited my clinic. She presented with serious inflammatory symptoms including muscle pain, brain fog, and fatigue. After examining her and conducting a full workup, I wasn't convinced she had multiple sclerosis. I noticed some of her symptoms overlapped with those relating to mold exposure. I also found it interesting that the neurological symptoms that put her in a wheelchair began right after she was diagnosed with multiple sclerosis. I suggested she get a second opinion, which confirmed my suspicion. Turns out, she had been misdiagnosed. She didn't have multiple sclerosis; she had mold toxicity. Within a few days of this realization, she saw a miraculous improvement and no longer needed her wheelchair. Her new belief acted as a sort of medicine for the mind. It's staggering to think how our physical bodies react to something that isn't even true.

One case of the nocebo effect had a devastating outcome. A man in the 1970s was diagnosed with end-stage liver cancer. Doctors told him he had only a few months to live. Sure enough, the man died within the predicted time frame. The results of his autopsy were shocking, though. While there was a small tumor in the man's liver, the disease was localized and not yet life-threatening. The tumor certainly did not warrant the short amount of time the man had been predicted to live. The doctors had been wrong, but the man still died.[7] Why? Classic case of the nocebo effect. Negative expectations prompted negative results.

Can you think of an area in life in which you are living out the nocebo effect? What limiting belief consumes and affects your outlook on your future, relationships, self-confidence, or willingness to risk and try new things?

The stories you tell yourself are powerful. As life coach Tony Robbins once tweeted, "The only thing that's keeping you from getting what you want is the story you keep telling yourself."[8] It's time to rewrite your life story from an empowering perspective.

Memory Transplant

After graduating high school with a 2.3 GPA, I learned of an opportunity offered through a summer program at the University of Kentucky. If you could maintain a 3.0 GPA during the program and meet the other admittance requirements, you could be accepted into the school.

I'll never forget what happened in English 101 in my freshman year of college, when I worked on my first paper. For the first time in a long time, I applied myself and worked hard on an assignment. When my English teacher, Mrs. Williams, returned my paper, it felt like déjà vu. I was mentally transported back to my high school freshman English class with Mrs. Nobel—I expected Mrs. Williams to announce her disappointment and express doubt that I'd finish out the summer school program.

Instead, as she handed my paper back, she said, "Josh, I was really impressed with your paper. You got an A+, the highest grade in the class."

I stood there, shell-shocked.

"Have you ever thought about becoming a writer or at least an English major?"

"Uh, no."

"Well," Mrs. Williams said with a smile, "you did a great job. Keep it up!"

In that moment, I had what I will call a "memory transplant." I became aware of a *limiting* belief and traded it for an *unlimited* belief. I thought back to what Mrs. Nobel had said. *She had to be wrong. Mrs. Williams is right.* And instead of thinking, *I'm not smart. There's no point in even trying*, I started thinking, *I am smart. I can do this.*

When a certain memory leads to a limiting belief (as in my case with Mrs. Nobel), it is as though you have an organ in your body that is full of disease, like a kidney riddled with kidney stones or a heart plagued with clogged arteries. These malfunctioning organs wreak havoc on your entire body and can threaten your very life. Your memories, beliefs, and mindsets are no different. One single limiting belief can choke your dreams and future. A memory transplant is the moment you replace the limiting belief with an unlimited belief, like what happened when I received Mrs. Williams's encouraging words.

After my conversation with Mrs. Williams, I started applying myself in school with the goal of finding a career path that would help people get healthy. I finished the summer program with a 3.5, got accepted into the University of Kentucky, and maintained a high GPA throughout my undergrad program.

The momentum swelled. I started to believe in myself and threw off the limiting beliefs that were holding me back.

I continued my education to earn a doctorate in chiropractic medicine, founded and led a health and supplement company that hit the Inc. 5000 list, earned a master's degree in leadership from a top-ten academic institution with a 3.9 GPA, and am now writing my seventh book. Best of all, I am enjoying a wonderful family life, and I am proud of the person I am becoming along the way. None of this would have happened if I hadn't let go of my limiting beliefs and replaced them with unlimited beliefs.

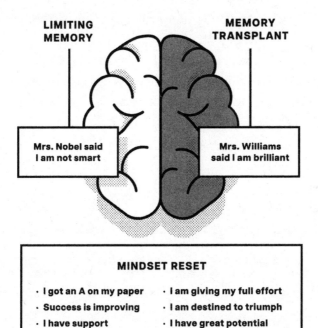

LIMITING MEMORY

MEMORY TRANSPLANT

Mrs. Nobel said I am not smart

Mrs. Williams said I am brilliant

MINDSET RESET

· I got an A on my paper
· Success is improving
· I have support

· I am giving my full effort
· I am destined to triumph
· I have great potential

Many people today are living in critical condition, their potential unrealized and unfulfilled because of unchallenged limiting beliefs. You may be one of them. If so, it's time to create your own memory transplant to help you become the person you are meant to be. Sometimes a significant event or conversation naturally sparks a memory transplant. Other times you must make the choice to do it on your own—which this book can help you do.

Go back to a moment when you stopped believing in yourself, or pinpoint when your false narrative about others or the world started. What is that memory? Where were you? Who were you with? What happened?

Today, you can make a memory transplant by creating a new memory that replaces the old one. What day is it? Where are you? Are you sitting on a crowded subway? At home with your dog, curled up on your couch? Remember this moment. Let today be the day you deactivate the power of the limiting belief that has kept you stuck.

If this feels overwhelming, don't worry. We'll walk through the process together.

As a word of encouragement, I'll tell you that as I've continued to confront limiting beliefs in my journey, I've become more courageous, gained more wisdom, and experienced more enriching relationships than I ever imagined. But it started when I decided to change the beliefs that were undermining my potential and my future. *Deciding to change is key.*

Identify Your Limiting Beliefs

The first step in creating a memory transplant is identifying what your limiting beliefs are. Everyone has them in some area of their lives, whether related to career, relationships, faith, finances, or health. Do any of these thoughts sound familiar?

I am not strong/smart/witty/caring/educated/talented enough.
I am too loud/wild/sensitive/passionate.
People are always trying to get something from me.
Nothing good happens to people in my family.
I've missed too many opportunities, and the doors have been closed.

In a nutshell, limiting beliefs are excuses that keep you from living your best life. Limiting beliefs often fall into three categories:

- **"I'M NOT ENOUGH."** People who struggle with this limiting belief feel like a fraud, not because of merit but because of some faulty perception. Also known as *impostor syndrome*, this is a common phenomenon successful people like Michelle Obama, Emma Watson, Sheryl Sandberg, and Howard Schultz have experienced.[9] Impostor syndrome is often associated with depression, anxiety, and social dysfunction.[10]
- **"WHAT I'VE DONE IS NOT GOOD ENOUGH."** Often, a statement like this stems from perfectionism. It's about striving to reach unrealistic or unachievable standards and basing your worth on whether you can reach those standards—and when you don't, it's the end of the world. Perfection, of course, is an illusion. Striving for an illusion, and inevitably falling short, leads to stress, burnout, fatigue, and low self-esteem.
- **"I WILL NEVER HAVE ENOUGH OF SOMETHING."** If you are convinced you will never have enough money, work, opportunity, love, or anything of value, you will develop a mentality of scarcity. You are constantly comparing what you have to others and always fall short. Who you are is tied up in how much you have—and it is never enough. You will hoard whatever you do have and engage in self-protective behaviors that will limit your potential, growth, and success.

Albert Ellis, a clinical psychologist from Columbia University, developed a tool called the ABCDE model to overcome his own limiting beliefs because he was incredibly afraid of talking to women.[11] It worked so well that he later used this same technique to help his patients overcome limiting beliefs associated with low self-worth, shame, and guilt. The ABCDE model helps people break free of false psychological perceptions.

ACTIVATING EVENT OR MEMORY: What triggered the limiting belief? (For me, it was my conversation with Mrs. Nobel.)

BELIEF: What is the limiting belief formed from the event or memory? (*I'm not smart.*)

CONSEQUENCES: What will result from continuing to believe the limiting belief? (*I will fail my class. I will not succeed. I will not even try.*)

DISPUTATION: How can you dispute the limiting belief and take a more rational approach? (*I can study harder and take more time to learn. I have succeeded when I've applied myself.*)

EFFECTS: The limiting belief has turned into a rational belief and has a healthier and more positive outcome. (*I get better grades. I improve my skills.*)

Studies indicate that this technique has tremendous benefits for lowering psychological stress. It reduces burnout at work and school, helps people overcome depression and anxiety, and improves job fulfillment and engagement. It's now being used in sports psychology to help athletes perform at a higher level.[12]

Spend some time right now thinking of three to five limiting beliefs about yourself that are stopping you from becoming who you could be. They might be one of the top three mentioned on the previous page. If you're not sure, consider what thoughts have kept you stuck in your personal growth, relationships, career, or health.

Here are some ways to identify whether a belief is limiting:

- Does the belief limit your potential or help you improve?
- Is it good for you and everyone around you?
- Is the story you're telling yourself completely true?
- What do the wisest and most successful people in the world believe about this?

Choose one category in the following table, and, in an empty space, jot down the lies that are limiting your potential:

My Limiting Beliefs

CAREER	RELATIONSHIPS	FAITH	FINANCES	HEALTH
Example: I could never get that promotion because I'm not smart enough.	Example: I don't deserve to be loved.	Example: God can't heal me.	Example: No one in our family has ever made money working for themselves.	Example: I'll never lose weight.

If you're unsure of whether a limiting belief carries weight, consider the cost if you continue to believe it. What is going to change a year from now if you continue to believe that you will never be successful or find love? Staying fixated on what's not possible will increase frustrations and result in a higher chance of failure. Focusing on the beliefs that lead to a healthier outcome will result in a healthier future.

Create Unlimited Beliefs

Now that you *recognize* your limiting beliefs, your next step is to *replace* them with unlimited beliefs. When you adopt a mindshift of unlimited beliefs, you unlock the door to becoming the person you were born to be.
Here's what this looks like:

LIMITING BELIEF: I'm too old to go back to college.
UNLIMITED BELIEF: I can get an education at any age.

LIMITING BELIEF: I've made too many mistakes.

UNLIMITED BELIEF: I can't change the past, but I can choose how to move forward.

LIMITING BELIEF: I can't become successful, because I have a learning disability.

UNLIMITED BELIEF: I can increase my potential in every area of life by growing my skills and in character.

Perhaps you have an easy time recognizing a limiting belief but struggle with finding a new belief to replace it. If this is you, think of someone you admire, someone who is thriving in the area of your life in which you're stuck. Maybe it's a mentor who's been happily married for thirty years or an entrepreneur who not only has experienced financial success but has channeled that prosperity into philanthropic impact. How have they produced the results you want in your life? Consider their way of thinking. This might mean asking them about their mindset, listening to someone else interview them, or reading their memoir. Zero in on their unlimited beliefs, and see if you can use them as a model for your own.

Then review the limiting beliefs you wrote down on page 15. Take a moment to determine alternative unlimited beliefs. What best serves you and your future instead? Write those down in the space below.

Unlimited Beliefs

CAREER	RELATIONSHIPS	FAITH	FINANCES	HEALTH
Example: I can work hard, dream big, and strive for what I want.	Example: I can be a loving person in a loving relationship.	Example: God has a plan and a purpose for my healing.	Example: I can earn money, save, and invest to build a secure future.	Example: I am responsible for my health.

Tips for Transforming Beliefs

Swapping a limiting belief for an unlimited one is not an overnight process. It will take energy, time, and some practice to cultivate your new belief. You'll need to do this over and over until the new belief becomes a habit.

Write it down somewhere you'll regularly see it. Put it on a mirror, your coffee machine, your water bottle, or a phone app. Say it out loud—do this often, especially when you hear the echo of your limiting beliefs. The more you see and voice your unlimited beliefs, the more you'll begin to absorb them.

After my memory transplant and adoption of unlimited beliefs, the limiting beliefs still crept into my mind. Every time I heard, *Josh, you're not smart*, I fought it off with the facts that I was capable and that I could learn what I didn't know. At one point, I even put the A+ paper Mrs. Williams gave me on my bathroom mirror so I saw it every day. I repeated these habits until the limiting belief lost its power over me.

A mindshift toward unlimited beliefs is also a progression, not a destination. After my conversation with my college teacher Mrs. Williams, I could have continued the false narrative that I wasn't smart, that I couldn't write, that college was just a way of following the crowd, but something about that moment stirred in me a truth I clung to. It leveled up my confidence. That one belief shattered a ceiling, which then shattered another ceiling, and so on. This shift is what creates a pattern of unlimited beliefs.

You don't have to know every single limiting and unlimited belief of yours right now to create a future of great potential. All you need to do is change *one belief at a time*.

Pleasure and Pain

One way to motivate yourself is to understand how pain and pleasure drive beliefs. Sigmund Freud developed the principle that human beings are driven to both avoid pain and pursue pleasure.[13] Everything we do in life comes from our desire to do one or the other. Most of us get more satisfaction out of avoiding immediate pain than gaining immediate pleasure.

When I was in high school, I kept a C average to dodge being disciplined by my father. The pleasure of the inner satisfaction of getting higher grades wasn't on my radar. After my memory transplant—thanks to Mrs. Williams—I forced myself to think of what was possible if I nurtured a more positive belief in my ability and my future. I linked *pleasure* to the goal of creating a career in which I could help people live healthier and more meaningful lives. And that helped override the *pain* of my limiting beliefs that I wasn't smart and I shouldn't even try.

Think about the pleasure you can associate with your new, unlimited belief. If you believe you can begin to make better food choices, think of how much more time you can spend playing with your kids without feeling tired or out of breath, or what it would feel like to get your blood test results back within the normal range and not need medication, or how great it'd be to pick up the new sport or hobby you've been wanting to do.

The more you think about the pleasure of what's possible, the more motivated you will be to keep tuning into that new belief. You'll be able to watch the cycle of progression of how beliefs "become your thoughts, your thoughts become your words, your words become your actions, your actions become your habits, your habits become your values, your values become your destiny."[14]

Take Action

There's one caveat when it comes to discerning your beliefs. You are not the things you *say* you will do; you are what you *actually do*. Beliefs are more than your feelings or deepest convictions. They align with your behavior; they demand action.

If you tell me your family is the most important thing in the world to you, but you log more hours in the office on the weekends than at home and are distracted when you are with your family, your claim is not accurate. The adage "Actions speak louder than words" is famous for a reason—it's true!

What's Possible

When former Denny's waitress Jamie Kern Lima began to pursue her dream of creating her own makeup brand, inspired by her own journey of dealing with rosacea, she struggled with two major limiting beliefs. One was that she wasn't good enough to succeed.[15] Another was that marriage would keep her from fulfilling her potential.[16]

When she met and fell in love with Paulo, a fellow student in grad school, Lima wasn't interested in becoming a wife; she wanted to build an empire. She wrote in her bestselling book *Believe IT*, "I grew up believing that men hold women back, and that belief transitioned into the conviction that I didn't want to get married."[17]

Yet she was so in love with Paulo that, sensing deeply that she belonged with him, she surprised herself by answering yes when he proposed. "My intuition [to marry Paulo] shocked the heck out of me. . . . I set aside my fear and doubt to follow it."[18] Together, they worked on the business plan for her company while traveling for their honeymoon in 2007.

As she worked to pursue her dream, she was met with a barrage of criticism that added to her self-doubt and insecurity about her own skin issues. One potential investor told her that no one would want to buy makeup from someone who looked like her. The statement hit hard. But it also ignited a challenge to get her mind right.

"While the logical part of my mind wondered if he was right," Lima said, "I felt this overwhelming gut instinct that he was wrong. And I also knew the journey of proving that would hinge first on me learning to truly believe it for myself."[19] While Lima worked to build her brand, she was determined to believe that she could be the woman, the wife, the mother, and the entrepreneur she was born to be. In her words, "I decided to believe that I could no matter what anyone else said."[20]

Lima's company, IT Cosmetics, is now one of the most well-known beauty brands in the US. In 2016, L'Oréal bought it for $1.2 billion. Lima stayed on as CEO of her brand and became the first female CEO in L'Oréal's 108-year history.[21] Today she's a bestselling author after stepping down as CEO in 2019. Lima says, "I'm just scratching the surface of what I have to give and what I have to do."[22] The future is unlimited for Lima because of the powerful beliefs that drive her.

What could be possible if you identify and eliminate your limiting beliefs? You may have to sit for a while and think about it, and that's okay. But if you choose not to identify and eliminate your limiting beliefs, someday you will likely wonder, *What if?*

What if I had pursued my dream?

What if I had developed the specific gift I have?

What if I started being more vulnerable in my relationships?

Imagine all the good that's possible instead of setting yourself up for regret.

Before we close this chapter, I want to tell you about one more mental exercise, one I use to help people get unstuck in business and life. It's called the "10x Strategy," and it entails visualizing what you want—but ten times bigger.

One of my clients, John, was an entrepreneur who held a limiting belief that the more he grew his business, the more work and less freedom he would have. I showed him the opposite was actually true. I told him that when I started my clinic, I was in charge of everything. Not only was I examining and educating patients, but I was also marking up X-rays, doing blood work, and even answering the phones and making Costco runs. The bigger the clinic became, however, the more employees I was able to hire, which allowed me to narrow my focus to leading my staff and treating patients. When John understood the possibilities that come with growth, he was able to remedy his limiting belief and imagine his business growing ten times—which is exactly what happened!

It's your turn. Sit for a moment and "10x" what you want out of life. What could your life look like if you moved the needle ten times further than where it is now? The marriage of your wildest dreams? A million-dollar company? To write the book that's been a blank document on your computer for the past five years? Break away from the limiting beliefs that tie down your life and your future. Then start believing in what's possible and keep building, one belief at a time.

Maybe your life is not what you once dreamed it would be. You've made mistakes. Maybe something awful happened to you. I want to remind you that you are not your past. You are not that event. You are a unique individual with vast potential who can use failures and even injustices to move forward and flourish.

It's time to shatter your limiting beliefs.

As you adopt unlimited beliefs and unlock unlimited potential, you'll likely begin envisioning what you might have been created to do. Before that becomes your focus, though, I want to show why and how you must first become who you were always meant to be.

Create a breakthrough by unlimiting your beliefs.

Limiting Beliefs → Unlimited Beliefs

REDEFINE SUCCESS BY *BECOMING, NOT ACCOMPLISHING*

"He was my best friend," a man in his sixties blurted out. The heartfelt cry was barely recognizable between the sobs.

I admit, I was skeptical. *I know this man, and he is* not *my grandfather's best friend.* My doubt began to subside, however, as I listened to the praise of other people ring out in honor of my ninety-six-year-old grandfather, whose life the packed crowd was celebrating in the funeral home.

"Howard gave me money when I lost my job."

"Howard showed me what a great father and husband looked like."

"Howard offered me wise advice that saved my marriage."

"Howard prayed for me when I felt like all my hope was lost."

After hearing these heartfelt statements, I realized that my grandfather likely was the best friend this man had ever had. I had a feeling that half the people in that room viewed my grandfather Howard as their best friend, their father figure, or the person who had the greatest impact on their lives.

I was overwhelmed by the nonstop tributes that people voiced for this

World War II veteran who had lived for almost a century. He embodied so many qualities that we all should aim for—integrity, honesty, wisdom, generosity, love, and compassion—but that so few live up to today. In that moment, I began to realize my grandfather Howard was the type of person I wanted to become. People could always count on him. He was acutely in tune with the needs of others, always ready with an encouraging word and a comforting hand on the slumped shoulder of a person struggling with life's problems.

After the funeral, I started thinking more about my grandfather Howard. What was it about him that made me want to become like him? It wasn't his wealth; he didn't have much money. It wasn't his online influence; he didn't even participate in social media, much less have a million followers. It wasn't his list of impressive achievements, at least according to society's standards; he had never been ranked on any *Forbes* lists. I had never considered my grandfather successful, and maybe that was the problem. I needed to reexamine my definition of success.

A False Notion of Success

Up until this point, I thought the definition of success was obvious—a growing list of accomplishments, influence, and financial prosperity. By our culture's gauge, I was traveling the trajectory of success. I was operating a successful wellness clinic and had just written my first book. I had a clear vision of myself and my future and had put strategies in place to achieve my goals. But something was missing. There was more to life than striving and accomplishing.

I began to think about the people I admired most. Why did I hold them in such high esteem? I noticed a common thread. Their goal wasn't only to reach certain milestones in their career or cross off a list of lofty ambitions; they aspired to be better men and women than they were the day before and to positively influence other people. This purpose manifested in their lives not only in words but in actions. It was embodied in the choices they made and how they led people, spent their time, and interacted with everyone. They were people of virtue who could be described as courageous, wise, just, and loving. They encapsulated the true definition of success, which was something I hadn't fully understood as a younger man.

I was reminded of one of my heroes when I was a triathlete in college, cycling champion Lance Armstrong.

In 2010, Armstrong was considered the most influential athlete in America, above Kobe Bryant, Tiger Woods, Serena Williams, Tom Brady, and Tim Tebow.[1] However, he had a questionable reputation. Rumors of his use of performance-enhancing drugs had circulated, and Armstrong had vehemently denied them throughout the years. In 2012, an investigation by the United States Anti-Doping Agency confirmed the allegations. As a huge fan, I was disappointed and felt betrayed when I discovered Armstrong had cheated and lied thousands of times.[2]

His cheating and lies forced him to resign as chairman of the board of his foundation and cost him his career, the loyalty of his fans, multiple sponsorships, millions of dollars in settling the false claims he had made, his personal relationships, and most importantly, his reputation and character.

It wasn't just Armstrong who suffered from his deception. Those around him felt the devastating repercussions, from the cancer survivors who looked up to him to his family and loved ones, to the nonprofit organization he founded, and to the millions of fans who esteemed his work ethic, perseverance, and supposedly "clean" method of reaching championship status.

When you don't live up to who you say you are, you and those around you suffer. It's a ripple effect. When have you known someone—an influencer, friend, spiritual guide, or someone you admire—to be one thing and then found out they weren't? It hurts, doesn't it? Even if it's not personal, it feels like you've been betrayed.

This duplicity can happen when people focus solely on accomplishing without paying attention to who they are becoming. When you accumulate accomplishments while ignoring your character, it's like building a house on sand. Eventually, your house will crumble and wash away.

If your idea of success has anything to do with how I once thought of it, and how most people define it, you've been lied to. You may have been told by your parents, a professor, a coach, your peer group, or a social media influencer that you will attain success when you get the trophy, acquire a position, make a certain amount of money, or buy the car of your dreams. This is false.

The Formula for Success

Let me set the record straight. It's when you *maximize your unique skills for the greatest good* that you achieve success. This definition of success is not a matter of meeting an end goal; it's a way of approaching your everyday life.

Success = maximizing your unique skill for the good of others

What is your unique skill? What is the one or two things you can do well? Is it writing, organization, innovation, athletics, leadership, communication, customer service? According to John Maxwell, talent itself isn't enough.[3] Great leaders recognize that the greatest returns actualize when they maximize their talent. The idea is not to rely on your natural skills alone to fuel your direction and momentum in life but to add effort and optimize them to a higher level. Focus on doing what you're good at—and getting better at it.

Honing your skill is a process, not a destination. And it's not instantaneous. The first time I did a radio show and listened to myself afterward, I was horrified. I thought I sounded dull and boring, and I'm positive I said "um" close to forty times. So what did I do? Practice, of course! I researched ways to improve my communication skills over the radio and spent hours and hours rehearsing in front of the mirror until I improved. There's always room for development, and while I've certainly not arrived, I've made tremendous strides since that first radio show.

If you're good at something, get even better at it. If you're a good writer, kick it up a notch and take a workshop or two, read books about writing, and interview top authors and journalists. Create a plan of growth so that in six months, a year, and two years from now, you will have excelled at your skill.

To become your greatest possible you, you need to excel in your character and your skill. The graphic below illustrates what happens when you move the needle in those two areas to the highest level possible.

WHO COULD YOU BECOME?

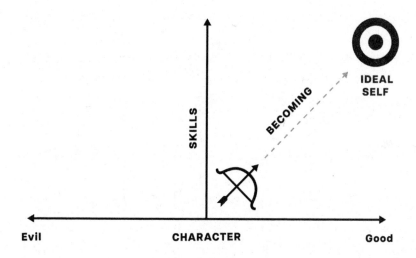

If you know what your unique skill is, great! But I wonder if you are using it for the good of others. Every person has their own idea of what that means, and we'll explore this in depth in mindshift 4. For now, consider your answer to the following questions: "How can I add the most value to others and to the planet?" and "What can I offer that can help others become the people they were born to be?"

There is a plethora of intelligent, savvy, creative, and talented entrepreneurs, artists, influencers, and financial tycoons who are maximizing their skills but not using them for the good of others. Just think of those celebrities who flood their social media pages with pictures of themselves, financiers who profit from illegal schemes, or politicians who favor power over the interests of the people.

When you begin to intentionally live with purpose, you experience *the reward of contribution*. You know that you have made a difference in someone else's life, whether it comes in the form of your parenting, innovation, or leadership. Adding value to others and to the world is something you can be proud of, which is the truest test of success.

Before you throw out your list of goals and aspirations, though, I want to remind you that accomplishments aren't bad—in fact, they can be used in a positive and meaningful way. The key is having the right mindset.

> **THINK THIS:** Success is about optimizing my skill to help others and bring good to the world.
> **NOT THAT:** Success is using what I'm good at to look good.

An Accomplishing Mindset

To understand this right mindset, let's first look at its opposite—the wrong mindset.

When what you *have* and what you *do* are your focus, you are guided by what I call an *accomplishing mindset*. If you zero in on reaching a certain level of material success without aiming to develop your character and enrich your relationships, inner satisfaction will always be out of reach.

When entrepreneurial legend and Apple founder Steve Jobs passed away from pancreatic cancer at the age of fifty-six, he left behind a legacy that revolutionized the computer, music, phone, and movie industries.

Founder of the world's first trillion-dollar public company, Jobs developed groundbreaking products like the iPod, the iPhone, and the iPad and transformed the way people listen to music and talk on the phone. When he died in 2011, Jobs was worth $10.2 billion.[4]

This visionary genius left more than a legacy of great wealth and world-changing innovation; he also left behind great regrets. Toward the end of his life, he said this to his biographer: "I wanted my kids to know me. I wasn't always there for them, and I wanted them to know why and to understand what I did."[5] In a way, Jobs held the world in his hands, yet in the process of accomplishing what most of us can only imagine, he paid a steep price: his relationship with his family.

What good is gaining the world but losing your soul?[6]

What good is growing a company but losing your family?

What good is gaining wealth but losing your health?

What good is being right but ruining your marriage?

What good is getting a promotion but losing your integrity?

An accomplishing mindset may lead to receiving an award, high esteem among people, or impressive accolades, but it rarely produces the type of person you are proud of becoming. Our culture may glorify talent, fame, fortune, and power, but accomplishments at the expense of character will always lead to disappointment, and sometimes a bitter end.

The accomplishing mindset focuses on things, not people. Are you truly a success if you build a great business but do it while sacrificing your employees' well-being and destroying your family life in the process? Of course not. When you build your life around metrics and outcomes outside of personal character and relationship building, you miss out on a meaningful future and life.

One study published in the *Journal of Research in Personality* followed 147 college graduates. Their goals and happiness were tracked twice—first at twelve months after graduation and then one year after that. There was a vast difference between the people who achieved extrinsic goals like wealth and fame and those who achieved personal growth and relationship-oriented goals. Researchers noted that the participants who valued material goals (e.g., a high salary) over close relationships and community involvement had less life satisfaction and well-being.[7] A meaningful life is anchored in developing strong character, creating deep connections with others, and adding value to their lives.

Many of us slip into an accomplishing mindset without realizing it. Answering these questions can help you see if that's where you are:

- Do you find yourself in a persistent state of frustration because no matter how much you achieve, it's still not good enough?
- Are you chasing dreams and goals but losing relationships and your identity in the process?
- Has trying to attain a false definition of success left you feeling empty and unsatisfied?

If you answered yes to any of the above questions, I've got great news for you—you don't have to live like this anymore. It's time to take the pressure off. There's a better way to think and be.

The Mindshift of Becoming

A *becoming mindset* is the key to living a life of success. This principle zeroes in on the most important element of who you are—your character. Rather than focusing on what you accomplish, aim to grow in wisdom, honesty, courage, and justice.

Becoming unlocks your full potential and positions you on the path toward being who you were born to be. Albert Einstein had it right when he gave the following advice to his son: "Try not to become a man of success but rather try to become a man of value."[8] People of great character adopt a regular habit of asking themselves, How can I be a better man/woman, son/daughter, spouse, colleague/leader, student/mentor, [fill in the blank]?

Becoming = growing in character

> **THINK THIS:** What's most important is who I become.
> **NOT THAT:** What matters most is what I accomplish.

As the father of a toddler, I am constantly striving to be a better dad. I don't know of a greater example to follow than my friend Isaac Meek, a third-generation local business owner and baker. I met him and his wife, Stephanie, in 2010, when they were patients in my clinic. Isaac loved two things: his family and baking. He worked as an accountant, and while he didn't care for his nine-to-five job, he was committed to providing for his family and never once complained.

Everything changed for him in 2015. After much prayer and reflection with his wife, Isaac admitted his job caused him to waste his true talents and set aside his dreams. It was also "crushing" his family, he said.[9] He and his wife decided the right thing for him to do was to step away from his corporate job and start a baking company. This did not come without a massive risk: 90 percent of entrepreneurial startups fail.[10] But Isaac and Stephanie both felt a conviction that Isaac was called to use his greatest skill of baking for a greater purpose.

My friend woke up at three o'clock every morning and made mouthwatering croissant-style donuts with the highest-quality ingredients. He began selling them to local coffee shops and in farmers markets before he opened his first location, Five Daughters Bakery in Franklin, Tennessee. It was a joy to watch him include his five daughters in the baking and selling process. As he mixed dough or handed out samples, his little girls were the best employees, helping however they could from the beginning. Isaac was devoted to the business and to his family, demonstrating that commitment by always putting his family first.

I learn from Isaac by watching what he does, not just listening to what he says. His character aligns with his actions. Isaac devotes time to serving and loving his wife by scheduling annual trips to New York City where they first met, taking dance lessons with her, and planning group activities for them and their friends, even though he is an introvert at heart. Isaac also plans monthly date nights for each of his daughters and is deeply involved in their lives, teaching them ethical principles. He leads his team at his company by example and through mentoring his employees. He donates proceeds from his monthly specialty donuts to raise money for charitable causes.

Isaac also constantly reminds me that an encouraging word goes a long way, whether it's to a stranger on the street or the people closest to you. This man lives by the mindshift of *becoming* because he knows who he wants to be, which is a good husband, father, son, and leader, and he acts on that knowledge. All those ingredients—pardon the pun—make great character.

What is character? Character is made up of traits at the core of our being. In other words, it is who we are on the inside. American entrepreneur Jim Rohn called it "a quality that embodies many important traits such as integrity, courage, perseverance, confidence, and wisdom. Unlike your fingerprints that you were born with and can't change, character is something that you create within yourself and must take responsibility for changing."[11]

Even the business world values character over performance. If you had to guess why most company executives are fired, what would you say the top reason is? Poor financial performance? Lack of skills? In fact, it's misconduct. Nearly 40 percent of CEO and company executives are fired due to moral and ethical failures versus only 35 percent fired for poor financial performance.[12] If we focus on accomplishing before becoming, the weight of achievement will eventually crush us.

This priority of character over accomplishment also applies to our relationships, our personal mission in life, and whatever it is we strive for.

None of us can claim the prize for perfect character, but how many of us are committed to being a person of moral value when no one is looking, when we know we won't get caught, or when it doesn't hurt anyone? Think of your behavior from an ethical standpoint in the workplace. Did you really work on that project over the weekend? Did you ask for permission to take supplies home? Would your spouse appreciate the conversations you're having with your coworker? Were you completely honest about being sick and unable to work or about how many hours in total you reported working per week?

Let's focus on lying for a minute. According to studies:

- 78 percent of job applicants lie during the hiring process.[13]
- 60 percent of participants in one study admitted to lying about being sick.[14]
- 41 percent of people who didn't like their job admitted to lying once or more a week.[15]

Most people who say they work more than sixty hours a week are lying or overestimating by eighteen hours.[16]

President Abraham Lincoln earned the nickname "Honest Abe" because of his commitment to fairness as a young man. According to one source, when he worked as a store clerk and realized he shortchanged a customer by a few pennies, he always shut down the store and walked, sometimes for miles, to the customer to deliver the correct change.[17] Because he consistently showed his strong character, he eventually was invited to mediate disagreements in town. "Lincoln's judgment was final in all that region of the country," reported one townsperson. "People relied implicitly upon his honesty, integrity, and impartiality."[18] By the time Honest Abe became president, he was already known and respected for being a person of value.

To me, this type of character display from Lincoln and others is a greater sign of success than any title, trophy, promotion, or accolade. It is a true indication of becoming someone great.

ACCOMPLISHMENT MINDSET	BECOMING MINDSET
What matters most is what I accomplish.	What's most important is who I become.
Whoever dies with the most toys wins.	"A good reputation and respect are worth much more than silver and gold."[19]
Achievements trump character.	Character development comes first.

Win at all costs.	Consider what is right over what I can gain.
Focus on looking good or doing what's right when others will notice.	Who I am in public is who I am in private.
Everyone else needs to change.	How can I become a better person?

Begin Becoming

Before you concentrate on your bucket list or determine your top ten goals for the next five years, focus first on becoming. If you do this, you will maximize your potential to live the most meaningful life possible and fulfill your potential for good. Investing in *becoming* by growing your character may not sound as important as investing in your skills, but there will always be a return on your investment.

Here's what that can lead to on a personal level, according to multiple research studies:

- improved leadership capabilities
- greater financial success
- stronger relationships and marriage
- lower risk of depression and anxiety
- increase in physical fitness
- increase in life fulfillment and meaning[20]

When you develop character, people learn to trust you. Trust is the foundation of relationships.

Navy SEAL Jocko Willink has found that trust is the primary attribute people look for in a high-quality teammate, friend, or partner. He considers it to be more important than any skill. When you are at war, in business, or with your own family, you need to be able to trust that each person has your back, will operate with integrity and honesty, and will take full responsibility for their role. If you can't trust a person, the relationship is weak, and you can't count on them. This, in turn, leads to feelings of resentment, distrust, and dishonor.

A becoming mindset is ultimately about us serving and adding value to the lives of others. It's about people, not objects or numbers. It's about helping others fulfill their hopes and dreams and become the best version of themselves. These tenets are central to becoming a person of great character.

Life is about relationships. This is the key difference in how Lance Armstrong and my grandfather Howard approached their lives. My grandfather always thought about others, while Lance's defining characteristic appeared to be his "ruthless desire to win at all costs."[21] It's more important to build up others than to build up things.

Character is the strongest foundation to build your life and identity on. It is the ultimate bedrock on which your talents, skills, and abilities can become even more powerful. As you grow personally, you will help others grow, and eventually they will become people who do the same for others.

It's important to note that character is not a one-hit wonder; it is not demonstrated in a single action or event. Who you are shows up in what you do day in and day out. It is not static, like DNA or your height. You become greater in character every day. It is also not something you will one day attain perfectly. The *accomplishing* mindset is a destination, but the *becoming* mindset is a lifelong journey.

So be committed to personal growth and forming your character. Ask yourself each day, Is what I'm doing hurting others and creating a more cynical and unhealthy world? Or is it building up others and causing the world to flourish?

Who Can You Become?

The late leadership expert Myles Munroe said this about untapped potential:

The wealthiest spot on this planet is not the oil fields of Kuwait, Iraq or Saudi Arabia. Neither is it the gold and diamond mines of South Africa. . . . Though it may surprise you, the richest deposits on our planet lie just a few blocks from your house. They rest in your local cemetery or graveyard. Buried beneath the soil within the walls of those sacred grounds are dreams that never came to pass, songs that were never sung, books that were never written, paintings that never filled a canvas, ideas that were never shared, visions that never became reality, inventions that were never designed, plans that never went beyond the drawing board of the mind, and purposes that were never fulfilled. Our graveyards are filled with potential that remained potential. What a tragedy![22]

Imagine what you can offer the world when you couple the mindshift of becoming with the accomplishments that come *as a result*. Imagine the loss you and others suffer when those gifts are wasted.

Your greatest potential is not just about *you*; it's about *us*. It's about influencing others. It's about becoming the greatest *you* so you have the greatest impact on helping someone else become the greatest *them*. Transformation like this starts in one place: recognizing what's possible.

I'm pretty sure that when you were seven or eight, you wanted to become something or somebody. A ballerina, the president, a firefighter, or a professional athlete. As adults, we're quick to dismiss what were likely nothing more than fanciful dreams, but scientific research tells us a person's future vision of themselves is a helpful guide to what they might become.[23] It can be a self-fulfilling prophecy.

Possible selves, a term coined by researchers Hazel Markus and Paula Nurius, describes how an individual thinks about their potential and future. An individual's possible selves are thought to be the link between past experiences and future hopes and fears. They represent what a person would like to become (future self) as well as what they dread becoming (feared self).[24] This principle aligns with the ancient proverb "As a man thinketh in his heart, so is he."[25] In other words, how you envision your future self determines how you make choices today.

Research tells us that the more connected we are to our future selves, the more emphasis we will place on becoming that person.[26] In one study, participants were given the choice to receive a smaller amount of money soon or a bigger sum later. The participants who had a stronger connection with their future self chose to wait for the larger amount of money. The researcher found that these same participants had a larger amount of savings than the participants who had a weaker connection with their future self.[27] The study discovered this principle holds true not just in finances but also in issues of health, relationships, and moral standards.

The lead researcher of the study, Hal Hershfield, refers to a scene in the hit TV series *The Simpsons*, which illustrates his point. Homer Simpson's wife, Marge, says to her husband, "You know, someday these kids will be out of the house, and you'll regret not spending more time with them."

Homer responds, "That's a problem for future Homer. Man, I don't envy that guy."[28] He then pours vodka into a jar of mayonnaise and guzzles it down.[29]

Don't be like Homer! When you're not connected to your future self, you make bad decisions that harm your future.

The clearer we visualize who we want to be and the better we nurture that connection, the more decisions we will make to become that person, and the more successful we will be. If you see your future self as kind and generous, you will be kind and generous right now. If you see yourself loving and enjoying fulfilling relationships, you will build a strong community now. (Mindshift 11 will bring you on a deeper journey into the tool of visualization.)

What is your future self like? Do you see yourself as an innovator in the health field? A person who will one day be happily married for fifty years? A political leader who uses her power for good? Envision your ideal future self. Who are your friends? What is your day-to-day life like? How are you using your skills and platform? What do you stand for? Now envision the person you would need to become for that to happen. What character traits do you need to develop to become your possible self? What needs to change?

Let's say you want to see yourself as a great parent. Visualize yourself going camping with your kids, playing tag in the backyard, or taking them out for ice cream (coconut milk–based, if you're a health nut like me) for no special reason. Picture having heart-to-heart conversations with them in which you share how important they are to you and how much you love them. Imagine yourself gently correcting them instead of lashing out when they make a mistake.

Think of your future self as an actual person. What steps can you take, starting now, to build that relationship that's important to you? Do you need to tweak your financial habits so you can enjoy economic security in the future? Get into therapy to focus on the emotional trauma you have been avoiding so you can be free of emotional dependencies? Spend more time with your children so you can build strong relationships with them in ten or twenty years? Pre-decide and visualize your ideal self, then live it out.

One more thing. Rather than focus on checking off the items on your to-do list each day, consider making a *to-be* list. At the start of every morning, for instance, set a goal to be more compassionate. Throughout your day, recognize a hardship someone may be enduring and ask how you can help. Think about it this way. Future selves aren't something we want to *do*; they are people we want to *be*.

Two Mindsets, One Choice

After my grandfather Howard's funeral, a group of family members and I went back to a recreational campground where we swam in the lake, barbecued, and shared memories. My grandfather had a special knack for bringing people together, even after he had passed. I remember taking a minute to myself at one point to walk on one of the beaten paths while there was still light. I wondered if, at the end of my life, there would be a roomful of people speaking highly of who I was and the meaningful impact I had on their lives, rather than reciting a list of what I had accomplished. I knew in that moment that I didn't want accolades about titles or things; what was most important was making a positive impact on others. I wanted to leave this world without regret, knowing I had done everything I could to be the best son, husband, dad, friend, leader, and person to others and to make the planet a little bit better than the day I entered it.

Take a minute right now and view your life through the lens of an *accomplishing* mindset. If you're focused on tackling your goals without first developing your character, building wealth without first forming virtue, or creating influence without first considering the good of others, you are headed for temporary satisfaction and a life absent of purpose.

On the other hand, if you live with a *becoming* mindset, you can look forward to flourishing in life. You are on the path toward enduring relationships, high life-satisfaction, and living with purpose.

Your greatest life accomplishment is becoming a better spouse, parent, friend, boss, daughter, or son. Think for a moment about who you could become. What needs to change?

The best way to act like your possible self is to start becoming that person today.

Redefine success by *becoming,* not *accomplishing.*

Accomplishing → Becoming

Click here (joshaxe.com/thinkthis) and you'll find FREE quizzes, exercises, and downloadable PDFs to help you grow.

BECOME SELF-AWARE TO GET WHERE YOU NEED TO GO

In the past, I didn't cry much. I'm not saying that to sound tough; it's just that I used to allow only a few things to move me to tears. My sister-in-law, however, cries as easily as Buddy the Elf smiles. It's natural to her. She's incredibly empathetic and can even shed tears while watching a car insurance ad. I used to wonder if I should be emotionally moved more. But after taking several mission trips around the world, I've become more empathetic and shed tears more easily now. One trip to Ethiopia noticeably heightened my awareness when I witnessed something that just wasn't right with the world.

In 2010, I traveled to Africa with the nonprofit Soles4Souls, an organization that collects and distributes shoe and clothing donations to the neediest places in the world. One day a group of us brought food and shoes to a giant landfill that doubled as home to hundreds of people. Makeshift houses haphazardly constructed out of plastic, cardboard, and tin sat on top of rolling hills of foul refuse. Men, women, and children combed through the garbage looking for something edible. Others hoped to find a treasure like a leftover scrap of soap.

THINK THIS, NOT THAT

When we got to the dump, nausea hit everyone in our group (and lingered in our stomachs for hours, even after we returned to our hotel). As strong as that stench was, nothing was as impactful as the people I met who lived and worked in that garbage dump. They were beautiful, kind, humble, and loving. We were honored to distribute shoes and even break bread with them (in the form of a goat) before we left. The entire experience was life-changing, but I didn't get a chance to process what transpired that day until a week or two after I got back to the US.

One day, when I was back home and alone, I sat down and wept. I kept thinking over and over, *It just isn't right.* The experience unlocked for me more than a feeling of mere sympathy for poor people living in an impoverished country on the other side of the globe; it developed a deep awareness that the type of suffering people experienced was real and unjust. They were living in cardboard houses that could collapse with the slightest weight of rain, gobbling up the crumbs of someone else's mostly eaten bread roll lying atop fly-covered banana peels, and sending their toddlers to climb the tallest peak of the dump to scavenge through trash. These people were made for more.

I began to think differently, approaching my life with a humbler and more grateful attitude. I became more intentional about alleviating the suffering of others by giving more of my time and money to serve organizations both locally and abroad.

My experience in Ethiopia forced me to feel compassion and sadness and then act on these feelings. This is the power of self-awareness at work, a living example of Socrates's wisdom to "know thyself." When we are self-aware, we understand what we feel—maybe anger, sadness, or fear—and we can transform it into productive behavior. How often have we exploded in anger instead of taking a minute to process our rage and then responding with careful thought and self-control?

Self-awareness is more than emotional self-regulation. It is the bedrock of "emotional intelligence," a concept popularized by Daniel Goleman's bestselling book of the same name. Emotional intelligence can be defined as "the ability to perceive, interpret, demonstrate, control, and use emotions

42

to communicate with and relate to others effectively and constructively."[1] Goleman defines self-awareness as "the sense of an ongoing attention to one's internal states" or "introspective attention to one's own experience."[2]

When you are self-aware, you are mindful of what is happening to you and in you, rather than letting it consume and overwhelm you. You can recognize your blind spots, weaknesses, and areas needing improvement. Self-awareness allows you to discover where you are *now*, so you can get to where you truly *want to be*. If you want to reach your potential and live a meaningful life, begin by cultivating self-awareness.

It's easy to assume that we already know who we can become and all the possibilities life has to offer. But chances are, we've had only a glimpse of what's possible. There is a saying aimed at business leaders: "Don't just work *in* your business. Also work *on* your business."[3] In other words, rather than do only the necessary daily or weekly tasks and mark off the checklist, it's also important to brainstorm opportunities, visualize, look at the big picture, research the possibilities, and then develop habits and strategies for implementation.

Consider doing this in your life. Do more than mark up your daily to-do lists; meditate on where you are, where you want to go, and what you need to change to make that happen.

The Mindshift of Self-Awareness

Organizational psychologist and researcher Tasha Eurich published a piece in the *Harvard Business Review* that featured a scientific study she conducted on self-awareness. One astonishing result struck me: while 90 percent of people believe they are self-aware, only 10–15 percent of people actually are.[4]

We like to think we are cognizant of our thoughts, actions, and behaviors, but the truth is, most of us are not. Without understanding our strengths, weaknesses, unique traits, and motivations, it is nearly impossible to improve and develop into the people we want to become.

Eurich defines self-awareness as "fully knowing who you are—your values, passions, goals, personality, strengths and weaknesses—and understanding how others perceive you."[5] By activating self-awareness, you can begin to answer questions like *Why do I feel like I always need to prove myself to others? Why can't I stop being a people pleaser? Why did this person try to undermine my character?*

Do you know anyone who makes every conversation about themselves? You could be telling a story of how your dog just died, and somehow they will hijack the conversation to make it about them. I'm not a fan of slapping labels on people, but there's a sociological term for these kinds of self-centric people: conversational narcissist. I'll call them "Mr./Mrs. Me."

You: It was a hard week. Saying goodbye to Otis was rough.

Mr./Mrs. Me: I'm so sorry. I know the feeling. I went through the same thing a few years ago.

You: Oh, that's terrible. When—

Mr./Mrs. Me: I can't tell you how long I cried over that little dog. I thought about getting another dog, but I didn't have the heart. I was also in the process of moving, though, so it probably wasn't the best idea. Did you know I lived in LA two years ago?

You: Um, no.

Conversational narcissists make terrible dinner guests and tiresome friends. Their manipulation of the conversation causes them to fail to listen, talk much longer than they should, and reveal their lack of interest in others; consequently, this absence of self-awareness blinds them to these traits.

My friend Dan is the opposite of this type of person. His level of self-awareness is on point. He is considerate, polite, engaging, and sincere. When my wife, Chelsea, first met Dan, the first thing she said to me after he left was, "I can tell Dan is an incredible friend and someone you can count on."

"Why such glowing approval?" I asked.

Chelsea told me Dan was a great listener, asked a lot of questions, and was genuinely interested in what she had to say. Self-aware people don't feel the need to constantly talk. They realize that listening to others and learning from them offers more value.

Are you self-aware enough for it to show in your life and relationships? If not, you can start moving in that direction. There's no shortage of online assessments to help uncover your character traits, relationship patterns, strengths, weaknesses, and leadership styles, to name a few. The Big Five personality test, Myers-Briggs Type Indicator (MBTI), DISC, and Enneagram are just a few tools that can help you learn more about how you're wired and why you do the things you do.

These tests helped Chelsea and me learn how to relate with each other better, as we improved our awareness of ourselves. According to Myers-Briggs, Chelsea is an introvert, so I've learned to recognize her need for alone time and, if she needs it, to help her to get it. The Enneagram showed us that I am an 8, a Challenger, and Chelsea is a 3, an Achiever. Knowing this personality archetype about me has helped my wife understand why I ask a lot of questions; she also helps me find the balance between challenging people and not setting unrealistic expectations for them.

Chelsea is a born athlete, competitive to the bone, and loves to play sports and board games. I make sure we do those things when we have spare time. As an Achiever, Chelsea also tends to be critical of herself. Knowing these traits about her has helped me over the years find (and fine-tune) a balance between helping her optimize her strengths by challenging her limits and not putting too much pressure on her or triggering her self-critical tendencies.

> **THINK THIS:** I am self-aware and choose not to lie to myself.
> **NOT THAT:** I would rather live on autopilot than face hard truths.

When we tune into our thoughts, emotions, and behaviors, incredible things can happen. We can build stronger relationships. We can have less stress in social interactions.[6] We can become more confident and accepting of ourselves.

The benefits of self-awareness materialize in the workplace as well. It improves job-related satisfaction and well-being, increases confidence in performance and promotion potential, boosts communication skills, and helps us become better leaders.[7] Self-awareness has the power to unleash within you something you never expected: your inner superhero.

The Batman Effect

In a groundbreaking study called "The Batman Effect," researchers wanted to determine what type of mindset would improve work ethic in children.[8] They discovered something fascinating. The practice of self-distancing, a type of self-awareness, had a big influence on their success.

In this study, a group of four- and six-year-olds were given a project to work on for ten minutes with the option of taking a break to play a video game. The first group was directed to act naturally, however they normally would. The second group was asked to think about themselves in the third person and be extra self-aware of their actions. The third group was invited to engage in a sort of identity swap—they could become their favorite superhero like Batman or a Disney princess.

The children who were not self-aware had the poorest performance. Children who operated with self-awareness had a 13 percent improvement in work effort. The children who took on a superhero identity had a 23 percent greater performance than the first group and evidenced more diligence and perseverance. This study solidly demonstrated the power of building self-awareness.

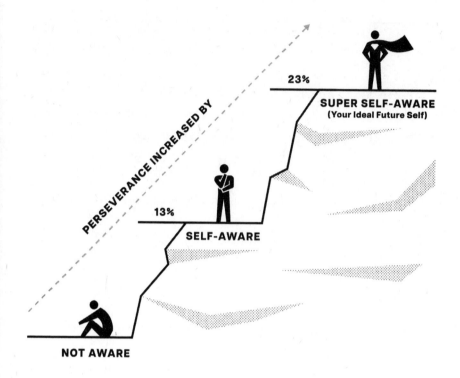

When you are self-aware, you reap the benefits of a special type of superpower—you can *interrupt* unconscious, emotion-driven reactions. For example, in a conversation, you can respond to a perceived threat with impartiality and compassion instead of retaliating in kind.

Do you remember the last time someone said something to you that was mean or that rubbed you the wrong way? Maybe a loved one snapped at you because you left dirty dishes on the table and began a rant of how disrespectful and lazy you are, and how they're getting tired of cleaning up after you.

A response without self-awareness typically goes something like, "What are you talking about? I just stepped away from the table for two minutes. I was coming right back. Why are you acting like such a jerk? It's not a big deal! At least I don't leave the entire house a mess all the time like you do!" A reply like that only fires up more anger, and the dialogue can escalate into much deeper and more volatile territory for both parties.

Throw on a cape of self-awareness, however, and a response to the "lazy and disrespectful" accusation can look something like this (using a nondefensive and sincere tone): "Oh, I'm so sorry. Of course I'll take care of those dishes. Is there anything else bothering you? How can I help?"

When you combine self-awareness and character, you can respond with empathy, wisdom, and love. You're not stuck in insecurity; you accept yourself, including your weaknesses and strengths. Because you're not caught up in defending yourself, you're more in tune with how your choices affect others and with what you want to offer them.

Self-awareness makes you more bulletproof and resistant to threats; it is akin to a superhero characteristic. It packs a special kind of punch. It provides the capacity and pathway to consciously think and act at your best.

Barriers That Block Self-Awareness

The mindshift of self-awareness takes courage and often feels uncomfortable. We may not like what we see when we view ourselves on a deeper level. But without it, our potential is limited. We don't know what we can't see. We can't fix what we're not aware of. And if we don't work on ourselves, we'll stunt our personal growth.

I see four common barriers to self-awareness:

- pride,
- busyness,
- character sabotage, and
- our constant demand to be entertained.

Pride

The first and greatest barrier to self-awareness is pride. When a person believes that they have already thought of or been exposed to all they need to know, they lock themselves into a position of stasis.

The adage "Experience is the best teacher" isn't always true. Studies tell us that the more power or experience a leader holds, the more likely they are to believe they are more virtuous than they actually are.[9] Simply put, power begets pride. Similarly, the same kind of leaders also are more likely to overestimate and overvalue their skills and strengths (including emotional self-awareness, empathy, and trustworthiness) when compared to others' assessment of them.[10] They have a puffed-up sense of their own abilities. Not only does pride come before a fall, as the ancient proverb tells us, but pride shows up because you don't even consider failing a possibility.

When a friend or a colleague talks to you about something you already know, how many times have you said, "Oh, I know," during the interaction? At least once? More times than you're willing to admit? I've made that same mistake many times. Even if I haven't said "I know" out loud, I've communicated it some other way. It can be my instinctive reaction to hearing about things I believe I know because I have studied and lived them out for decades.

I have been guilty of acting like a know-it-all in other ways too. Health and fitness have always been important to me, and I take great pride in knowing the importance of having proper form while lifting weights. A few years ago, I hurt my back doing a dead lift exercise. Turns out, I *didn't* know. While I was recovering, Chelsea respectfully told me I had been doing the exercise with poor form. It was a miracle I hadn't hurt my back earlier. My wife showed me how to do a dead lift the proper way, and I was reminded of a reality I now will never forget: I'm not the only health and wellness expert in our house.

Shoshin is a concept that comes from Zen monks, meaning "beginner's mind,"[11] and I like to think of it as a key quality in self-awareness. Instead of assuming you know something, assume you know nothing. When you do this, you can explore the world with curiosity, awe, and wonder, and learn new things. This is true even if you have some familiarity with a topic. The fact is, *we don't know what we don't know.* Not acknowledging that truth only puffs us up with pride.

There's another truth that might be hard to swallow, but it is critically necessary to grasp. In the previous chapter, we talked about our great potential for good in our pursuit of becoming. And if *that's* true, then the flip side is just as true—you and I also have potential for evil. Admitting we are capable of not-so-great behavior and action demands vulnerability, humility, and courage.

Pride keeps us from being aware of our capacity for good and evil and thus prevents us from becoming the people we want to be. A healthy understanding of our capacity for both evil and good is necessary. Jordan Peterson, bestselling author and professor emeritus of psychology at the University of Toronto, said, "I don't think that you have any insight whatsoever into your capacity for good until you have some well-developed insight into your capacity for evil."[12]

When we refuse to take responsibility for our vices and avoid painful self-reflection, we will find ourselves on a destructive path.

Imagine your worst qualities, dependencies, or habits. Let's say you're hot-tempered. Or maybe you're drawn to the occasional cocktail that's recently become much more than occasional. You may think, *Well, my anger issue is not that bad.* Or *I only drink after five o'clock.* Now magnify those things times ten. Play out in your mind what might happen. Could you end up divorced? Or perhaps an alcoholic? Or, if you don't get a handle on your drinking, even get behind the wheel drunk one night and get into an accident that claims the life of another person? Bringing to light both the good and bad parts of ourselves diminishes pride and illuminates what needs to be changed so we can grow.

It is crucial, even if it is shocking, to realize the evil we are capable of. When combined with the realization that you also have the potential to do extraordinary things to bless the world, it empowers you to make better choices.

Busyness

The second barrier to increasing your capacity for self-awareness is busyness. Chances are, if you ask someone how they are doing on any particular day, their response will be some form of "Good, just real busy." We're running to and from something all the time. We're dropping the kids off at soccer practice, then running home to finish the project for work, then running to the school to deliver cookies for the bake sale, then running around the block to get in some exercise, then running to the downtown office to catch the team meeting. With all this movement, who has time for self-awareness?

The answer is simple—*you*! No one can afford *not* to make time for self-reflection. Stop. Be still. Reflect on whether you are working on the right things at the right time. Are you focusing your energy on the tasks that are most important, or are you in the vicious cycle of constantly putting out fires? Sit with your answers for a bit. Then make the shifts you need to make.

Character Sabotage

Third, character sabotage (or being overwhelmed by vices) is another barrier to self-awareness. We discussed how important character is in the last chapter. Open any news site, and you're bound to find a high-profile figure with great talent or many accomplishments who lost it all because of a moral failure or an addiction that spiraled out of control. When your character is compromised, self-awareness is out of reach. If you tend to gossip about a coworker, are married but look at other people with lust, have an unhealthy attachment to money or achievements, or have a tough time controlling your temper, it's a sign that your capacity for self-awareness is being threatened.

These vices are much like blinders. Just as blinders restrict a horse's vision, vices restrict who you really are and limit you from reaching your full potential. (We'll get into this more in mindshift 8: Bust Vices by Building Virtues.)

Our Constant Demand to Be Entertained

Finally, our culture prioritizes entertainment, which limits the time and energy necessary for increasing self-awareness. For instance, according to one survey, 60 percent of people use social media not to connect with others or to learn but to be entertained.[13] And do we really need

THINK THIS, NOT THAT

studies to tell us about the countless hours that are wasted playing video games, binge-watching television shows, or going down a rabbit hole of YouTube videos because the spike in dopamine feels so good in the moment? When people lack purpose (which we'll discuss more in the next chapter), they're more inclined to trade their love of learning and personal growth for immediate gratification.

What's your biggest barrier to self-awareness? Is it any of the big four I mentioned? Be honest with yourself so you can start becoming who you were meant to be.

Activate Self-Awareness

Now that you know the barriers to self-awareness, I want to present you with three tools to overcome them.

First, *create your version of peace and quiet.* Multiple studies have linked chronic exposure to noise to serious health and learning problems in both children and adults. Gary Evans, a Cornell University psychologist and expert on environmental stress, conducted a study on hundreds of children who lived near an airport compared to those who lived in a quieter area. He and his colleagues concluded that the children who were exposed to excessive noise, like planes flying overhead, had a noticeable deficit in their reading ability and long-term memory.[14] Even the noise of everyday commuting, whether it involves the chorus of hundreds of speeding motor vehicles, honking horns, or the thunder of subways, is enough to trigger stress pathways in the brain that can lead to inflammation and even heart problems.[15]

Duke University regenerative biologist Imke Kirste agrees that silence is golden. She discovered that two hours of silence per day encourages cell growth in the hippocampus, the part of the brain related to memory development.[16]

Start now by getting off social media and turning off distractions like screens, television, unnecessary outside static, and internal dialogue, and be still, even if only for a few minutes a day. Take a deep breath and just be. It may be awkward at first, but you'll soon find it to be regenerative.

Second, *recognize your thoughts by writing them down.* Dr. James Pennebaker, professor of psychology at the University of Texas, has led the modern writing therapy movement since the late 1980s. He has written several books about the cathartic experience of writing, advocating for its potential to help people heal from trauma.[17] Pennebaker discovered that those who wrote about highly emotional experiences were happier and less anxious.[18]

Try taking a few moments to reflect on and write down any memories that still bug you today. What is that event, conversation, or experience that has stuck with you and negatively impacted your mindset and decision-making? What bothers you about it? What can you learn from the experience that can influence your life and the lives of others in a positive way?

Finally, *create purposeful exposure.* I've found when we intentionally expose ourselves to experiences outside our comfort zone, we cultivate more humility and a greater appreciation for what we have. My experience in Ethiopia opened my eyes to a world outside of the comfortable one I was familiar with. One of the best ways to cure entitlement is to serve others who truly lack, whether it be volunteering for an organization like Habitat for Humanity, going on a mission trip to provide basic needs for people (like food, clean water, or education), or learning facts, like how 13 percent of people in the world live without electricity[19] and how more than 2.2 million people in America alone do not have running water and basic plumbing in their homes.[20] Exposure to harsh realities awakens us to act for the good of others. It's not about shock value; it's about being moved from ingratitude to compassion, from idleness to action.

Living on autopilot is easy. But you can gain so much more from facing hard truths that can open your eyes to new and better possibilities. It's time to become aware of your strengths, weaknesses, and opportunities, and figure out what is standing in your way.

An Exercise in Building Self-Awareness

As the leader of a company, I can't help but make the association between what it takes to grow a healthy, thriving organization and what it takes to grow a healthy, thriving internal life, and I've come across tools that help with both.

For instance, I've used a business tool called SWOT that was developed at Stanford in the 1970s to help identify the internal and external aspects of a company needing improvement. Turns out, this tool is just as effective when applied to character and personal development. Whether you need to decide on a different career track, improve your relationship skills, become a better parent, or find some momentum to catapult yourself out of stagnation, this tool can help get you closer to your target. I've found it to be a valuable asset in unlocking self-awareness and, in particular, uncovering blind spots.

SWOT stands for:

- **S**trengths
- **W**eaknesses
- **O**pportunities
- **T**hreats

I've adapted this tool here for your personal journey, beyond the business aspect of life. As you think of each component of SWOT, think of your answers in terms of both character and skill.

1. *List your **strengths**.* Ask yourself the following questions to help gauge your answers: What abilities and skills do I have? What am I better at than most people? What do others see as my

character and skill strengths? What positive personality traits do I have?

2. *Know your* **weaknesses**. Ask yourself, What are my bad habits? What would others say I can improve? What valid criticism have I received? What do I usually avoid doing because I lack the confidence? Brutal honesty and courage are necessary to effectively answer these questions. If you're having trouble thinking of your weaknesses, think of the most successful people you admire who have strong character and list qualities in them that you lack and you'd like to emulate.

3. *Look out for* **opportunities**. List the positive factors that can give you an advantage and improve your situation. This could look like opportunities to serve in your local community, be around people with similar values and goals, gain more knowledge through attending a workshop or finding a mentor, or even apply for a new job.

4. *Avoid or eliminate* **threats**. List the external forces that hinder your personal growth and keep you from fulfilling your potential. Threats could come in the form of people, situations, life events, even yourself. Ask yourself, Are there people in my life who exacerbate my weaknesses? What reduces my motivation and productivity? What is the biggest external barrier to becoming the person I want to be?

Your threats may be related in some way to your weaknesses. Becoming aware of both can help you identify and eliminate what is preventing you from growing and moving forward. You may realize you've been hanging around the wrong crowd and need to find more supportive friends who will encourage you and lovingly tell you the truth. You may realize you need to give up previous commitments, spend your time differently, or avoid distractions in culture that are leading you away from high-level character (threats can also come as distractions). The key is awareness.

THINK THIS, NOT THAT

This SWOT analysis will help you open the portal to self-awareness. You may uncover things about yourself that are tough to look at and to envision changing. Welcome to the jungle of growth. It's certainly not an easy space to explore, but it is worth it.

For some of us, engaging a self-awareness mindset comes naturally. For others, it demands a conscious decision to step outside what's familiar and explore the subconscious mind through lots of effort and struggle. Don't let the hard work intimidate or stop you. According to Socrates, "The unexamined life is not worth living."[21]

As you work through SWOT, you might notice something unexpected. The exercise may ruffle the feathers of your pride. But pride doesn't bolster personal growth; it stunts it. Like we said earlier, you don't know what you don't know. If you sense your pride being threatened, know that it is a positive thing; it means humility is making her debut appearance. That is what happens when we are willing to see ourselves with accuracy. We realize, in the spirit of humility, that we don't like everything we see and that some things demand change.

Erwin McManus wrote, "Humility is not about having a low self-image or poor self-esteem. Humility is about self-awareness. . . . If you see yourself for who you are and embrace it honestly, humility is the natural result."[22]

Don't mistake humility for an open door to shame or self-loathing. It is, in fact, a portal of opportunity to change, grow, and increase your capacity to become a better person by becoming aware not only of yourself but of others.

Greater Self-Awareness Leads to Less Self-Interest

When you become self-aware, you start to realize you aren't the only "self" out there. Honest self-awareness leads less to navel-gazing and more to noticing others and what they are going through, as well as our roles in community life. It's what Goleman's emotional intelligence model calls *social awareness*. My trip to Ethiopia reminded me that life is bigger than just myself. When I came back to the US, I became more aware of people in need, noticing and looking right in the eyes of people panhandling at stoplights and giving them some money for a meal, recognizing that most of my complaints (like having to wait in line for thirty minutes for a Five Daughters Bakery donut) were first world problems.

A friend of mine takes his three children on mission trips all over the word so his children can witness the suffering of others and do something about it. This has developed in them a compassion they wouldn't otherwise possess. I aim to do the same with my children one day.

> **THINK THIS:** Self-awareness can motivate me to change things for the better.
> **NOT THAT:** It's easier to ignore what's really going on because I can't do anything about it anyway.

Being aware of yourself and others compels you to stop and look at the needs surrounding you, not turn the other way. It frees you from the grip of self-interest. It helps you view humanity through a bigger lens rather than the microcosm of the familiar world you live in.

Better still, awareness prompts you to do something about the plight of someone else. You don't want to miss the opportunity to alleviate the suffering of another person, so you take action. You give up your seat on the subway. You hold someone's hand and listen. You volunteer at your community food bank. You tutor someone for free. You become aware of the needs of others, and you fill in the gaps. When you are aware, you immediately become positioned to do meaningful things. Don't just think of what becoming more aware can do for *you*; think of what it might do for *others*.

Step outside yourself and examine your level of self- and others-focused awareness. What is it that you are not aware of? A hidden skill in someone you know? The emotional needs of a loved one? Maybe even the presence of the divine?

Do you spend any amount of time numbing out? Is there something you haven't been aware of—maybe an opportunity? Your potential? A person in need? Shift your life forward by awakening to truths you may have been overlooking or trying to forget—they're often the same truths that bring you closer to becoming the person you are meant to be.

Become self-aware to get where you need to go.

Ignorance → Self-Awareness

FIND A WHY OR RISK
WASTING IT ALL

When I was in eighth grade, my mom was diagnosed with stage 4 breast cancer that had spread to her lymph nodes. This came as a shock to my family and me. We couldn't understand how my forty-one-year-old mom, a swim instructor and gym teacher, the picture of health and wellness, was sick with a life-threatening disease. My mom chose the conventional route of treatment—a mastectomy followed by four cycles of chemotherapy. I'll never forget seeing clumps of her sandy-blonde hair fall to her bathroom floor and noticing she looked like she'd aged twenty years in two weeks. I almost didn't recognize her. I remember thinking three things at the time: (1) I wanted to help her get well, (2) I didn't want anyone else to suffer the way she was, and (3) there must be a better way.

Although Mom was declared "cancer free" after the harsh treatments, her health continued to spiral downward. While she recovered from chemotherapy and returned to her job, she still felt lousy. Mom struggled with a weak immune system and was diagnosed with chronic fatigue syndrome, and she also suffered from a mood disorder and was prescribed antidepressant and antianxiety medications.

Seeing my mom struggle with her health inspired me to begin

studying nutrition and functional medicine (as opposed to conventional medicine), which focuses on finding the root cause of disease. This became my purpose in life.

Ten years after my mom's cancer diagnosis, I was twenty-five years old and close to graduating and opening my own clinic when I received a call from her.

"I've got bad news, Josh," Mom said in tears. "My oncologist told me they found a tumor on my lungs that was two and a half centimeters. He wants to do surgery and start radiation right away."

I encouraged my mom as best as I could and prayed with her. The next day, I flew from Florida back to Ohio to help Mom with a health program to treat the root of many of her issues. The goal was for her to change her diet, overcome toxic thoughts, reduce stress, and cleanse her system.

For the next four months, my mom stopped eating processed food and instead juiced fresh vegetables, took numerous nutritional supplements (turmeric, astragalus, reishi, vitamin D, etc.), spent time outside every day, and started the practices of gratitude, visualization, and prayer. All these new protocols helped her form a positive mindset. My mom followed this regimen for four months and then returned to her oncologist for blood work and imaging. The doctor's response was astounding.

"What's happened is highly unusual," he began. "We don't see cancer shrink very often." Mom's largest tumor had shrunk by 52 percent. The oncologist told my mother, "Keep doing what you are doing, because whatever it is, it's working." Her medical team decided to hold off on surgery, and nine months later my mom was cancer free and in complete remission.

At the time of this writing, my mom is sixty-eight years old and incredibly active. She water-skis, hikes with her friends, and takes her grandkids to Disney World. My mom had a mindshift that her cancer diagnosis was not a death sentence but instead an opportunity to be more intentional about her health and inspire others with her courage and faith.

The experience of helping my mom heal crystallized my life's mission as a medical professional. Years later, I opened my own clinic in Nashville, Tennessee, and brought what I learned with my mom to my work there, helping thousands of patients heal using natural medicine.

Mom showed me that a crisis can either paralyze and destroy you or unlock an opportunity within you. Helping her also led me to identify one of my individual purposes—to use food as medicine—under my grand purpose. I believe that all of us share a grand purpose, which is to love others (people and God) and to turn this planet into a paradise.

Before you can become the person you were born to be, you must determine your purpose. The best version of yourself always starts with the *why*.

> **THINK THIS:** My life has value, meaning, and a specific purpose to make this world a better place.
> **NOT THAT:** I have no purpose and no power to make a difference.

Why Your *Why* Matters

Why do you exist? Why do you do what you do each day?

The answers to these questions have everything to do with purpose. Purpose is "the reason for which something exists or . . . is made."[1] Simply put, it is the *why* for existence.

In the big picture, we all want to live a life that matters and makes a difference. How do we do this? By alleviating suffering in the world and helping others reach their full potential. This principle can be seen in the top tier of the hierarchy of needs developed by Abraham Maslow, one of the founders of humanistic psychology. He saw the needs of a human being as a pyramid, ranging from the foundational basics (our personal needs to sustain life, such as food and water) to the top level of *self-transcendence* (becoming the best version of ourselves, which pour into others and help them grow). According to this pyramid, our purpose includes helping people fulfill their needs.

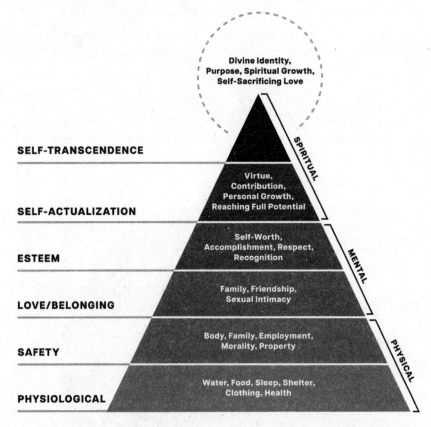

DIVINE IDENTITY, PURPOSE, SPIRITUAL GROWTH, SELF-SACRIFICING LOVE

SELF-TRANSCENDENCE — SPIRITUAL

SELF-ACTUALIZATION — Virtue, Contribution, Personal Growth, Reaching Full Potential

ESTEEM — Self-Worth, Accomplishment, Respect, Recognition — MENTAL

LOVE/BELONGING — Family, Friendship, Sexual Intimacy

SAFETY — Body, Family, Employment, Morality, Property — PHYSICAL

PHYSIOLOGICAL — Water, Food, Sleep, Shelter, Clothing, Health

If you've ever suffered from depression, a physical ailment, or the loss of someone or something you loved—or have walked beside a friend on that path—you know what a desperate and agonizing experience it is. When you see others hurting, you can help ease their burden by offering an encouraging word, bringing a bowl of chicken soup, or simply showing up regularly.

A big part of your life's purpose is seeing the pain or potential in others and acting with compassion to meet their needs. It is also helping them ascend to the top of Maslow's hierarchy and equipping them to help *others* rise to this higher mindset. When you can motivate people to engage in high-level living, in which they add value to others, you are in essence changing the world, one person at a time.

I believe that God gave humanity a common purpose—to love others and to turn this planet into a paradise. This was revealed in my study of the Judeo-Christian faith. It may surprise you to hear that biblical philosophies played a pivotal role in helping to eliminate slavery, reduce poverty, and expand women's rights.

Universal Purpose = to love others (God and people) and to turn this planet into a paradise

We also are created with individual purposes that include the combination of our character development (becoming) and our skills. We have different individual purposes in the myriad roles we play in our lives—as a spouse, parent, leader, manager, friend, caretaker, professional, artist, and so on. My individual purposes center on my roles as a husband, father, mentor, and business leader, to name a few. For instance, one is "to raise purpose-driven leaders." Another is "to be a husband who supports my wife and helps her dreams come true." Here is a simple formula:

Individual Purpose = grow in character and skill to alleviate suffering and help others reach their full potential

Let's imagine this formula in action. Have you ever been feeling down but then you heard a song that put a smile on your face? The composer, musicians, and performer of that piece of music did more than just write, play, and sing a song. Through expressing their natural giftings and love for the arts, they brought joy to others—at the time, you. That's purpose!

Think about a teacher you had in elementary school who not only helped you pass a test but also helped remedy a learning disability you struggled with and optimize your abilities to continue succeeding in school. Or the coach who stressed the importance of integrity and gave you life advice you use to this day. They had purpose!

Consider what this world would be like if some of the greatest world changers like Mother Teresa and Mahatma Gandhi had not fulfilled their purpose by using their unique gifts.

At the same time, don't think of purpose as something that's solely consigned to people who initiate global movements or are household names. Purpose can be found anywhere, in whatever job you hold or roles you have. There's a story told about President John F. Kennedy during a visit to the NASA space center in 1962. When the president noticed a janitor carrying a broom, he stopped what he was doing and approached the man.

"Hi, I'm Jack Kennedy," he said. "What are you doing?"

"Well, Mr. President," the janitor responded, "I'm helping put a man on the moon."[2]

The janitor was doing more than mopping up the messes of others; he was helping history unfold. That's the power of knowing your purpose.

No matter what you do, even if it's sweeping a floor or ringing up a purchase, if you recognize your *why*, you add value to the people, the community, and the world around you every single day. And that makes each day worth living.

The Japanese word *ikigai* is translated into the English words "alive" and "worth" and signifies purpose.[3] In Japanese culture, purpose is fulfilled when the following four facets intersect in what you do in life—not just in your career but in the contributions you make as a human being to the people around you: (1) what you love, (2) what you are good at, (3) what your family/community/world needs, and (4) what brings the greatest reward (i.e., personal satisfaction, money). If you live without purpose, you are likely not using your skills, which means not only do you miss out on the joy of contribution, but the world misses out on the value you bring with your existence. There is less love, service, and leadership, and fewer ideas, songs, books, and art in your family, in your community, and on the entire planet. What a terrible thought.

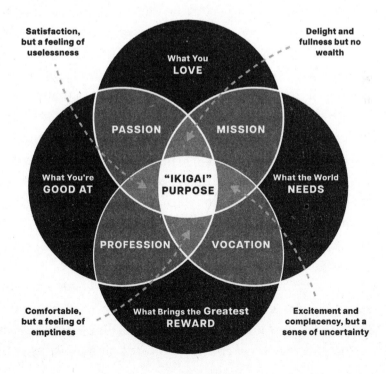

Don't think that your life is pointless; think about what you can offer that can bring purpose into your life and into the lives of others. Finding your *why* is more than an empty platitude. It is a tool to help others and impact the world that, sadly, many people don't even use.

Levels of Purpose

Did you know that, according to one study, only about 25 percent of Americans have a clear sense of purpose? Forty percent don't know or have no opinion on the matter.[4] I find this mind-boggling considering the amount of research that points to how important purpose is for a fulfilling and physically healthy life.[5]

I see individual purpose (or lack thereof) being engaged on five levels:

LEVEL 1: I am nothing. My purpose is inconsequential and unimportant. Much of my existence revolves around sitting on the couch and binge-watching TV shows/movies or playing video games. All my goals are self-serving.

LEVEL 2: I do the bare minimum to survive. I work to pay bills and provide a roof over my head. I look forward to coming home and relaxing. I get done what I need to but lack joy. My energy and enthusiasm levels are low. All my goals are self-serving.

LEVEL 3: I don't hate my job, but I don't love it either. I enjoy family time and barbecue with friends on the weekends. I have fun on occasion but lack meaning and significance. (This is equal to a neutral level of purpose.)

LEVEL 4: I add value to others. I have an idea of my purpose and do things that matter. I know my worth and contribute my skills to benefit my family and my community. I seek to better myself.

LEVEL 5: I maximize my potential by fulfilling my purpose in all areas of life. I know what my unique skills are and use them to better the lives of others. I get excited when I wake up in the morning. I regularly revisit my purpose and adjust my priorities accordingly. I have great hope in my future and the future of the world.

We all should strive for Level 5. Where do you see yourself? What needs to change for you to start transforming into a Level 5 purpose of living?

Often what stands in the way is a plateau, a season where personal growth has been interrupted or is stagnant. This is what Level-3-or-under living looks like. You stop working toward a goal. You become more focused on yourself than other people. You are bored most of the time. Passion and excitement seem like things reserved for influencers and others in the spotlight. You feel restless and sometimes on edge. A lack of motivation makes it hard to figure out how or what to change.

If that's you, I have good news for you. But first, I want to close the loop on what happens if you don't change. You can expect much of the same dull existence we just discussed, along with some serious physical problems, such as depression,[6] high incidences of sleep disturbances,[7] a higher risk of strokes and heart attacks,[8] and even premature death.[9] Having purpose can literally be a matter of life or death.

Now for the good news. You can change. You don't have to wait for a big event or spend money on an expensive retreat to break out of your purpose plateau and ascend to a higher level of living. You can design your own breakthrough by determining your *why* and begin living at Level 5. The key to adopting a mindshift of purpose is to understand the two fundamental components of purpose: (1) meaning and (2) an emphasis on serving others.

The Right Kind of Happy

Many people seem to be attached to the idea that purpose relates to being happy. This happiness involves a feeling of temporary pleasure that comes from short-term gratification and pain avoidance, or what philosophers and psychologists term the *hedonistic* approach. Think of the dopamine hit that comes from hitting the slot machines, impulse buying, or eating your favorite cheat food.

The problem with the spike of this feel-good chemical is that it doesn't last. The idea that purpose is found in pleasure fixes can't be further from the truth. Studies prove that trying to manufacture this feeling of happiness actually leads to lower well-being and depression.[10] So what's the answer?

It's not indulgent happiness that will bring us purpose but rather a meaningful life—having a positive impact on someone, on even your own life, or on the planet.

Imagine for a minute the way this feels: You finish a tough workout you didn't feel like doing in the first place, but that was forty-five minutes ago. Now, as you're stretching and beads of sweat drip down the sides of your face, your muscles fatigued, you feel on top of the world. Within you beats a deep sense of accomplishment. You are proud of yourself, energized, and motivated to continue your day. That's what meaningful feels like. You committed to something hard for a good cause, and you did it.

Have you ever found the perfect gift for a friend? Maybe you spent weeks or even months searching high and low for this very special thing and finally you found it. You can't wait to see the look on your friend's face when he opens the package. When he does, his surprise and gratitude are even better than you envisioned. You feel much joy and gratification in that moment. Your friend's smile and gratitude are truly the best thanks you could ever get. That's deeply meaningful because you stepped outside of yourself to bring joy to another person.

If you look around and consider the people who are the happiest with how their lives turned out, chances are they are the ones whose lives had the most meaning. True life satisfaction boils down to a commitment to cultivating meaning.

> **THINK THIS:** Purpose is about building a meaningful life.
> **NOT THAT:** Purpose is about being happy.

Meaning—and Even Suffering—Builds Purpose

In *Man's Search for Meaning,* a book written in an astounding nine days, Austrian neurologist and psychiatrist Viktor Frankl tells the story of how he survived the Holocaust in Nazi concentration camps by finding meaning through the experience. Before and after the war, Frankl dedicated his life to the theory of psychology called *logotherapy,* Greek for "will to meaning," or desire to live a meaningful life. He used this system of thinking to survive the horror of being imprisoned in four concentration camps over three years. And even more remarkably, he was able to help others survive the nightmare.

Frankl believed that all human beings need to find meaning in what they do and experience. Once we do that, he posited, we will be able to endure even the worst of things. Frankl wrote, "If there is a meaning in life at all, then there must be a meaning in suffering. Suffering is an ineradicable part of life, even as fate and death. . . . The way in which a man accepts his fate and all the suffering it entails, the way in which he takes up his cross, gives him ample opportunity—even under the most difficult circumstances—to add a deeper meaning to his life."[11]

If we do not attach meaning to our lives, we will not be able to function at our best, sometimes not at all. Living with meaning is having a mindset that you, and what you do, matters. Even your pain matters and can be used for good and to further your life purpose. In Frankl's book, which has sold more than sixteen million copies to date, he made the connection between the prisoners who began to lose their purpose and those who were the first to die: "The prisoner who had lost faith in the future—his future—was doomed. With his loss of belief in the future, he also lost his spiritual hold; he let himself decline and became subject to mental and physical decay."[12]

When my mom got cancer the second time, I was afraid she might lose hope and purpose, so I dropped everything to work with her to create her own. One of the things that means the most to her is her family. Although my mom didn't have grandchildren at the time, she pictured what it would be like to nurture and spend time with them and even take them to Disney World. I helped my mom envision a future of doing just that, which gave her a "why" to fight and beat a deadly disease. When she felt depressed or anxious, the very thought of being able to care for and influence her family gave her the will to live and do whatever it took to persevere.

Frankl was convinced, from his research, experience as a prisoner in the Nazi concentration camps, and loss of many loved ones in the Holocaust, including his wife, that pursuing a sense of meaning in life was necessary not only to maintain the will to live but also to thrive and avoid chronic boredom and aimlessness.[13] In his book, Frankl often echoed the words of Friedrich Nietzsche, "He who has a why to live for can bear with almost any how."[14]

What does a life of meaning look like? These elements are common in those who know their *why* in life.

LIFE VALUE: You know that you and others are valuable, worthy, and have significance.

PRINCIPLED LIVING: You have life principles and a life philosophy that guide your decisions and life path.

GOALS AND ACHIEVEMENT: You have goals, and when you've achieved those goals, you enjoy a sense of satisfaction.

EXCITEMENT: Your life has a sense of excitement, curiosity, and wonder.

GROWTH: You are progressing in life and feel like you are experiencing personal growth or career growth.

COMMUNITY CONNECTION: You have a group of people you

feel connected to and share similar values and passions with. You feel like you have a family or tribe that has your back.

CONTRIBUTION AND IMPACT: You are doing something that feels meaningful at work, in your home, or as a form of service that is making the world a better place.

BIGGER THAN YOU: You are living for something bigger than yourself, something that fulfills your life purpose and truly matters.

Read through this list one more time, this time reflecting on your own life. Which areas need some attention? Do you need to deepen your social connections to gain a sense of belonging? Maybe you need to start focusing on volunteering your time and effort to a local cause. Perhaps you're stuck in a cycle of anxiety or apathy and long for more joy.

Pick one or two areas in which you feel stalled. What is one action you can take, starting now, to strengthen that area and begin to build meaning into your life? As you continue reading this book, we'll discuss the building blocks that will help you connect to your purpose.

Purpose Centers on Others, Not Self

In the previous chapter, we explored how self-awareness leads to awareness of others. Similarly, our purpose is linked to our relationships with others. Human beings are wired for relationship and community. (We'll discuss this more in mindshift 6: Assemble a Team to Fulfill Your Dreams.) In order to live a life of purpose and meaning, you have to shift from being self-focused to others-focused.

Many of us approach life with self-oriented goals, such as gaining a certain number of followers on social media or earning a certain amount of money. But, according to research, self-oriented goals can often have a negative effect.[15] If you believe that having one hundred thousand Instagram followers will make you happy for the wrong motive (because you think it makes you more popular and liked, not because it gives you the platform to use your influence for good), you may hit that goal and realize you don't feel any more connected and consequently get depressed. If, however, you set goals that are family- or community-focused, like seeing your kids work hard and achieve something difficult or giving your time to serve others, you will experience a deeper sense of meaning.

Another study demonstrated how college students who had a desire to help others were found to have greater well-being (including personal growth, integrity, and purpose) years later compared to students who did not.[16] The results illustrated the words of American writer Leo Rosten: "The purpose of life is not to be happy—but to matter, to be productive, to be useful, to have it make some difference that you lived at all."[17] Helping others brings purpose to life.

I think of my grandfather Howard and how he often went to the hospital to visit with someone who was sick, just to talk to them, pray with them, or bring them their favorite meal. He brought me with him a few times. Watching him love on those who were suffering, I learned the value of empathy and compassion. I also witnessed purpose in action and realized that serving others is one of life's biggest blessings.

Consider the last time you did something altruistic or met the need of another person. Maybe you spent a weekend volunteering at a local food pantry. Maybe you opted to forgo your night of relaxing to encourage a neighbor who'd been going through a crisis. How did it make you feel? Chances are, you experienced a heightened sense of well-being, a feeling of belonging, a renewed perspective on life, and a boost to your self-confidence.

Psychologists refer to this as the "helper's high." Altruism has been shown to produce the same chemicals in the brain as a mild version of a morphine high.[18] When someone gives, the part of the brain that lights up in an MRI is the same region that is activated in response to pleasure or receiving rewards.[19] We are created to help others.

When my mother got cancer, I wanted to help her and others who go through a similar journey. As I got older and began to define my own individual purpose, I was excited to be working toward something. Having a purpose motivated me through school and kept life exciting. But at one point my schedule became extremely busy, so much so that I lost sight of my purpose for a time. It took a serious accident for me to pause and not only reawaken but further develop my individual purpose.

A Renewed Sense of Purpose

I doubt most of you reading this book have zero sense of purpose. More likely, what I've found is that most people get distracted from their purpose. Perhaps you would benefit from better defining and prioritizing your *why* amid a life of responsibilities and an overbooked schedule, like I did.

In my first year of studying to be a doctor, I started losing sight of my purpose. I started thinking more about the extrinsic benefits of the career I'd chosen, like how much money I would make, vacation time, and the golfing and waterskiing I could do with a shortened workweek. As a result, I became a little lazier in school.

One day, while training for a triathlon, I was out cycling. I got hit by a truck from behind and sustained serious injuries. As I recovered in bed, a friend brought me a book about health and wellness to read. I'm not being dramatic when I say that the book changed the trajectory of my life. Although my mom's cancer had put me on the path to my purpose, I needed a reminder that my purpose wasn't about making my life more comfortable or easier; it was about helping others get healthy.

Being immobile gave me time to pause and reflect on my purpose. I started to think about how I was spending my time and whether I was doing things that really mattered. I realized I was doing good things, but I could do greater, more meaningful things during my time in school.

Lying in bed, I returned to the thought that I was alive to love others and turn this planet into a paradise and determined that I could make a bigger impact than I had been envisioning. Sure, I could help people and

THINK THIS, NOT THAT

still take a few days off to play golf and water-ski—there's nothing wrong with fitting in recreational activities. But I realized I wanted to do more.

I started doing two things: (1) volunteering for a local doctor, whom I respected and admired, and (2) mentoring high schoolers at a local church and leading a growth group. When I did these things, my purpose reignited, and my life became full of meaning.

My vision expanded and presented new missions I had never imagined possible. Instead of settling for one career path, I began to think bigger. I didn't want to just be a doctor; now I wanted to open my own clinic to help save and transform lives. Over time, this mission unfolded into a bigger mission of starting a website to educate people on natural health, then building a supplement company to widen access to the world's greatest superfoods, and now helping others be their best in the areas of servant leadership, business, purpose, and personal growth.

This experience has taught me that our individual purpose is not something we just think about once, write down, and put away. Instead, we must constantly keep it in focus, nourish it, and expand it, knowing it likely will evolve and change over time. Who knows where your individual purpose may lead you?

What's Possible?

Imagine a world in which every single human being on the planet operated in the fullness of their grand and individual purposes. What would that look like? Paradise.

It is no mistake that the story of humankind as recorded in the ancient Scriptures begins in a garden[20] and ends in a magnificent garden city with creation restored.[21] Think about what that heaven on earth would look like. Picture before you a land bordered with towering mountains that slope into green valleys. Pristine clear-blue lakes dot golden plains. Waterfalls rush down mossy cliffs of limestone and granite. Groves of trees with silver bark and golden leaves glow as they bask in the warm sun. I envision it almost like J. R. R. Tolkien's Lothlorien or Rivendell, the picturesque Elven town and realm.

Your home is an oasis of your choosing, a house cut into the slant of a lush hillside or nestled on the shore of a translucent lake. This is your dream haven. Not only does this paradise look breathtaking and defy your imagination with its natural beauty, but the land is bountiful. The soil is rich and fertile, and every kind of fruit and vegetable you crave lies within your grasp.

The land is not the only thing that flourishes. People thrive as well. They are the best version of themselves, operating in their unique gifting and becoming extraordinary.

Does this sound like a pipe dream? I don't believe so. I see it as the vision of what we are meant to move toward.

My friend and business partner Jordan Rubin and I own four thousand acres of organic land on which we practice regenerative agriculture and are building a forest of superfood trees to feed people in need. We've already planted one million of them, including moringa, mulberry, and goji. When Jordan and I bought this land, much of it was rocky soil, not ideal for farming. When we implemented silvopasture (combining trees, forage, and animal grazing trees), for example, the soil's quality and fertility increased. This is one way we are doing our part to turn this planet into a paradise. Research demonstrates that you can turn deserts into rainforests through regenerative agriculture.[22] This farming practice can enhance ecosystem biodiversity, produce nutrient-dense food, and even improve climate health.[23]

Most of us want to make this world a better place. Practically speaking, this can be as simple as recycling your trash, buying organic, not using chemicals in your home or office, or starting a garden in your backyard. Remember that you don't need to make a grand gesture or have a global platform to make a difference. You just need to use your skills to serve, love, lead, teach, create, and innovate within your family and community. As you continually become a person you are proud to be and live with purpose, your actions will have ripple effects that leave a legacy.

What can you do to fulfill your role in bringing paradise a little closer to earth?

What's Your Why?

Decades ago, a nineteen-year-old outdoor adventurer and self-taught blacksmith named Yvon Chouinard began creating his own rock-climbing gear. Though he had never aspired to become a businessman, he started selling parts out of his car so he could continue doing what he really loved: surfing and climbing. Chouinard's small business grew beyond his expectation. By his early thirties, what became known as Chouinard Equipment was the largest climbing tool company in the US.[24]

In 1973, Chouinard founded Patagonia, an outdoor apparel company. He was resolute in doing business his way, with sustainability at the forefront of his mission. Chouinard was determined not only to use Patagonia as an avenue to make money but also, according to their purpose statement, to be "in business to save our home planet."[25] He did this by establishing local and global efforts to help protect the environment and each year giving away 1 percent of sales to nonprofit organizations.

In 2021, Chouinard began to plan for his succession. Rather than pursuing the conventional approaches of selling the company or taking it public, he created a third option. In September of 2022, Chouinard announced that, instead of "going public," Patagonia would "go purpose,"[26] which for him meant giving away the entire company to a trust and nonprofit. Outside of money reinvested into the business, all future profits would be used to help fight climate change and defend nature. In an open letter, Chouinard wrote, "Instead of extracting value from nature and transforming it into wealth for investors, we'll use the wealth Patagonia creates to protect the source of all wealth."[27]

Chouinard is not the only businessperson to initiate such a bold philanthropic move. In an op-ed piece published the following month, Hobby Lobby founder and CEO David Green announced that, inspired by Chouinard's purpose-driven initiative, he would give up ownership of his business. His reason? "I chose God," he said.[28]

"I was just a steward, a manager of what God had entrusted me," Green continued. "God was the true owner of my business. That steward-ship gave me a greater responsibility. I wasn't supposed to take the profits of the business and use them for myself. I also had a responsibility to the employees that God had put in my charge. This is why our company pays a minimum wage of $18.50 per hour, why we close on Sunday (which had been our most profitable day of business), and why we close by 8 p.m. every day."[29]

"Going purpose" isn't something only rich businesspeople do. It is what every human being is created to do.

Think back to the five levels of purpose we talked about on pages 68 and 69. Where did your level of purpose fall on that scale? Are you between two levels? I challenge you to reach Level 5. Living at Level 5 will help you sleep better,[30] be physically healthier,[31] have a lower risk of depression,[32] better manage stress,[33] and even live longer.[34]

Hold on, there's more. When you contribute your character and use your unique skills to help ease the suffering of others, you also will enjoy a deep sense of meaning that is more fulfilling and lasting than a dopamine hit or fleeting pleasure. Getting out of bed in the morning will be met with optimistic anticipation instead of a groan or the slap of a Snooze button.

Isn't it time to start getting excited about waking up and imagining what's possible? You can begin to write a new life story by moving toward your purpose.

If you don't know your purpose, take a few minutes and try answering the following question:

Why do you exist?

To: _____

_____

THINK THIS, NOT THAT

Remember the formula I mentioned earlier in this chapter for discovering your individual purpose?

Individual Purpose = grow in character and skill to alleviate suffering and help others reach their full potential

Think about your strengths related to your character, skills, and talents. Any insights you gained in the last chapter, on self-awareness, can come into play here, especially if you've discovered your strengths in a personality test. Using the formula above, determine your individual purpose in each area of life listed below. If necessary, write down more than one. (Don't be afraid to write it down if you think it might change. Just think about one for the time being.)

Career: _____

_____

Relationship: _____

_____

Faith: _____

_____

Finances: _____

_____

Health: _____

_____

Now that you have your purpose written down, how does it feel? How can you let that motivate you?

I hope it helps you remember that you deserve so much more than watching your life trickle away while merely existing, doing the bare minimum to survive, or living solely for pleasure or comfort. You were not created to live a life that counts for nothing. You are on this earth to contribute, to add value, to use your skills to alleviate suffering, and to help others unlock their potential—and to know the deep joy each of these things brings.

Watching my mom battle and overcome cancer taught me priceless lessons. This matriarchal hero used her suffering to create a more meaningful life. Her choice to step into the fight with hope and purpose unleashed a robust intention of making moments count. Realizing time was precious, she stewarded it wisely and with great purpose. My mother modeled for me the significance of creating memories and not wasting time.

If you want to experience deep fulfillment, long-term happiness, and positive life impact, you must determine your purpose. When you are armed with purpose, you become powerful. By unleashing this power, you become a hero far greater than any actor in a cape and costume. You were born for this.

What are you waiting for?

Find a *why* or risk wasting it all.

Pointless → Purpose

REWRITE YOUR ROLE
IN THE STORY

I first met Donald Miller about seven years ago, when I went to a dinner hosted by Michael Hyatt, a close friend and leadership expert. We were part of a small group of local leaders gathered that night. Donald had recently moved to Nashville from Portland, Oregon, and was pivoting from writing bestselling books to starting his own marketing company, StoryBrand. Both mission-minded, Donald and I connected over our passion to help rescue sex trafficking victims through organizations we serve.

Several years later, I visited him at his house, and as we exchanged life experiences, goals, and dreams, he told me how he had used the power of story to change his life.

At one point, I asked this master storyteller, "How does one create a great life story?"

His answer was simple: "Put yourself into a challenging story."

Donald explained how he himself had done just that years beforehand. At the time, he was struggling with limiting beliefs in three areas of his life: weight, relationships, and finances. Donald weighed almost four hundred pounds. His relationships suffered. And every penny of his savings, including the money he had made from the recent sale of his house, was gone after a failed short-term investment. He felt stuck, unmotivated, and disappointed with his life.

Donald decided the only way he was going to change was by putting himself into a challenging story. He began a quest to lose weight and to create a meaningful life.

For him, this included cycling across the country to raise awareness and money for a charity that provided clean water in Africa. Hopping on a bike for hundreds of miles did more for my friend than get him in shape and raise money for a good cause, though; it sparked transformation from the inside out. It motivated him to take ownership of his life and take massive action to change what wasn't working. He not only overcame his limiting beliefs about his weight and health but also tackled his self-lies about being bad at relationships.

Fellow author and mentor Bob Goff continually affirmed the truth that Donald was capable of being great in relationships. Though he once had been convinced he would never get married, as Donald worked to change his story by facing and conquering his limiting beliefs, he reconnected with a friend, a beautiful and kindhearted woman named Betsy, and married her. They now have a wonderful child together, Emmeline Laurie.

I love what Donald wrote in his book *Hero on a Mission*, which I highly recommend: "When a story demands transformation, you are much more likely to transform."[1] No matter what your current story is or what character you are playing, you don't have to stay in a plot that's not working for you. You can edit it and invite more meaning and transformation into it. And you can use your experiences, both bad and good, to help others in their own journeys.

Only one thing is required: you must take ownership of your life and accept the challenge of rewriting your story.

> **THINK THIS:** I can own my story and edit my role.
> **NOT THAT:** I am a helpless victim; everything is out of my control.

What Character Are You Playing?

If you feel unsatisfied with your life, it's time to start living a better story by identifying and changing the role you choose to play.

In my conversation with Donald, he broke down for me the four characters we play (which he also shares in his book): a victim, a villain, a hero, and a guide.

A *victim* is helpless and powerless—a refugee forced to flee her country or the target of a cruel bully.

A *villain* is akin to the evil dictator who aspires to take control no matter how many might be destroyed in their path.

The *hero*? This is the person who summons the courage to make a change, the one who storms the castle or topples the evil regime. The greatest heroes even sacrifice their lives for the greater good. Heroes are made, not born.

The *guide* is a bit less obvious. Guides typically have a supporting role as they help others become the best version of themselves. Yoda in *Star Wars* and Gandalf in *Lord of the Rings* are classic examples.

Do you see yourself as a victim, overwhelmed with hardship and certain there is nothing you can do about your role and the direction of your story? Or is it a villain you play, making excuses for poor behavior because of how poorly someone else treated you? Are you confident that you are living a challenging story, making a difference as a hero or a guide? During a single day, you might play all these roles. The goal, however—the big mindshift—is to transcend whatever uncontrollable events emerge and to rise above the struggle as the character who creates an epic journey and ending.

With the right mindshift, you can be the hero and the guide, facing trials and refusing to let them keep you down. You can progress with *all* the mindshifts we've been talking about so far in this book by creating and practicing *unlimited beliefs* that enlarge your potential; focusing on *becoming* and strengthening your character instead of wasting time on striving for what's meaningless; becoming aware of what's working and what's not and change; and engaging your *purpose* by helping to build others up and bring beauty back on earth.

Now *this* is a story worth living.

If you want to know the surest way to stop yourself from bringing your epic story to life, here's what you need to do: play the victim or villain.

What Is a Victim?

At some point in each of our lives, we will experience an event or situation in which we are threatened, treated unfairly, or at the mercy of something beyond our control. It happens every minute, every second. A hurricane wipes out an entire community. An orphan in Africa is malnourished and lacks clean water and medical supplies. A teenager is kidnapped from her home to be used in a human-trafficking ring.

A true victim is helpless and needs to be rescued. But no matter how much pain they endure, they are not meant to stay in that place. Their story involves healing and a greater quest in which they can uncover meaning and purpose and bring light to others.

Note that in the context of this book, when I use the word *victim*, I am referring only to a person who has embraced a "victim mentality," making victimhood part of how they perceive themselves and their future. A true victim is powerless; when you hold on to a victim mentality, you become powerless within your own mind.

If you consider yourself a victim, you have two choices: you can stay a victim, or you can use your experience to help others. The second choice will help you move forward and create a story worth telling; the first will keep you stuck in a sad story.

Learned helplessness, a theory psychologist Martin Seligman coined in the late 1960s, has become synonymous with a victim mentality. It enforces the negative belief that if we can't do anything about our situation, we might as well give up. Consider a child who is being repeatedly bullied at school. The constant verbal assaults may trigger a feeling of powerlessness over the situation, and the child may stop resisting or fighting back. This may develop into a pattern; when they get older, they may respond to conflict with others the same way. They have learned to be helpless.

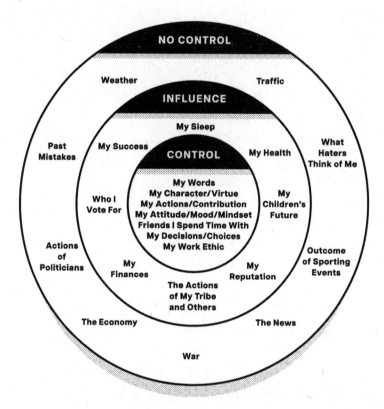

You might know someone who seems to always struggle in the same area of life, like relationships, but instead of accepting responsibility for their actions, they blame someone or something else. Learned helplessness can keep you stuck as the same person and keep you from becoming the best you can be.

Now let's look at the flip side of helplessness. If you are a *Spider-Man* fan, you know the Peter Parker principle: "With great power comes great responsibility." I would say it is actually *great responsibility* that gives you *great power.* When you choose to be responsible, you gain the power you need to fulfill your potential.

Think of that power as a light switch you can flip on (or off) whenever you want. Chances are a circuit breaker in the form of limiting beliefs prevents the switch from staying on. When you eliminate the limiting beliefs, you eliminate the tripped wires. What does this mean? Anyone can stop playing the victim the minute they choose to accept responsibility. Still, sometimes it's more comfortable to keep playing the victim.

Why does anyone want to play a victim? Well, there are plenty of benefits if you think about it—but none include being able to write your own epic adventure.

When someone plays the victim,

- they are free from accepting responsibility; how they feel or where they are in life is everyone else's fault, after all.
- they enjoy the attention, sympathy, and pity of others.
- they probably get what they want (because people feel sorry for them).
- they get the "right" to complain and feel entitled to get what they want.
- their relationships are focused on them, their needs, pains, desires, and wants.
- they are involved in much drama (excitement in the moment) that leads nowhere.

These "benefits" are hardly characteristics of a life well spent. They are certainly not going to get you close to storming the castle or saving someone in distress. They will, however, strain your relationships because everyone around you will be forced to constantly cater to *your* emotional needs, *your* condition, *your* disease, *your* pain, *your* loss, *your* heartache, *your* void. If you continue to live as a victim, I have bad news for you: your negative fixations will suck the life, energy, creativity, and joy out of the space you're in and the people you're around. You have so much more to offer than that.

REWRITE YOUR ROLE IN THE STORY

Whenever I'm tempted to fall into a victim mentality, I force myself to think of true victims—orphans, children who live in food-insecure homes, survivors of war, genocide, sex trafficking, violence, the Holocaust. I think of people who have overcome tragic life circumstances yet have chosen to strive beyond their victim state, overcome all odds, and help others along the way. When you live as a victim, you may get people to pity you, but you will stay unsatisfied and miserable because you were made for more.

Every victim has the choice either to take ownership and act toward their new role as a hero or to choose a darker route that feels empty and involves many people getting hurt. It's a simple choice, but one that needs to be made on purpose.

What Is a Villain?

When you think of evil, maybe you think of Adolf Hitler, for propagating the Holocaust and killing six million Jews and millions of others,[2] or Joseph Stalin, for murdering an estimated six million to as many as twenty million during his reign of terror through forced starvation, labor camps, and execution.[3]

Each of these men is exactly how we personify a villain—a raging, vile, vicious monster. We would never compare ourselves, even on our worst days, to villains, but here's the reality: there's a villain in each of us. We may not strive to annihilate an entire group of people, but at times, we inflict pain on others in more subtle ways, like raging at a driver on the way to work when we're running late or barking orders at our spouse because we're not feeling well.

Villains punish others for where the villains are in their stories. One time I had the opportunity to coach an individual who owned his own business. He was concerned because the company wasn't delivering its projected outputs and he was convinced his employees didn't respect him. I shadowed him for a day and observed his interactions with his staff. I noticed he acted like a villain to his employees. He often raised his voice, made belittling comments, and hardly showed them any appreciation. Later, I learned he'd struggled with feeling disrespected in his past. Seeing that he was acting out this aggression on his employees, I gave him some advice. I told him that when bosses love, encourage, invest in, and stay positive with their staff, their staff will love and care for their customers and the business will naturally grow. It's an organic formula that works. But first, he had to set the example of being respectful. He had to overcome his inner villain.

When was the last time you were angry and lashed out at an innocent stranger? I remember being on the phone with the cable company once for more than an hour. By that point I had been shuffled around to at least three different agents who were supposed to help fix my problem. By the time I was connected to the fourth agent—and I'm ashamed to say this—my impatience erupted into a mini meltdown. I said a few things to the person on the other end of the phone that probably were not the most encouraging, to say the least. It wasn't their fault, of course; they just happened to be collateral damage for my irritation. That was the villain in me! (I did manage to collect myself enough to apologize by the end of the call, but I sure didn't like the person I'd been to that phone rep.)

Most villains don't start out as evil schemers. Villains usually start out as victims. Think of Anakin Skywalker from *Star Wars*, Gollum from *Lord of the Rings*, or *Breaking Bad*'s Walter White. Villains are victims who have not worked through their pain. They take on a mission of what they believe will help remedy their pain by trying to gain control, force their agenda, and do whatever is necessary to get others to do their bidding. Villains often have a warped worldview, believing that, in order to succeed, they must use other people as tools.

Consciously or subconsciously, villains create pain in the lives of other people, in hopes that those people have no choice but to succumb to their demands. The adage "Hurt people hurt people" certainly applies to villains. Resentful of their pain, they inflict it on others.

But there's good news for both victims and villains. Both characters are redeemable. Both can transform into something greater. Victims and villains can become heroes and guides, not only changing who they are on the inside but also using their newfound power to influence others for good.

Think of what happened to Gru from the movie *Despicable Me*. A supervillain who has stolen the likes of the Times Square Jumbotron and the (Las Vegas) Eiffel Tower goes on a mission to steal the moon but, in a delightful and compassionate twist, ends up becoming a dad to three orphaned children. Another example is Harry Potter and Voldemort. Both characters start out orphans. Yet Voldemort, known as Tom Riddle in the orphanage, chooses to use his power for evil on the path of villainhood, and Harry, choosing to use his power for good, becomes the quintessential hero.

If you are a victim, a villain, or a little bit of both (and we all have been at some point in our lives), you have the power to change. It's simply a matter of saying yes to the hero's journey, one quest at a time.

A Hero's Journey

When you accept responsibility for your circumstances and take radical action to change, you automatically step into the shoes of a hero. That is how you begin to write your best story possible.

Consider Minty, who was born into slavery in Maryland in 1820. Hardship was all she knew. When she was five, Minty was rented out as a nursemaid and was beaten whenever the baby she was hired to watch cried. Two years later, she was used to set muskrat traps and later worked in the fields. When she was twelve years old, Minty stepped between a slave owner and a slave he was about to hit with a blunt object. As a result, she sustained severe head injuries and suffered from headaches, hallucinations, and seizures for the rest of her life.

Minty got married in 1844 to a free Black man, but she was still enslaved. Upon hearing rumors that she was about to be sold to another owner, she escaped to Philadelphia in 1849 via the Underground Railroad.

Though she tried to make a new life for herself, she was consumed with thoughts of her family members still enslaved hundreds of miles away. Filled with conviction, Minty returned to Maryland and risked her life to help them gain freedom. She became a conductor for the Underground Railroad and, through this antislavery network, helped guide approximately seventy enslaved people to freedom. You probably know Minty by her adult name, Harriet Tubman. Also known as "Black Moses" and "General Tubman," she later became the first woman to lead an armed expedition in the Civil War, which freed more than seven hundred slaves.[4]

We hail Tubman as a hero because she helped free African Americans from slavery and gain traction in the women's rights movement. What she did is, in a sense, something we all can do—see a need, fill it, and keep saying yes to that cycle of action. We create our future with a story worth telling by continually choosing to act.

Tubman had every right to remain a victim. As an enslaved, abused, disabled woman, she was an unlikely hero. Since Tubman was born into oppression, injustice marked and shaped her future. When she finally escaped, she realized there was no point to her freedom if she couldn't use it to help others. So she returned to the place of oppression, but this time on a quest to rescue her loved ones. She went back to slay the dragon.

The first trait of a hero is accepting responsibility and acting accordingly. The hero knows that, while you can't control everything, you *can* influence certain aspects of your life, one by one, for the good. Even if the odds are stacked against you, you resolve to take ownership and create a life worth living for yourself and for others. It's when the doctor gives you bad news, but you refuse to take the diagnosis lying down, and you fight for your health with everything you've got. It's when the dream has shattered, but you choose to rebuild.

So are you ready to become a hero? Author Joseph Campbell, in his book about scriptwriting called *The Hero with a Thousand Faces*, broke down the heroic journey into seventeen stages and three major phases.

Inspired by Campbell's model, I've come up with a simplified version with eight stages that can be applied to our lives: comfort, awaken, assemble a team, quest, trials, transformation, triumph, and return with wisdom.

1. *Comfort*: Life feels utterly ordinary and mundane. You live to be entertained and comfortable. You watch from the sidelines (or online) as everyone else lives their lives. The purpose of your life is to have an easy experience.

2. *Awaken*: In this stage, you become aware. (Think mindshift 3: become self-aware to get where you need to go.) You notice something broken that needs fixing in the world, something bigger than yourself. You may have been invited to see this via a guide.

3. *Assemble a Team*: You can't win life alone. You'll need a guide and a team of heroes to fight alongside you if you're going to make the greatest impact. (We'll be talking about that in the next chapter, mindshift 6: Assemble a Team to Fulfill Your Dreams.)

4. *Quest*: You accept responsibility and embark on a mission—one of your own making, or you join forces with one already at work to remedy the problem. (This is akin to mindshift 4: Find a *why* or risk wasting it all.)

5. *Trials*: You encounter obstacles and challenges that deter you from your quest, but you persevere and keep your focus on your mission.

6. *Transformation*: Through self-sacrifice, you allow the trials to transform you on the inside by building your character and self-confidence. This inner transformation helps you to make external changes in your quest.

7. *Triumph*: You overcome, reach your goal, and accomplish your quest. You slay the dragon.

8. *Return with Wisdom*: You become a guide. You use what you have learned to help others slay their own dragons and become heroes.

BECOMING A HERO

COMFORT

RETURN
(With Wisdom and Gifts)

AWAKEN TO PURPOSE
(By Guide or Mentor)

ASSEMBLE A TEAM

QUEST BEGINS

TRIUMPH
(External)

TRIALS & TEMPTATIONS

TRANSFORMATION
(Internal)

SELF-SACRIFICE

Recognizing this template of a hero's journey can help us understand the stories that shape our lives. Where do you see yourself? Are you in the comfort stage, or have you felt a shift as you've started reading this book and are beginning to awaken? If you are ready to take on a quest, stay tuned later in this chapter for what steps you need to take to do it.

The most inspiring stories are those where a character experiences the greatest degree of transformation. A slave girl becomes a conductor of a historic movement to save slaves from oppression. Bilbo and Frodo shed their comfortable hobbit skins to become risk-takers, dragon chasers, and world changers. Luke Skywalker transforms from a farm boy shooting womp rats on Tatooine to the most powerful Jedi in the galaxy. Katniss

Everdeen evolves from a young girl barely able to take care of herself and her family to a powerful leader who starts a revolution to overthrow an evil empire. It is inspiring to see someone ordinary, like us, who accepts responsibility and transforms into someone who does extraordinary things; it means that we can do the same.

Another trait of a hero is the willingness to risk their life to help others and sacrifice for the greatest good. In the movie *Iron Man*, we see Tony Stark as an obnoxious billionaire playboy. Over the course of his life through the cinematic lens, he grows in maturity as he accepts more responsibility. In *Avengers*, we see him at his best self as a superhero, one who ultimately gives his life to save the planet. Stark demonstrates the self-sacrifice of the hero archetype in a similar way that Aslan in *The Lion, the Witch and the Wardrobe* and Gandalf in *Lord of the Rings* do when they give up their lives for the sake of others. When heroes accept responsibility and begin to transform, they become willing to give the utmost sacrifice to save someone else. Self-sacrifice generates self-rebirth. When we are willing to give of ourselves for the betterment of others, we become stronger, wiser, and more insightful versions of ourselves. It's an extraordinary story to live and tell.

After you have spent years as a hero helping others become the best version of themselves, you rise to an even higher level of living. You become a guide.

We will examine the role of a guide in the following pages, but first, let's take a closer look at becoming a hero.

Characteristics of the Characters in a Story

VICTIM	VILLAIN	HERO	GUIDE
Self-focused	Resentful	Willing to transform	Focuses on helping hero transform and win
Helpless	Hurts others	Accepts responsibility and grows in virtue	Has compassion, humility, and wisdom

Full of excuses	Narcissistic	Uses pain for good	Gives credit away
Doesn't change	Doesn't change	Wants more out of life	Helps others to reach their full potential

How to Become a Hero

If you're thinking your life doesn't amount to anything even remotely resembling an epic hero's adventure, don't worry. Heroes come in all shapes and sizes. They are not defined by how gargantuan their quest. You don't have to topple an evil regime or pull off a brave rescue to become a hero. Just focus on doing two things: (1) discover your quest, and (2) take ownership and action. These are the first steps of living mindshift 5.

Discover Your Quest

Heroes and guides don't live a treadmill existence. They purposely see how they can better someone or something else—and then they do it. Tubman helped run an underground network to liberate people. You can stand up to something that is wrong in your town and strive to make it right, join a local philanthropic effort, regularly visit with an elderly neighbor who never gets any visitors, or make the conscious choice to raise the kindest, most loving, most compassionate children you can.

Some of the greatest heroes in your life are probably ones who have done the simplest things, like shown up when you needed it, encouraged you when everyone else walked away, or stood up for you when others did nothing. A quest doesn't have to be a nearly impossible mission. It means showing up and paying attention to what you can impact to build a better world.

When I was in chiropractic school, I was in a comfortable place. Outside of the stressors of studying and working, my life was steeped in comfort. I wasn't fighting for a greater cause or championing on behalf of others. I was checking off my mostly self-oriented goals on my five-year plan. One day, I listened to a doctor give a lecture on the opioid crisis.

He talked about the tens of thousands of people who die every year from opioids and other prescription medication. My heart sank. This doctor's words were a much-needed reminder that I was born to do more than work as a medical professional simply to make a comfortable living; I wanted to change and save lives. I began my quest by shadowing this doctor in his clinic and learning about the value of food as medicine.

Think of the mindshifts of self-awareness and purpose we covered in the previous two chapters. With those two tools in mind, see if you can discover your quest by thinking of that meaningful cause or injustice that is whispering your name and seeking your undivided attention right now. Next, find or create an opportunity to get involved. If you are unsatisfied with the current curriculum in your local school system, join the PTA and see how you can help make a change. Maybe there is another need you can help meet by starting an online support group or by joining forces with an organization that is already addressing it. Break out of your cozy comfort zone and start making a difference.

Think of your quest as a giant red *X* on a treasure map. Now visualize the dotted or dashed lines that lead to that *X* from where you are right now. That path is your journey of goal-setting you need to take to complete your quest. Try the STARS method that I've created to help you navigate your way to your *X*.

- **S**pecific—Goals must be well-defined and clear and have a precise date.
- **T**rackable—Whether you use an app or a journal, monitor your progress. Tracking will help you measure your progress and ensure you accomplish your goals.
- **A**ccountable—Find someone who will help hold you responsible for completing your goals.
- **R**ealistic—Set reasonable goals you can achieve. Choose things you can begin doing now.
- **S**ignificant—Your goals should be purpose driven, help stretch and transform you, and get you excited.

When will you start? Hopefully today!

Remember that commitment is key, but so is flexibility. The goal is to keep heading in the direction of that *X*.

As you begin to map out your quest, know that quests can change. When I was forty years old, my goal in life changed. It evolved from the health and nutrition space to focus on a new quest in the leadership and personal growth space. I loved my previous quest of using food as medicine in clinical practice. But as I got older, I became more attuned to the absence of quality leadership in our current government, businesses, media, and education system. I had a deep desire to influence leadership growth in a virtuous way, to help others focus more on becoming than accomplishing. Therefore, I shifted my quest in a new direction by starting my leadership, business, and personal growth website, leaders.com.

One more thing: it's okay to have more than one quest at a time. When I was on a quest to create the number-one natural health website in the world (which took seven years to do), I also was on a quest to become the right spouse to get married to the right woman. When I married Chelsea and we started a family, I created new quests to become a better husband and a father. Don't think of your role in your story as a "one-stop shop." You are a multidimensional individual who can impact your family, school, workplace, community, country, and world. It makes sense to have multiple quests!

Take Ownership and Action

Responsibility makes life meaningful. Without accepting responsibility, you remain powerless. If there is something in your life you don't like or that isn't working, change it.

> **THINK THIS:** Owning responsibility gives me power.
> **NOT THAT:** Taking ownership just means more work and headaches.

US Navy SEALs refer to this idea as "extreme ownership." In their book with the same name, SEAL officers Jocko Willink and Leif Babin explain how true leadership arises from the fundamental truth that "the leader is truly and ultimately responsible for everything."[5] If something goes wrong on a mission, the only person to blame is the person in charge. This principle doesn't apply solely to military elite; it is applicable to each human being. Think of it this way: you are the leader of your life. Enacting effective leadership means taking responsibility and fixing the problem—not making excuses or pointing to someone else, saying, "It's their fault."

Taking ownership means you will have to give up your victim mentality, complaining, and excuses, but in turn you will power on the potential to live a life of meaning, increase your confidence, and approach each day with intention. It won't be easy, but I promise it will be worth it.

A Guide's Job

As a hero grows in years and experience, the natural progression is to become a guide and share wisdom with others. After all, heroes need guides. Where would Luke Skywalker be without Yoda? Would there even be a Karate Kid if there wasn't a Mr. Miyagi?

After my mom beat cancer, she taught other people who were battling the disease the methods that worked for her to get healthy. Using her own journey, she was able to offer other cancer patients comfort and guidance. She took responsibility for her story, faced her fears, made the necessary sacrifices, and then became a guide for others.

When you grow and become the person you are meant to be, you want to share what you've learned with others. You want to see those around you grow and succeed and become who they are meant to be. This is one way you become a guide.

Another way to think of a guide is as a great coach. A guide's job is to find potential in others and help them fulfill it. Gandalf believed Bilbo Baggins was capable of great things because he'd been watching the hobbit. The old man saw something in Bilbo and chose him for an unexpected journey. A guide focuses on helping the hero transform and win. They are selfless, expecting nothing in return while graciously providing empathy and compassion to those they serve. A guide also helps the hero slay the dragon and lets the hero get all the credit.

A parent is a built-in guide to a child. Each day is an opportunity to pass along understanding and wisdom right in the comfort of your own home. The same is true for a pastor, a boss, a growth group leader, or a mentor. If you are involved in any of those practices or something similar, you are already guiding others.

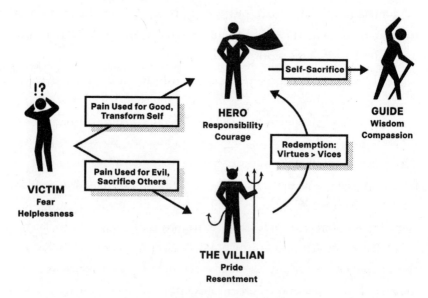

Mindshift 6 (assemble a team to fulfill your dreams) will provide you a roadmap to find a guide (or mentor) for your journey.

Do you have something to offer the next generation or a desire to raise up leaders in a space where there aren't any? Be a guide. Be quick to offer advice and be a sounding board when someone with less experience asks something of you. Here are four ways to become a powerful guide:

1. **Recruit heroes and give them a quest.** Guides look for people with good character who are humble and hungry. Then they guide

the hero (and team) toward a quest where they can use their gifts for the good of the world.

2. **See potential and call it out.** A friend from a growth group once told me that one of the most impactful exercises they experienced was when I went around the group and highlighted the potential I saw in each person. I called each individual by name and said, "I see _____ in you," whether that was a future as a CEO or the creator of an innovative product. Guides see who others can become and help them identify it.

3. **Model.** When guides *do* the right thing, it speaks volumes. It teaches more than simply *telling* someone what to do ever could. Guides focus on becoming over accomplishing and demonstrate heroic behavior for the hero to model.

4. **Inspire the hero to sacrifice and transform.** Guides instruct others on how to improve in both character and skill. They know when to push and challenge, and when to encourage and pat someone on the back. Guides help others grow and support them in their quest; sometimes they even assign the quest. I once mentored a young man who had a lot of pride. I was honest with him without discouraging him, affirming his incredible skill and potential yet also pointing out that he was constantly boasting about his accomplishments. He was open to my helping him tame that beast, and I offered a few books he could read to begin to change his attitude. Quests help people grow.

The goal for all of us is to be a guide. We find meaning and value in helping people write their own stories. And it's something we can do only after we have learned how to rewrite our own story and become a hero.

Choose Your Own Adventure

Consider the story of your life right now. What does the ending look like? If you choose to remain in victim mode, transformation is impossible.

Your story is not going to get much better than this. When you choose to stay a villain, you choose the same story of hurting others as a way of processing your own hurt. You are heading into a future of hurt and more hurt.

But then there's the better way. The minute you take ownership of your current life and your destiny, you accept a new role as a hero that ushers in great change from the inside out. This change is the key ingredient in creating an epic adventure.

Choose a story that demands your transformation, and put yourself in it. The goal must be bigger than you. Be ready for the challenges you will face—unmotivating days, relationship difficulties, and detours. And know that overcoming these obstacles will strengthen and build you up as you become who you are meant to be, a slayer of life's dragons.

Heroes and guides realize not only the great potential and power they possess but also their frailties. They need help. If you want to do great things, you can't make the journey on your own—you're going to need a team. It's hard, if not impossible, to write a great story when you are the only character in the story. However, when you step into a community that's a galvanizing force, the only thing waiting for you is an epic journey. That's where we'll focus next.

Rewrite your role in the story.

Victim → Hero/Guide

ASSEMBLE A TEAM TO FULFILL YOUR DREAMS

Heroes need a team. Maverick needed Goose and even Iceman. Frodo needed Sam and the Fellowship. The Avengers wouldn't be the Avengers with only Iron Man. To survive and thrive as you take on different quests in work and in your personal life, you're going to need other people by your side who challenge, motivate, guide, and encourage you (and you them). Think of this as a team of world changers.

After Chelsea and I got married, I realized the necessity of being surrounded by what I call a "community of greatness." Before we settled down in Nashville, Tennessee, we lived in Florida for a while. While the weather was great, one thing was missing: community. We didn't feel connected to couples our age who shared the same values and were motivated to think big and make a meaningful impact on the world. After praying about this deficiency, we moved back to Music City, where we had lived when we met and I had operated my clinic.

One morning in a Nashville coffee shop, Chelsea and I saw Shawn Johnson East, a former Olympic gymnast, and her husband, Andrew, an NFL player, a few tables over. Our agents had been trying to get the four of us together for a collaboration, but we hadn't officially met yet. I took the opportunity to introduce myself, much to Chelsea's dismay.

"Don't be weird and bother them," she begged. After promising my wife I'd be my normal nonweird self, I introduced myself, and within minutes, Chelsea came over and the four of us were talking and laughing like old friends. Unbeknownst to all of us, we even lived three blocks away from each other.

Chelsea and I were amazed to learn months later that the day we met Andrew and Shawn, they were planning on moving to Los Angeles. Boxes and bags were already packed. The couple felt a move was necessary in order for them to find deeper and more meaningful community, the same reason Chelsea and I had made our way to Nashville.

Coffee turned into dinner later that week, then regular workouts together nearly every Saturday morning, and then brunch, plus multiple handstand competitions among the four of us. (Shawn crushed us every time.) Not only did we have a blast getting to know one another while doing game nights, going on couples' vacations, and having kids during the same time, but we became stronger in character, better in our marriages, and grew as parents and as entrepreneurs in business. To this day, the four of us share a purpose to serve each other and others. We are heroes on a quest together. Our community has grown since then, but meeting this couple has confirmed one of the greatest principles I've learned: life is better with people who make you better.

> **THINK THIS:** Life is better with people who help me grow.
> **NOT THAT:** Life is better on my own.

Who We Are With = Who We Can Become

Doing life with the right people matters because we become like the people we spend the most time with. Our social network influences what we believe, how we act, what we think about, and what we prioritize. Science backs up the truth that you adopt the habits of your peers.

According to psychological scientists at Duke University, one of the most effective ways to stay on track and reach your goals is to surround yourself with people who are more disciplined than you.[1] You may lack self-control, but being around people who excel in that virtue will improve your level of self-control. Can't keep from impulse shopping online or gossiping with your friends over a glass of wine? Hang out with people who don't do those things.

In a 1993 study, British anthropologist Robin Dunbar surmised that, thanks to the size of our brain's neocortex, human beings can maintain an average of 148 stable social relationships. This magic number boils down to:

- 5 loved ones / close support group
- 15 good friends (including the 5 loved ones)
- 50 friends (including the 5 loved ones and 15 good friends)
- 150 meaningful contacts[2]

Consider the first group of Dunbar's number, the five people in your loved ones / close support group. This mirrors the numeric makeup of the original six superheroes in the Avengers, the six friends in the hit TV show with the same name, and the four people in a Navy SEAL Fire Team. This core group consists of people who know practically everything about you and love you anyway.

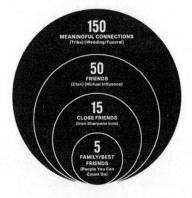

Think of the top five people in your circle. What kind of impact do they have on your life? Do they encourage you to work out when you don't feel like it? Are they merely a sounding board for your problems, or do they help you do something about your troubles? Can you rely on them to always do the right thing, even when no one is looking? The community you choose will either push you forward in life or hold you back.

Who you can become has everything to do with what your community can become together. Without a solid community, made from the right people who will help you learn, change, and grow, it will be almost impossible to become who you were created to be.

Imagine what your life could look like if you were surrounded by people who are purpose driven and who pushed you to be your best. How much more would that improve your life? How much could your presence serve and add value to the community?

We Is Better Than Me

For tens of thousands of years, people lived in groups. Community was about survival, so isolation was a rarity. Families locked arms with other families to hunt, farm, and share food. Groups joined forces for protection against enemies. People who were part of a community felt responsible for one another, so they cared for, protected, and helped each other. We see this bond in team sports. It's not about individual competition but teamwork and cohesion.

Modern and Western societies tend to value the individual above the community. In an individualistic society, the qualities of self-reliance and independence are more favored than the characteristics bred by communities, such as connection, support, and shared responsibility. Dependence is seen as a weakness. Pursuits are driven by ego and personal achievement. In her book *The Gifts of Imperfection*, Brené Brown noted how culture mistakenly values doing life solo. She wrote, "Somehow we've come to equate success with not needing anyone."[3] But that doesn't make sense—not even physically.

Here's an incredible example. Did you know that draft, or working, horses are known for pulling two or even three times their weight? Do you know what's even more powerful than one workhorse? Two of them. Say one horse can pull a load of six thousand pounds—you would assume two horses can pull double that, or twelve thousand pounds. Wrong. Together, two workhorses can pull eighteen thousand pounds, or *three times* the load of one horse. Pairing up these powerful steeds increases their load capacity. Partnership does more than double; it multiplies!

The same principle applies to human beings. You can go further and accomplish more with others than if you were on your own.

While being your own person, and a competent one, is a necessary ingredient of personal development, doing life on your own is a recipe for sadness and meaninglessness. In fact, people who live in individualistic societies tend to be lonelier than those who live in societies that value groups such as a family.[4] Chances are, if you're in the West, you live in an individualistic society. And you can see its effects around you.

The feeling of loneliness is on the rise, with rates having doubled since the 1980s.[5] It's a paradoxical twist considering how modern technology and social media have allowed us to be more connected than ever. Research even tells us the higher the social media use, the more pervasive loneliness is.[6] Just how prevalent is the loneliness epidemic? Studies show that nearly half of Americans report feeling alone or isolated.[7] Four in ten say "their 'relationships aren't meaningful.'"[8]

Sometimes we feel disconnected because of a job transition or a move to a new city, but most often it's because our friendships are superficial and lack purpose.

Former surgeon general Dr. Vivek Murthy relayed a shocking discovery in an article he wrote for the *Harvard Business Review*. He reported that having weak social connections is as harmful to our health as smoking fifteen cigarettes a day.[9] We all know the harmful effects of puffing on cigarettes; being lonely is just as unhealthy.

The antidote to having weak social connections? Community.

Community here refers not just to the people who attend the same place of worship or gym you go to. Community consists of meaningful relationships that help you to thrive and maximize your potential—and help others to do the same. Together, you build toward a common good, like raising kids with character, talking about deep spiritual ideas, or dreaming about entrepreneurial ventures.

I can look at every success I've ever had and point to community as a major driving force behind it. Chelsea and I have a strong marriage because we have been intentional about surrounding ourselves with couples who are just as serious about the sacredness of marriage as we are. These couples fought *for* their marriages, not against each other. They encouraged each other instead of tearing each other down. Gleaning wisdom from these like-minded couples helped my wife and I strengthen our own marriage.

When you position yourself in purpose-driven communities, you naturally become a better person. If you want to overcome failure and to flourish, it's time to intentionally build community.

The Power of a Community of Greatness

There is no shortage of programs and gurus that teach "how" to do, be, or have something. I'm convinced, however, that instead of seeking out the "how," we need to find the right "who."

Aristotle recognized this; he divided friendships into three types, based on utility, pleasure, or virtue. A friendship of utility is one in which a benefit is shared (when you're friends with the parents of your child's classmates or teammates with whom you carpool). A friendship of pleasure is one in which both parties get fun out of it (these are the people you hang out with to unwind and have fun). A friendship of virtue is one based on shared values, a similar purpose, and a deep respect for each other's standards and goals in life. It's the kind of friendship Chelsea and

I found in Andrew and Shawn. This is the highest level of friendship, or what I call a "community of greatness."

A community of greatness is a group of peers linked through a shared purpose of doing good in the world and the common goal of transforming into the people they were born to be. Imagine being surrounded with friends of virtue, people who are around not only because it's fun, convenient, or transactional, but because they, like you, want to be and do better than the day before. These friends support and encourage your personal growth. They challenge you to explore new opportunities you wouldn't otherwise have even entertained. They encourage you to not give up. They inspire you to change through the way they live. And, of course, you do the same for them.

King Solomon taught that "just as iron sharpens iron, friends sharpen the minds of each other."[10] If you're a culinary enthusiast, you know that without regular sharpening, a knife can become dull and bend out of its original shape. Ever try slicing or chopping a tomato with a dull knife? It's not fun and doesn't produce a good result. The only way to maintain the strength of a knife and optimize its purpose is to regularly sharpen it against another piece of steel. In the same way, having the right relationships can help us improve as individuals as we share ideas, constructive feedback, and encouragement to keep going when our own motivation falls flat. This is why top athletes become better by competing against other elite athletes. You become your best by playing against the best.

Contrary to popular belief, J. R. R. Tolkien's literary achievements were not the result of solitary genius. His close friendship with C. S. Lewis played a pivotal role in bringing Frodo's epic journey to life. In the late 1920s, Lewis and Tolkien, both professors at Oxford University, bonded over Norse mythology, philosophy, and politics and regularly shared their writings over pints of beer. As Tolkien faced the daunting task of building the intricate world of Middle-earth, Lewis provided unwavering support and urged him to complete *The Lord of the Rings* series. Tolkien later acknowledged that without Lewis's encouragement he never would have finished. This friendship's impact is astonishing, considering it birthed the bestselling trilogy ever. The duo later formed the Inklings, an informal group of writers and academics who offered feedback on each other's works, including Lewis's Chronicles of Narnia and Tolkien's masterpiece.

When like-minded people who share the same purpose engage in a community of greatness, their synergy sparks innovation, creativity, and personal growth. Great leaders, artists, and world changers never flourish in isolation; they thrive in the environment of other great leaders, artists, and world changers. Any major change in history was initiated by a community of greatness. Think of great Italian artists like Leonardo da Vinci, Michelangelo, Donatello, and Raphael. Not only did these household names spark the Italian Renaissance movement of the art world, but they also make up the Ninja Turtles, some of my childhood heroes.

Just imagine what's possible and who you could become if you were plugged into an intentional community who committed to developing high character and optimizing their skills.

Michael Hyatt, a mentor of mine, taught me how to create a community of greatness and said that starting a group with this mindset was one of the most fulfilling endeavors of his life. After finding out what worked for Michael and his group, I started one of my own, aiming to live out the proverb that "iron sharpens iron." This group would consist of six to eight men who served in some form of leadership capacity and—this was critical—shared the same purpose. The purpose of our group was to grow as servant leaders and have a positive impact on the world. Each of us strove to have a stronger marriage and family, grow spiritually, and lead purpose-driven businesses.

Some of these men were already my friends, some were recruited, but all were hungry to grow and rise to the next level. This was more than just a group of buddies hanging out and getting to know each other better. We were accountable to one another in every area of our lives, because there is no greatness without accountability. We even made it official, and each signed a document pledging our confidentiality and commitment. Unless there was a dire emergency, like the birth of a child or serious illness, we were committed to attending (in person or through video or calls) monthly group meetings, one-on-one meetings, and in-person retreats; memorizing Scripture; and reading books that helped us grow. Also, we gave donations together and participated in fundraising events, like a clay-pigeon shooting contest our friends Mike Fisher and his wife, Carrie Underwood, put on to benefit inner-city kids in Nashville.

To illustrate how seriously we took the commitment to showing up for the group, I'll mention a time when the retail chain Target wanted to schedule a meeting with me about including a supplement of mine in their stores. This meeting was the same time as a men's group retreat. Which meeting do you think I prioritized? That's right. Target had to wait. This might seem extreme, but we do not become the people we are born to be unless we take our commitments seriously and first invest in our communities.

The community of greatness I formed was a true success, and we are still going strong today. This group has helped me become a better husband by teaching me how to serve and love my wife better, how to be a better dad to my daughter by being present when I'm with her, and how to inspire those I work with toward excellence and growth. Starting this group has been one of the most fulfilling decisions in my life.

THINK THIS: Who can my community become?
NOT THAT: Who can only "I" become?

How to Create a Community of Greatness

You may have the beginnings of a community of greatness in your life. Maybe you have a friend or two with whom you share the same purpose and values, and through that relationship you organically help each other grow. I want you to think of stepping into a new level of friendship and broadening that circle. Who could be part of your own community of greatness and help you fulfill your quests? Consider the relationships of iron you could build to generate your own development and pursue your missions.

Here are four steps you can take to begin to build your tribe.

1. Write down the purpose, core values, and priorities of your potential community of greatness. To give you an idea of what this can look like, my group consists of:

   GROUP PURPOSE: grow as leaders, grow our businesses, change the world for good

   GROUP CORE VALUES: servant leadership, excellence, vulnerability, courage, love

   GROUP PRIORITIES: business, spiritual, family, leadership, personal growth

2. Write down the names of six to eight people you know (friends, family, colleagues) who currently embody these key qualities and would flourish in your potential community of greatness.

3. Think through some possibilities of how this new community can grow together. For example, our group gets together over dinner, reads books that advance our growth, and participates in fun activities like golf.

4. Create a weekly, monthly, and yearly format for meeting and pursuing growth together. Think through what would happen in these meetings, what you plan to teach/discuss, methods of accountability (like the document I talked about earlier that we all signed). Consider what I call "growth assignments," or homework that is done in between meetings. Below is a format of our monthly in-person meetings from 5:00 to 9:00 p.m.:

- Teach: A group member talks for about ten minutes on a subject of choice.
- Discuss: Each person spends about five to seven minutes responding—sharing their biggest takeaway, something that surprised them, or why X is important.
- Accountability: Each person reviews what they said they would do over the previous month, about one to two minutes each.
- Dinner: We eat and hang out.

Below is a sample of our monthly meeting agendas, which we plan out a year in advance. (Told you we were intentional.)

#	TOPIC	DATE	DISCUSSION	BOOK TO READ	ASSIGNMENTS FOR NEXT MONTH
1	Vision & Goals	January	Share your life vision and your biggest goals for the year.	*Your Best Year Ever* by Michael Hyatt	Visualize your ideal future. Write your top 5 goals & strategies.
2	Mindset	February	What are your limiting mindsets? How has that limited your life?	*Mindset* by Carol Dweck	Identify your top 3 limiting beliefs and replacing truths.

3	Love	March	What is love? How do we love God and people?	*The Four Loves* by C. S. Lewis	Write your spouse 10 Things I Love About You.
4	Character	April	How do we eliminate our bad habits and grow in character?	*15 Invaluable Laws of Growth* by John Maxwell	Make 3 Character Cards and meditate on them 3x a day.
5	Business	May	How do we build purpose-driven businesses and leave a legacy?	*Built to Last* by Jim Collins and Jerry Porras	Write down your company values and vision statement.
6	Marriage	June	What is the purpose of marriage? How do we become better spouses?	*The Meaning of Marriage* by Timothy Keller	Write your spouse a poem.
7	Wisdom	July	How do we create a life of meaning and have the greatest impact?	*12 Rules for Life* by Jordan Peterson	Write down 10–15 lessons you will teach your kids.
8	Focus	August	What are your life priorities and what do you need to eliminate?	*Essentialism* by Greg McKeown	Time management exercise: Stop, Start, Keep
9	Faith	September	What is prayer and how should we pray? Share answered prayers.	*The Circle Maker* by Mark Batterson	Create a vision board w/ spouse. Pray w/ spouse for 30 days.
10	Courage	October	Have you been a villain? What can you do to become the hero?	*Hero on a Mission* by Donald Miller	Write down 1–3 habits that will help you become a hero.
11	Purpose	November	What is the purpose of your life and your business why?	*Start with WHY* by Simon Sinek	Write down your personal why. Write down your career why.

12	Identity	December	Who are you and what is identity? How does culture impact identity?	*And David Perceived He Was King* by Dale Mast	Write down a personal identity statement.

If this feels intense to you, don't be put off. I call our group a top-tier, or Level 1, community of greatness in its format, requirements, and frequency of meetings—basically as involved as it gets. If you are new to this, or life's responsibilities are particularly full in this season, consider creating and facilitating a community of greatness on a less intense level, what I call a Level 2 or 3. These meetings tend to be more manageable with most people's schedules.

Level 2 could look like this: meet every month for an informal dinner and a more formal discussion of a book's teachings.

Level 3 could involve this: meet every other month for a group dinner with friends and family who share the same values, and let conversation flow naturally, without planned readings and teaching.

No matter what you choose, know that creating intentional community can be one of the most rewarding parts of life; you'll be glad you put in the effort.

Practical Tips for Your Group

As you think about how you might facilitate your own community of greatness, here are some tips to keep in mind.

Prioritize including people with shared purpose and values. While each person will have their own individual purpose and mission in life (and have varying occupations, backgrounds, and experiences), like-mindedness across the group is essential. If that is not the case, you set the stage for discord and division.

Size matters. You don't want a group that's too small or too big. Six to eight people is just right.

Look for people who are:

- hungry—fully want to grow
- coachable—will accept feedback and make changes
- humble—have an awareness that they always can grow and get better
- virtuous—follow the same moral and ethical principles in public and in private
- ready to pay it forward—will take what they learn and invest in others

Below are examples of what to look for in and keep out of your community of greatness.

WHAT YOU NEED IN A COMMUNITY OF GREATNESS	WHAT YOU DON'T NEED IN YOUR COMMUNITY OF GREATNESS
Listens attentively	Doesn't really hear you
Laughs and cries with you	Doesn't show compassion
Encourages you	Puts you down to build themselves up
Challenges you to grow	Unwilling to change themselves
Shares the truth in love	Dishonest, tells you what you want, not need, to hear
Celebrates your victories	Always trying to one-up you
Supports you in hitting your goals	Sabotages your goals and habits
Focuses on becoming (growing in character)	Prideful, jealous, unkind, selfish, and lazy
Makes you feel secure and included	Has low self-esteem and makes you feel insecure

Know when your community needs a change. The truth is, not everyone wants to do the work to change. Becoming the person you were born to be takes time, energy, and effort. Sometimes people aren't willing to invest these commodities. I remember an individual who used to be a part of our group who, over time, became a negative force. The other men in the group and I brought this up to him in a loving and respectful way multiple times, but he was not willing to change. It was obvious that it was time for him to leave the group. This is never an easy decision to make and requires much prayer, reflection, and constructive conversation.

I want to remind you that having a community of greatness doesn't mean you don't have other friends. A community of greatness is an intentional tribe created for a specific reason.

Mentorship Matters

One of the most impactful aspects of a community of greatness is mentorship. Teams play best when they are driven by a coach. Mentors, like coaches, help facilitate the growth of others in reaching their full potential. They point their team toward purpose, initiate a quest, and ask the questions, "Who can we become? What can we accomplish as a team?" In the previous chapter, we discussed the characteristics of a guide (or a mentor) and how one helps someone else become a hero. Now let's look closer at the impact a mentor could have on you and how you might act as a mentor for others.

Moses Maimonides, a revered Jewish scholar and philosopher from the 1100s, stressed the importance of *tzedakah,* a moral obligation toward others. *Tzedakah* can be translated into English as "charity," which is rooted in the Latin word for love.[11] Paraphrased, Maimonides's understanding of the highest form of charity was helping a needy individual become self-sufficient. For example, instead of just giving someone money, you teach them how to make money on their own. This paints a beautiful picture of mentorship. When you mentor someone, according to the Jewish faith, you practice the highest form of love.[12]

One of the secrets to my success in business has been learning from multiple mentors. From my father to my grandfather Howard to coaches and doctors and business leaders like Michael Hyatt and Jordan Rubin, a series of incredible men have invested their time, energy, and experience in me, and I'll be forever grateful.

In the first two years of college, however, I found myself lacking both a community of greatness and a mentor. It showed in the quality of my life. I felt unfulfilled and lost without purpose. While I was getting good grades, I also was wasting a lot of time on meaningless activities, like parties, that only stunted my potential. Knowing I was meant for more, I sought out a mentor to help me bring purpose back into my life. I met someone at a faith-based meeting who invited me to be a part of his community of greatness. Not only did I find a new group of friends who shared the same values and principles as I did, but I finally had a coach. He encouraged me in the areas I got right and pointed out the flaws I needed to improve.

There is nothing more transformative than being in a community of greatness and being mentored. It's how you grow the fastest.

Studies show that while 76 percent of people believe in the importance of mentors, only 37 percent of people have one.[13] The benefits of having a mentor are far-reaching. People in business who are mentored report a 70 percent improvement in their decision-making skills and are promoted five times more often than those not in a mentoring program.[14]

Mentorship is so powerful that it can help build a strong identity in someone who has had an absent parent. The most humbling and honoring statement I've ever received came from mentees who have said, "Josh, you've been like the father I've never had." Many people haven't been told that they matter and add value to the world. A big part of being a mentor is calling out the greatness in someone else. It's being a Gandalf to a Frodo.

Receiving Mentorship

If you don't have a mentor, here's what I recommend. Identify one to three people you respect and want to learn from. Maybe it's someone within your network, business associations, nonprofit organizations, college, family, church, synagogue, or community groups such as business chambers of commerce. Also consider looking into mastermind groups, life coaches, and counselors. Remember that a mentor may or may not be on the same career track as you. At certain points in my life, I've had multiple mentors, each with a different focus (business, family, spiritual growth).

Once you have a potential mentor in mind, set up a meeting with them. It can be at a coffee shop, on the phone, or over lunch. Remember, if you are requesting the meeting, lunch or coffee is on you. Explore the possibility of connecting regularly to discuss issues that will help you grow.

As a student of a mentor, the two most important characteristics you need to have are to be humble and hungry. You must be able to humbly learn and take action. Remind yourself that you don't know what you don't know. Be respectful and mindful of your mentor's time and expertise. You must also be hungry for growth. The greatest way to honor your mentor is to precisely follow their instructions for transformation. Doing this will also motivate them to continue investing in you!

Also, know what you want to know from them, whether it's asking, "What are the top three books that have had the biggest influence on your life?" or "How do you balance home and work life?" or "What are the biggest things I can do to support my self-development?"

While having in-person mentors is important, technology has made it possible to access and be virtually mentored by the most brilliant and admirable individuals. Make a list of people you want to emulate. Read their books, listen to their podcasts, watch their YouTube videos. Write down the principles they live by and mindsets with which they approach life. Then follow their examples. By modeling their mindsets and actions, you will experience many of the benefits of mentorship.

Bring a mentor into your life and watch how fast you grow.

Offering Mentorship

Research shows that 89 percent of mentees mentor others.[15] Socrates was Plato's mentor. While spreading Socrates's teaching, Plato became Aristotle's mentor, who in turn became the mentor of Alexander the Great. Just as mentors have discovered potential in me that I had never noticed, I seek to find potential in others that they cannot see.

Don't let the idea of mentoring others intimidate you. You don't have to be a Yoda or sage to impart wisdom, encouragement, and guidance to others; you just need to know a little more than your mentee.

A surprising and powerful component of mentoring others is the growth it brings *you*. Research shows that teaching others material you know causes you to retain 90 percent of that information.[16] It's yet another reason to start carving out time in your schedule to teach others the skills you are growing in.

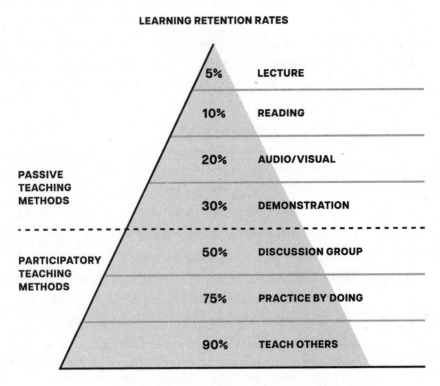

LEARNING RETENTION RATES

5%	LECTURE
10%	READING
20%	AUDIO/VISUAL
30%	DEMONSTRATION
50%	DISCUSSION GROUP
75%	PRACTICE BY DOING
90%	TEACH OTHERS

PASSIVE TEACHING METHODS

PARTICIPATORY TEACHING METHODS

Adapted from National Training Laboratories. Bethel, Maine

To think through the details of how to become a mentor, revisit the previous chapter's discussion about becoming a guide to a hero. (Give a quest, point out potential, model, and inspire transformation.)

Investing in others produces a multiplication effect. The meaningful connection Chelsea and I share with Andrew and Shawn naturally led to a series of other communities of greatness and mentoring opportunities initiated by the four of us as individuals. I started a local leadership group that Andrew was a part of, a circle of close-knit friends who were committed to excellence, growing in character, inspiring one another toward greatness, and living out our values. Then Chelsea and I started a group. Shawn created her own women's group and Andrew his own men's group. This is the multiplication formula, 1+1=3, the power of community at work.

Don't make the mistake of thinking you are better off alone or that the "friends" you have on social media are enough to complete your community. Instead of simply casting a wide net, go deep with your relationships. Don't settle for having only online social media conversations or waving hi and bye to people in the school car line. Invest in communities of greatness, find a mentor, and be a mentor. We can only become who we are meant to be through the people who surround, come alongside, lead, and follow us.

Don't just think about who *you* can become. Think of who your *community* can become.

Assemble a team to fulfill your dreams.

Solo → Community

MINDSHIFT 7

BUILD AN UNSHAKABLE IDENTITY SO NO ONE ELSE DOES IT FOR YOU

Growing up, I was a huge Michael Jordan fan. To me, he was a real-life superhero. I was in the fourth grade through eleventh grade during his run of winning six NBA championships. During that time, I wanted more than anything to be like Mike. I was one of the countless kids drinking the Kool-Aid (or should I say Gatorade) of wanting to model His Airness. Jordan's iconic commercial advertising the sports drink featured a jingle about the dream of being like Mike: "Sometimes I dream that he is me. You've got to see that's how I dream to be. I dream I move, I dream I groove, like Mike . . . if I could be like Mike."[1]

Of course I wanted to be like Mike! Most boys did. I played ball with the neighborhood kids on a suburban cul-de-sac or with my dad in the driveway and pretended I was performing Jordan's signature fadeaway jumper a second before the buzzer went off to hit a game winner. I wore Air Jordan shoes and Chicago Bulls shorts and, of course, drank Gatorade because the commercial made me believe that if I did these things, I would be like the man I greatly admired.

Our identity—who we are—is shaped by many things but particularly by the people we revere. Everybody has a hero or North Star in their life—a person, idea, or thing that validates their path in life and offers them security. It might be a celebrity or high-profile figure (like Michael Jordan was to me), a system (perhaps the government or a political affiliation), an ethnicity (being European, Asian, or American), or a higher power (God). It might even take the form of a title or position, like being an attorney, musician, or CEO.

If I asked you right now, "Who are you?" I'm confident your answer would come from one of three places (maybe even all of them): your name, your job, or your relationship to someone. It's hard not to reply with one of those answers when it comes to pinpointing your identity.

In this mindshift, the focus is not just uncovering *who* you are but unearthing the *roots* of your identity because that is what shapes who you are and what you will become in the future.

There are three main ways people establish who they are, and they have varying degrees of dependability. These categories are based on the work of Charles Taylor in *Sources of the Self.*

- **MODERN IDENTITY** is formed through self-focus and aligning yourself with current popular culture. I liken it to building your identity on sand.
- **TRADITIONAL IDENTITY** forms from prioritizing family, anti-selfishness, and duty, and revolves around the idea that "what has worked before will work now." It's more like building on soil.
- **DIVINE IDENTITY** means you discover who you are by first knowing who God is, and this knowledge informs your beliefs, morals, and values. This is like building your identity on stone.[2]

What would you rather build on? Sand, soil, or stone, steadfast and eternal? When you don't determine who you are, or what your identity is founded on, you rest your values, principles, and self-worth on shaky ground.

THINK THIS: Figuring out who you are is important because it determines your future.
NOT THAT: My identity changes depending on social constructs, the opinions of others, and my background—and that's okay.

Who I Am—and Why It Matters

Identity dictates your purpose, beliefs, and values. It is where you find security. It is also the source of your self-worth, value, and recognition. Your perception of yourself rules your life; it governs your success, potential, and relationships. If you are a people pleaser, struggle with low self-esteem, or suffer from a distorted sense of self, the root of your problems is likely an unstable identity.

The following three elements embody identity, and they draw from and build on each other:

1. Identity is connected to something or someone.
2. Identity feeds your roles and responsibilities (as part of a community).
3. Identity drives purpose, helps determine your value, and adds meaning to your life through fulfilling your roles and responsibilities.

Let's look at these a little closer.

Identity is connected to something or someone. What you connect your identity to is evidenced by what is most important to you. Think of identity in terms of a hierarchy. Look at the list on the next page and choose the top three words (in order of importance) that you say establish your identity:

Nationality	Race	Gender	Family
Character	Religion/Faith	Political affiliation	Economic status
Career	Sexuality	Achievements	Possessions
Health	Heritage	Community	Talents
Appearance	Morality	Ethnicity	State/City/Town

Out of the three words you've chosen, which one holds the trump card? Is it your career? Political affiliation? Family heritage? Your choice will influence your beliefs, decisions, and actions.

Consider what name you enter on a voting ballot come election time and why. Do you vote for a candidate based on their race, gender, morality, or merit? Your answer will tell a lot about your identity.

If your identity is based on your economic status and a stock market or crypto crash happens, what will that say about who you are? Will your identity shatter and your value plummet because you have less money in your bank account? If your identity is based on who you vote for, and the candidate you helped elect disappoints, what then? It's important to know what your identity is connected to so you can put priorities in their proper place.

Identity feeds your roles and responsibilities (as part of a community). Identity helps to identify, define, and establish the roles, and responsibilities, you have in life and with others. Your role is always tied to people. My role in my family is a husband and father; in my friend group, it's a challenger and community creator; in my profession, it's an educator and leader. Each role presents specific responsibilities and aspects of identity that must be managed.

Identity drives purpose, helps determine your value, and adds meaning to your life through fulfilling your roles and responsibilities. When you root your identity in the right things and take ownership of your roles and responsibilities, you will affect the lives of other people for the good. This is what gives your life meaning. What makes your life most fulfilling is not a specific talent, career, or accomplishment; it's about growing in character and in your unique skill to alleviate suffering and help others reach their full potential. In other words—purpose!

So why all this talk about what makes up our identity? When you aren't consciously aware of who you are and why it matters, your foundation is too easily movable. Carl Jung said, "The world will ask you who you are, and if you don't know, the world will tell you." A lack of clarity on the roots of your identity will force you to become a slave to culture and its ideas, beliefs, and values. You'll find yourself living for other people and letting them determine how your life plays out.

Think about who you are for a minute. Who gets to say that you are valuable? Who convinces you of your roles and responsibilities in this world? Who determines what you believe and how you live? Do you allow the latest social movement to dictate your beliefs and values because it is the voice that's screaming loudest? You might think your identity is completely self-based, but that's only partly true. Every person's identity is influenced by something or someone. You can consciously choose where your identity comes from and build your identity on solid ground.

No matter how you see yourself now, and no matter what you've done wrong or who your parents were, you can forge a new identity that will be the foundation for who you can become.

But first, let's determine whether your identity lies in the modern, traditional, or divine realm. If you find yourself reeling with anxiety most days because you feel good only when you are validated by others, or not enough people liked your posts on Instagram, or you're bombarded by pressure to have a family, run a business, and maintain a particular physique all at the same time, I have news for you—you are suffering from a modern identity. While the sad truth is that you have been force-fed lies by society, the good news is that you can choose to stop accepting those messages and build a better foundation.

The Pitfalls of a Modern Identity

The first billion-dollar film for Walt Disney Animation Studios was the hit movie *Frozen*. The movie was also the first to receive an Academy Award for Best Animated Feature. My two-year-old daughter loves *Frozen*, which means I've watched it hundreds of times. There's a slight issue I have with the film—its ideology. Take, for instance, "Let It Go," the song that's been in our heads since 2013.

After the iconic piano prelude, Elsa sings about being liberated from being a "good girl" and having had to hide her true self for fear of judgment. The queen is free to be herself and be by herself, all others be damned. She croons, there is "no right, no wrong, no rules for me."[3] This is freedom for Elsa—running away from her inner fears and responsibilities instead of facing them and following her emotions where they take her, into isolation.

Is Elsa a hero according to this song? We sure applaud her as if she is. Yet I don't see true heroism here, which I define as inner transformation, growing in character, and sacrificing yourself to save the lives of others.

This message of "Let It Go" runs parallel with the modern identity. A modern identity is created from arbitrary standards set by the individual. In other words, what works best is what works for you. If you want to know your value and your significance, look no further than inside yourself.

Modern identity is wrapped up in "expressive individualism," an ideology in which a person intentionally conforms to their own notions of identity (instead of one prompted by their family, past generations, and community) because they view external models of identity as oppressive.

Of course the starring role in modern identity is "me." It's all about me and my feelings. People with a modern identity find strength and security in the adage "Follow your heart." To validate their feelings, they look to social trends, people, and ideas that reinforce their desires. They expect everyone else to serve their needs and adapt to their desires, feelings, and preferences.

In a modern identity, there is no objective or absolute truth. This self-centered ideology is born out of the idea that there is no God, so it's modern society's job to decide what is true and moral. Anything goes—or rather, current popular opinion leads the way.

Often, people who adopt a modern identity crave constant recognition and praise, even if they haven't done anything innovative or noteworthy. You can smell modern identity from a mile away because it reeks of entitlement, disrespect, and ungratefulness.

The undertones of modern identity are seen in "cancel culture." When a failure, a mistake, something someone said two decades ago, a misinterpreted word, even an act that is rightly deemed immoral or unethical is exposed, there is only one option: ostracize and demonize the person. There is no call to redemption other than forced apologies and shaming, and even then, there is no space for repentance. There is no forgiveness or second chance.

Where did this all start? Way before our time. I believe four movements have led up to and created the modern identity: irreligion, rationalism, romanticism, and relativism.

IRRELIGION—summed up in Nietzsche's statement in his book
 The Gay Science that "God is dead," or rather, the idea of him
 post-Enlightenment was no longer valuable or necessary.[4]
RATIONALISM—the view that determines "reason as the chief
 source and test of knowledge."[5] This idea was established by the
 famous quote by René Descartes: "I think, therefore I am."
ROMANTICISM—this philosophy, hailed by Jean-Jacques
 Rousseau, projected the importance of feelings and
 individualism. Your feelings will lead you to the truth.
RELATIVISM—promoted by Jean-Paul Sartre, the philosophy of
 relativism alleges there is no absolute truth, just the truths of
 what an individual believes.

In essence, the fundamental belief here is that God doesn't exist, so self and others must fill that void and decide what is right, true, and moral, and, ultimately, who we are as human beings. These four movements led to the foundational principle that undergirds the modern identity—that our life purpose and mission should flow *only* from within ourselves and should satisfy whatever we think will make us happy, typically in a materialistic and hedonistic way.

No God = No Good/Evil = No Morality = No Truth = No Purpose = No Meaning = No Self-Worth = Weak Identity

My research indicates that the key problems with modern identity are that it is delicate, divisive, drowning, and deceptive.

Delicate. In modern identity, the individual attempts to find self-worth and validation in themselves and searches for viewpoints that build up their self-imposed ideas. Any opposition to their beliefs is seen as a personal attack, and they respond with a victim mentality. This is the person who lashes out at you on social media if your belief contradicts their own.

Divisive. In modern identity, because life is all about the individual and not the community, many relationships fall apart. Modern identity politics has been reduced to an Us-versus-Them mentality. If you don't agree with me, I will walk away, quietly quit, or cancel you.

Drowning. Modern identity is based on the mindset of accomplishing (remember our discussion of becoming versus accomplishing?). You must be successful at all costs, but it still won't be enough. Women, for instance, must do more than just raise children or have a career. They must have kids, be the class mom, build their own company, slay as a CEO, maintain a killer physique, and look at least ten years younger—all at the same time. If you look to what society says is important to focus on accomplishing, you will be playing a role for which you were not created, one that will inevitably lead to exhaustion and burnout. It's no wonder anxiety disorders are on the rise.[6]

Deceptive. The modern identity is all about self-assertion. You become your true self when you follow your feelings and do what is best for you, and you alone. The only one who defines you is you. And yet, an innate need of all humans is to be validated. People want it. They need it. And thanks to the surge of social media, they seek it through a flurry of likes and comments online. They think they are free to be themselves when, in reality, they are chained to the approval of others.

The modern identity is a foundation of sinking sand. If you build your house on it, it's going to sink. This movement gets props for recognizing our uniqueness as individuals. Of course it is true that there is no other person like you on the planet! But the fact that we are each unique doesn't mean life is all about us.

You may believe you are living for yourself while actually allowing culture to determine how your life plays out. In the words of a *New York Times* commentator, "The great challenge of our moment is the crisis of isolation and fragmentation, the need to rebind the fabric of a society that has been torn by selfishness, cynicism, distrust and autonomy."[7] I couldn't agree more.

> **THINK THIS:** Who I am is constant and unchanging despite what others say or think.
> **NOT THAT:** Society, friends, and family must adapt to my identity in order for it to be valid.

Traditional Identity

A traditional identity differs from a modern identity in that it focuses on community and the tested beliefs of the past, not on the self. A traditional identity forms from prioritizing duties, traditions, and the roles you play in fulfilling your responsibilities to your family, community, and country. The goal is to fit in and create harmony within the group you are part of and help it survive and thrive.

While people with a modern identity look *inward* to determine who they are, those with a traditional identity look *outward* and *backward* to figure that out. In a traditional identity, you encompass the values, morals, beliefs, and attitudes of your tribe, for better or worse. You sacrifice your own wants for the needs of others. The good of your community supersedes the interests of other communities.

On the surface, it's easy to see positives in traditional identity—putting others before self, believing in your community, fighting for your heritage. We see this in films like *Braveheart*, in which William Wallace fights for and sacrifices his life so Scotland, his country of origin, can be free from English rule.

We also see traditional identity roles in the Disney film *The Lion King*. King Mufasa is the leader of the Pride Lands, and his son, Simba, is the rightful heir. Mufasa's evil brother, Scar, plotting to take the throne, kills King Mufasa and convinces Simba he is to blame. Simba flees his homeland and adopts a carefree philosophy (a modern identity). Years later he runs into his childhood friend Nala, who reawakens his sense of duty.

Nala reveals Scar's tyranny and pleads with Simba to reclaim his rightful place. At first, Simba refuses, but he changes his mind after encountering the spirit of his father, Mufasa, who tells him, "You have forgotten who you are. . . . You are more than what you have become. . . . Remember who you are. You are my son and the one true king. Remember who you are."[8] Simba then returns to his homeland, reclaiming his true identity as king and leader of his pride.

You may notice how in Disney movies the roles and responsibilities of the female lead characters have evolved over time. Though they once showcased traditional roles, in today's films it is common to see a heroine broadcasting her lack of dependence on men, who are commonly portrayed as mindless oafs.

What traditional identity gets right, as we've said, is the significance it places on community. It shows us that our identity is tied to our tribe and whatever role we can play that adds the most value. For example, part of your identity and value might be found in the role of friend, spouse, parent, leader, performer, therapist, or engineer. Your various roles carry responsibilities, and fulfilling those responsibilities gives your life meaning as you contribute to the success of your community.

There are, however, a number of problems with traditional identity. It positions duty and tradition over feelings—directly contrasting with a modern identity, which is ruled by feelings. Both identities share an imbalanced relationship to emotions. Feelings are not the problem; they are part of our humanity. That said, it is not advantageous to swing to either extreme of devaluing them or of allowing them to rule our lives.

Another drawback to the traditional identity is that adopting and aligning your values with what your family or community has always done in the past limits positive change and progress. Consider arranged marriages, limited women's rights, the pressure to have the same vocation as your parents, and religion without relationship.

In addition, focusing on only your group can often lead to prejudice and discrimination against others. This danger is evidenced in extreme nationalism. While the focus of supporting your own family and community should be a priority, there also should be a focus on helping others outside of your community even if they don't share the same values and customs.

I compare the traditional identity to building a foundation on soil; it can wash away over time. While it is a better foundation than a modern identity, there is an even better foundation in which to anchor who you are. If you are looking to build a rock-solid identity, look no further than our third option: a divine identity.

A Divine Identity

When you live with a divine identity, you believe that human beings are made up of more than flesh and bones; we are also spiritual beings. Not only that, but having a divine identity offers us a lens with which to see people. When we view others through that unique perspective, we are more likely to treat them with value, honor, and respect. In *Weight of*

THINK THIS, NOT THAT

Glory, C. S. Lewis wrote, "It is a serious thing to live in a society of possible gods and goddesses. . . . It is with the awe and the circumspection proper to them, that we should conduct all of our dealings with one another, all friendships, all loves, all play, all politics. There are no ordinary people. You have never talked to a mere mortal."[9]

When you have a divine identity, you also believe in a higher power and an afterlife, both of which influence your identity. A Gallup poll found that 81 percent of Americans still believe in God.[10] Studies demonstrate that when someone's identity is linked to their religious beliefs, they contribute more to society and are more charitable in their giving. They volunteer more with acts of service. They are also more virtuous in character.[11] As you can see, your spirituality can greatly impact your actions.

I am convinced that people who live shy of a divine identity question their purpose and meaning in life, leading to

- a lack of character and values,
- adhering to others' definitions of success,
- feelings of insignificance and uncertainty, and
- falling into social conformity and other types of peer pressure.

A divine identity answers the question of who you are by first knowing who God is and building your beliefs, morals, and values around that knowledge. One of my all-time favorite authors, C. S. Lewis, pointed out that people who have achieved the greatest good in all human history have had one thing in common: their identities were rooted in a relationship with the divine.[12] Think of Moses. Jesus. Michelangelo. Leonardo da Vinci. Galileo Galilei. Wolfgang Amadeus Mozart. Johannes Gutenberg. Martin Luther. George Washington. William Wilberforce. Abraham Lincoln. Harriet Tubman. Sir Isaac Newton. Thomas Edison. Florence Nightingale. Viktor Frankl. Anne Frank. Mahatma Gandhi. Martin Luther King Jr. Mother Teresa. All of these influential heroes, plus millions of other world changers, made a difference because they had an identity that was tied to the divine.

What you believe about the Creator will influence your personal belief system. For instance, not believing in God will often lead you to limiting beliefs that everything is relative with no absolute truth and that life has little meaning. Believing he is a tyrant can lead to limiting beliefs about how you see yourself and the world around you. Believing that God is benevolent can lead to a more optimistic outlook on your future.

Martin Luther King Jr. is a prime example of someone who lived with purpose and an identity connected to God. As a Christian Black man and an American from Birmingham, Alabama, his greatest influences were Jesus, Moses, Gandhi, Martin Luther, his professors Benjamin Mays and Howard Thurman, his wife, Coretta, and his father and mother.[13] He took on the roles of preacher, husband, father, and civil rights leader and fulfilled those roles with moral excellence. He chose to have high-character people influence him and took on the responsibilities that allowed him to make the most meaningful contribution in turning earth into a heavenly place.

In the last speech King gave before his assassination, he said, "I just want to do God's will. And He's allowed me to go up to the mountain. And I've looked over. And I've seen the Promised Land. I may not get there with you. But I want you to know tonight, that we, as a people, will get to the Promised Land."[14]

When you have an identity like King, you have positioned yourself to live with purpose and to have an eternal impact. If you don't have a strong identity, your life will feel meaningless. Faith and character were at the very top of King's identity hierarchy. While attributes like nationality, gender, and race are aspects of your uniqueness, they are not the most foundational elements from which to build your identity because they don't directly help in loving others and doing good in the world. Faith and character, both of which spring from a divine identity, stand at the top of the identity hierarchy for two reasons. Unlike the simple facts of birthplace, ethnic or political affiliation, achievements, or gender, *faith* and *character* are what lead people to make good decisions and create a more meaningful future. The great news is that, while you can't change some simple facts about yourself, you always can grow in faith and character and continue to become a better version of yourself than you were yesterday.

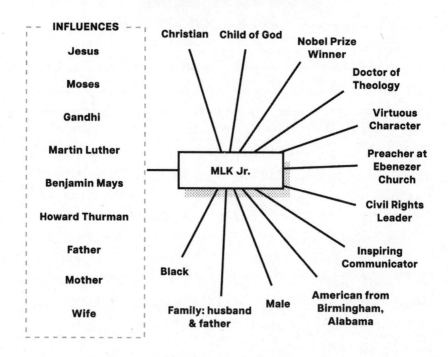

Divine identity isn't consumed by feelings like a modern identity is, nor does it treat feelings as irrelevant, like a traditional identity does. Emotions are important in the realm of divine identity. They serve as a barometer, indicating that there's an issue at the root of them we must attend to. If we are fearful, we need to determine where it is coming from, why, and what needs to change in light of our divine identity.

Comparison of Three Identities

MODERN IDENTITY	TRADITIONAL IDENTITY	DIVINE IDENTITY
Moral Compass: desires and feelings	Moral Compass: duty to family and tradition	Moral Compass: to please God and the Golden Rule
Self is the center.	Community is the center.	God is the center.

Truth is based on current popular opinion.	Truth is based on historical evidence.	Truth is based on ancient Scripture.
Purpose: happiness and personal success	Purpose: to be a good person and care for family	Purpose: to love God and people and to redeem the planet
Comes from within	Comes from community	Comes from God
Community sacrifices for you.	You sacrifice for your community.	You sacrifice for God and community, and they do the same for you.
Stand out by amplifying your individuality.	Fit in.	Stand out by loving God, people, and the planet.
Here and now (the present)	The past (what's worked before)	The present, what's possible in the future, what will last (eternal)
Marry for love/lust (love is a feeling).	Marry for the sake of looking good to others and strengthening your family name and reputation.	Marry for purpose and agape love.
Religion: self-actualization or atheism	Religion: tradition	Religion: relation to the divine

A modern identity is focused on the here and now. *What will make me happy in the moment?* A traditional identity tends to gravitate toward the past, keeping you from looking ahead. A divine identity, on the other hand, honors the lessons of the past, cherishes the present, and emphasizes a perspective that drives you to develop a type of character to serve and love everyone. The choice is yours. Which identity do you believe will help you become the greatest you?

Building a Rock-Solid Identity

In 1666, a great fire destroyed most of the city of London. One of its structural victims was St. Paul's Cathedral, which had been a fixture on Ludgate Hill since 604.[15] Famed architect Sir Christopher Wren was tasked with designing and rebuilding the cathedral. A story is told that he observed three bricklayers working on the reconstruction.[16] He asked each of the workers the same question: "What are you doing?" Each bricklayer gave a different response.

"I am cutting this stone," said the first.

"I am earning three shillings and six pence a day," said the second.

"I am helping Sir Christopher Wren build this great cathedral," said the third.

Each worker had the same task. To one, the answer was just the task itself. To another, the task was simply tied to making a living. But the third worker connected the task to a greater and meaningful purpose. This is similar to a divine identity. When you know who you are and who you are aligned with, what you do carries significance.

Think of what it means to be a parent. At the minimum, you may think that your existence makes little difference to your child. Or you can consider that your contribution matters and, at the same time, your kids exist to serve and make you happy. Finally, you can set the bar higher and think of yourself as a spiritual being with a divine calling to serve your family, which means bringing out the best in their character and helping them multiply their talents to impact future generations. Which of these perspectives on the identity of a parent do you think is the most powerful and gives life the most meaning? When who you are is built with a divine identity, you move past the self-centric and unsteady ideologies of a modern identity and the limited perspectives of a traditional identity into a future worth living for. You are able to develop a rock-solid identity, one that is deep and meaningful and will stand the test of time.

Everyone has a god, something or someone that provides the most meaning and security and warrants the most attention in their lives. This could be a person, a movement, or a community like family or the government. Take notice of what that god is for you. Whatever holds that divine and highest position, be sure it is virtuous and worthy of building your identity on. If it lacks depth, significance, and timeless value, your identity and anything else you construct on that foundation will fall in sinking sand.

Here are ways you can construct a rock-solid sense of self:

- Consider the limiting beliefs that are robbing you of your divine identity and substitute them with unlimited beliefs that embrace who you are as a spiritual being.
- Look at the identity hierarchy list near the beginning of this chapter. List your top five in ranking order, then write an identity statement of who you are (or will become) and the impact you will have.
- Connect with a positive community. Researchers at Vanderbilt University found that people who attend religious services at a mosque, synagogue, or church live longer and have less stress.[17]
- Identify and fulfill roles and responsibilities in which you can add the most value and to which you attach the most meaning.
- Read, watch, and listen to content that promotes a divine identity.
- Follow people on social media who prioritize character, spirituality, and values.
- Incorporate daily habits like meditating, praying, and focusing on gratitude into your schedule.

When you build your life on a rock-solid foundation, you can be confident that your life matters and that your actions, big and small, have eternal significance.

When I was practicing medicine, many of my patients introduced themselves to me as having this or that sickness. People who struggle with chronic illness often connect their disease with their identity because a great deal of their life is wrapped up in the many horrible details of the disease. Yet the illness is not who they are. Just as you are not a diabetic or arthritic sufferer, you likewise are not a mistake you made. Nor are you that lapse in judgment, the bad thing that happened to you, or whatever your mother or father did twenty years ago.

The power of a divine identity funnels down into your community, your purpose, your values and beliefs, your goals, and how you spend your time. All these things are influenced by who you are.

IDENTITY FUNNEL

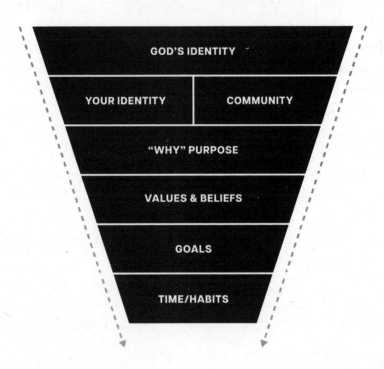

Before we close this chapter, I want to point out one more important distinction between the three identities. The modern identity embraces a mob mentality by aligning *supposed* individual beliefs with whatever happens to be trending and trying to force everyone else to defer to their preferences. The traditional identity espouses a domineering and rigid perspective, refusing to practice anything other than tradition. A divine identity, however, is the most inclusive. All are welcome. All have a purpose. All are loved. The goal of a divine identity is not to establish dominance or lay down the law but to influence other people and the planet via virtuous action.

I may have wanted to be like Mike when I was a kid, but I've since been reminded of the most important Person who informs who I am. Like Mufasa told his son, Simba, "You are more than what you have become. . . . Remember who you are. You are my son and the one true king. Remember who you are."[18]

When you think about who you are, consider whether the identity you choose will keep you flailing in your fleeting emotions, chained to the past, or moving forward into your best possible self. When you build your identity on solid rock rather than on sand or soil, you position yourself to live the most meaningful and fulfilling life.

Build an unshakable identity so no one else does it for you.

Traditional/Modern Identity → Divine Identity

MINDSHIFT 8

BUST VICES BY
BUILDING VIRTUES

Chelsea and I love traveling. In 2012, I had the honor of working with the US national swimming team and traveling to Europe to watch them compete in the Olympic games. Chelsea joined me in London, and then we decided to take some time off together and tour Italy for a week. While strolling the cobblestone streets, meeting warm and friendly locals, savoring the incredible food and wine, and reveling in the country's breathtaking art and architecture, my wife and I quickly fell in love with the place. It was one of the most awe-inspiring settings we had ever visited.

As lovers of art and history, we roamed the country admiring the art and architecture of historic masterpieces like the Colosseum, Duomo, St. Peter's Basilica, the Trevi Fountain, and Vatican City. I was most struck by the Sistine Chapel. On the outside, the rectangular brick building is unassuming—bland, even. The interior, however, is a different story. It is entirely covered in splendid frescoes (mortar-based paintings on walls and ceilings), most of which were designed by Michelangelo. On the walls of the chapel, this groundbreaking Renaissance artist painted a religious narrative through multiple scenes, from the creation of the world to the birth of Christ. In total, Michelangelo created five thousand square feet of frescoes.[1] Millions of people from all over the world visit each year to gape at the most well-known painting, *The Creation of Adam*, which depicts God reaching out and touching the finger of Adam.

Staring up at this ceiling masterpiece, Chelsea and I were silenced by wonder (even as we were smothered by hundreds of other tourists and heard security guards reprimanding people for taking pictures). It was hard to imagine what it took to create such breathtaking art. I later learned that Michelangelo toiled away at what some say were eighteen-hour days for more than four years while painting from a hanging scaffold.[2] Being forced to work in such an awkward position caused Michelangelo permanent eye damage.[3]

It's said that while the master artist once was painting in a dark corner of the chapel, a friend came to see him and noticed him paying painstaking attention to a detail no one would ever even see. When the friend asked him why he even bothered with it, the artist replied, "God will see."[4]

Michelangelo possessed a strong divine identity, which drove him to create masterpieces such as *The Creation of Adam* along with his painting *The Last Judgment*, which is also in the Sistine Chapel, and his sculptures of the *Pieta* in Rome and the statue of *David* in Florence. Michelangelo's life was a series of setting and meeting the highest standards for himself. This sixteenth-century artist was committed to excellence even if no one, other than God, noticed or recognized him for it.

Imagine the masterpiece you can create in your own life if you adopt a high standard of excellence.

> **THINK THIS:** A divine identity will motivate me to live and create with excellence, no matter who is watching.
> **NOT THAT:** I do my best when someone notices.

The Greatest Level of Character

When I was studying for my Master of Science in Leadership at Johns Hopkins University, I did in-depth research on ethics and virtues and gained a greater awareness of how essential they are to success in every area of life. I saw this confirmed in the classic *Nicomachean Ethics*, Aristotle's most important and widely read work on personal morality, where he connects excellence with virtue. The Greek word the philosopher used for virtue is *arête* and can be defined as "excellence of any kind."[5]

I define *virtue* as excellence used for the greatest good. Virtues are qualities or characteristics that are considered morally good, like wisdom, courage, honesty, kindness, forgiveness, and fairness. Virtues make up our character. They teach us how to act and help us lead fulfilling and meaningful lives that contribute to the flourishing of society. Virtue is knowing good, doing good, and moving others toward good.

When you live with a virtuous character, you are motivated to uphold a high moral standard and strive for human excellence. And you *become* the virtues you consistently practice.

Ancient saints adopted what became known as "the seven divine virtues" as a moral guide to teach others how to live the most excellent life possible. These seven virtues consist of four virtues identified by Aristotle, Plato, and the ancient Jewish writings of King Solomon and three proposed in the Bible: prudence (wisdom), justice, temperance (self-control), fortitude (courage), faith, hope, and love.[6]

Whatever our political views or religious stances, most of us would agree that these virtues dictate our moral framework. Acting with honesty, gratitude, and humility, for example, lead you to become a better person and build a better world. Think of these seven virtues as a compass to lead you to your personal true north, the best version of yourself.

The Seven Virtues

WISDOM (honesty, awareness, seeking truth, principled thinking, creativity)

JUSTICE (integrity, fairness, honor, responsibility, leadership)

SELF-CONTROL (self-discipline, patience, humility, forgiveness, work ethic)

COURAGE (perseverance, confidence, action despite fear and consequence)

FAITH (spiritual devotion, commitment, trust in God, obedience)

HOPE (joy, gratitude, positive outlook, awe, curiosity)

LOVE (kindness, self-sacrifice, compassion, generosity, charity)

This virtue compass is more than the sum of its parts. Virtues do not operate independently of each other; rather, they complement one another and work synergistically. Consider the symbiosis of love and truth (wisdom). Truth without love can be harsh. Sharing a hard truth with someone by shouting verbal attacks coated in judgment usually doesn't end well. Likewise, love without truth often does little to add value or growth. It's what happens when we watch someone self-destruct because of an addiction and we never say anything about it, or when we tell someone what they *want* to hear all the time rather than what they *need* to hear. Loving without saying what needs to be said restricts development and leaves no room for improvement. Like all virtues, love and truth work best when they work together.

If you want to make your life a masterpiece, you must be virtuous. It is the only way to create a life of beauty that inspires, that is meaningful, and that moves the world forward in a positive direction.

What masterpieces are you looking to create in your family, physical health, ministry, or career? You will make them happen when you build a virtuous character.

One problem we have today is that people perceive virtue and character as boring, old-fashioned qualities. Yet they are the most powerful and awe-inspiring practices on the planet. How did Martin Luther King Jr. create change? Justice. How did Michael Jordan become the greatest athlete of all time? Discipline. How did Elon Musk pioneer electric transportation? Wisdom. How did my mom overcome cancer? Courage.

How will you become the greatest you? By taking aim and growing in the seven virtues.

> **THINK THIS:** Virtues lead you to your personal true north, the best version of yourself.
> **NOT THAT:** Virtues are outdated and boring.

Ready, Aim, Fire

To build a strong, virtuous character, you must have a target, something to aim for in life. A target creates clarity, certainty, and a greater purpose—all of which are essential to living optimally and reaching your highest potential. As the saying goes, an archer cannot hit the bull's-eye if he doesn't know where the target is.

Aristotle used an example of archery to describe moral excellence, likening our ability to live a virtuous life to how an archer aims at his target.[7] Before Aristotle, the Torah (which means "to take aim"[8]) used similar language to describe sin, something that is morally wrong. The Greek word for "sin" is *hamartanó* and means "missing the mark."[9]

When it comes to taking aim at a virtuous life, a great target to strive for is the Golden Rule: treat others the same way you want to be treated.

I like to think virtuous character is asking the question, What is the most loving thing I can do for this person right now? because *love* is the ultimate bull's-eye. Love, as proposed in the ancient Scriptures and by Augustine, is the greatest of all the seven virtues.[10] I consider it to be the meta virtue.

Love is a rich and robust word that we in modern society have dampened with fleeting ideas of romanticism, hedonistic pleasures, and self-indulgence. The Greek language, however, offers four types of love.[11]

- *erōs*: romantic love or erotic desire (*I love my spouse.*)
- *philia*: brotherly love; friendship (*I love my best bud.*)
- *storgē*: affection, especially of parent to child and child to parent; picture a mother nursing a newborn (*I love my son/daughter.*)[12]
- *agape*: unconditional, self-sacrificial love; God's unconditional, self-sacrificial love for humankind and humankind's love for God and others (*I love you so much that I will do what's right by you, even though it will cost me.*)[13]

The highest form of love, *agape*, is action-oriented. It involves sacrificing your own needs and preferences for someone else's without expecting anything in return. The character Steve Rogers illustrates this well in the first scene of the *Captain America* film. To prove his heroic ability, he leaps on a grenade to potentially save the lives of his peers.

Agape is not a feeling; rather it is a choice.

Agape in action is offering to watch the children of a parent who must attend an important appointment but cannot afford to pay for a sitter. Or bringing chicken soup and supplements to a friend who is sick. It is how Dave, a great friend of mine and master handyman, helps those less fortunate to build local playgrounds and fixes what needs to be repaired in orphanages and organizations in his community. It is offering supplies, donating money to a charity, using your life experience and wisdom to mentor someone, and—how Tim Tebow defines his life purpose—fighting "for those who cannot fight for themselves."[14]

In *Lord of the Rings: The Return of the King*, Sam and Frodo are climbing up Mount Doom in the final moments of their quest. Their faces are sooted with dirt and ash, lips cracked from thirst, and limbs heavy as lead. At one point, Frodo collapses. Unable to take another step, Sam steps up and announces with great conviction that, although he cannot carry the ring, he can (and does) carry Frodo up and over the mountain.

This is how Thomas Aquinas described *agape*, as willing the good of another.[15] You take the burden of another upon yourself and fight for them with all your heart. You sacrifice your time, talents, and treasures so that others can reach their full potential. The breadth of *agape* is what makes love one of the seven divine virtues.

The first four virtues (prudence, justice, temperance, and fortitude) were formed from Aristotelian virtue ethics. Based on logic and reasoning, and practiced by the Stoics, the four virtues were guided by the question, What would a virtuous person do?[16] However, spiritual giants like Aquinas surmised that logic and reasoning only go so far. In his writings on virtues, *Summa Theologica*, Aquinas conjectured that faith and hope in an afterlife are necessary to practice the most purposeful and powerful form of virtue ethics and to have the highest level of character.[17] The first four virtues are incomplete in the absence of faith, hope, and love.

Having a virtuous character runs deeper than just being a good person; it is doing the greatest good, which is the *most loving* thing you can do *for everyone* around you and *for a lasting impact*. The greatest good is only possible to accomplish with the underpinnings of the virtues of faith, hope, and love.

During World War II, Corrie ten Boom and her family opened their home as a hiding place for Jewish people who were being hunted by the Nazis. The ten Booms were willing to put their lives in danger because of their faith. As a result of their heroic efforts, an estimated eight hundred Jews and other refugees were saved. But the freedom of these people came at a price. Corrie, her sister, and their father were arrested and sent to a concentration camp. Only Corrie survived. She spent the remaining years of her life spreading the message of faith, hope, and love.

This is a faith that flies in the face of reason. Logic alone cannot tear down injustice, hatred, and violence.

How to Determine What Is Good

Pursuing the virtues involves pursuing the greatest good. But how do we know what good is? That's the question of the ages. There are typically four questions most people ask (even unknowingly) to determine whether what they are doing is "good."

- Do I follow the *rules*?
- Do I have the right *motives*?
- Will my actions lead to the best *outcome*?
- What would the most *virtuous* person I know do?

Let's explore these.

Do I follow the rules? If a person did what they were told, they often conclude their actions were good. But is following the rules always the right thing to do?

The German people were told by the Nazi regime to rat out their Jewish neighbors, and we know where that led. It is obvious that edict was an immoral rule; not all rules are good ones. Other times, there are no rules at all. So this is not the best question to ask to determine what is good.

Do I have the right motives? The second way most people evaluate what is good is by asking if they meant well when they made a certain decision.

Motives are typically tied to fulfilling your duty, but when you have multiple duties, which one takes priority? If a parent chooses to work overtime instead of attending his daughter's basketball tournament and justifies the decision by having the right intentions of providing for his family, it doesn't necessarily equate to a good decision. His motives might be in the right place, but it may have been better for his daughter in the long run to see her dad cheering from the bleachers. This is another question that leaves us unsatisfied as we search for the good.

Will my actions lead to the best outcome? Asking this question determines right from wrong based on outcome. Specifically, whatever does the greater good for the majority is the way to go.

Another way to think of this is through the idea that "the end justifies the means." An example is pharmaceutical companies or billionaires testing drugs on people in impoverished countries for safety and efficacy yet causing them harm at the same time. This question does not provide a reliable gauge.

What would the most virtuous person I know do? You've heard me say this in different ways in this book, but it bears repeating. Following the footsteps of a mentor, your best possible self, or a superhero is the most effective way to hit the mark.

This is the question I find most helpful in discerning what is good.

You might ask, What would [insert the name of someone who has virtuous character] do? How would they think? If you're running a business, consider how Jamie Kern Lima, founder of IT Cosmetics, or Dan Cathy, CEO of Chick-fil-A, would handle the situation. By superimposing yourself into their thought process, you can move closer to your target.

If you want to become your greatest you, model people who are virtuous. Remember the mindshift of becoming? Grow to the greatest degree in your skill and character toward the greatest good.

WHO COULD YOU BECOME?

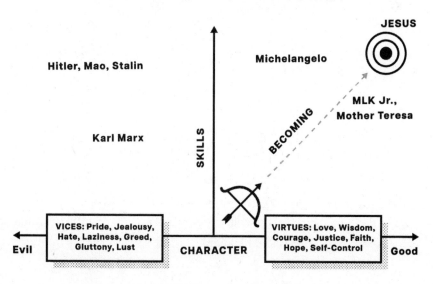

Tim Tebow may have been one of the most polarizing athletes in the NFL, but something most people can agree on is his virtuous character. Six years ago, Tebow created a global movement called Night to Shine where he puts on "an unforgettable prom night experience for people with special needs."[18] Teens and adults who are considered less-than, ignored by society because of their disabilities, are cheered on as they make their way down a red carpet. They dance all night, are extravagantly loved on, and by the end of the evening are given a crown or a tiara to wear as they are declared kings and queens.[19] Tebow's target is communicated in his purpose statement: "To bring Faith, Hope and Love to those needing a brighter day in their darkest hour of need." This is the same guy who each year auctions off his most prized possession, his Heisman Trophy, for children in need, raising more than one million dollars as of 2022.[20]

As you strive to become the person you were created to be and create masterpieces in all areas in life, it is important to ask not only, What is good? but also, Do I know my target? Are you aiming toward racking up trophies, titles, and accomplishments? Or are you seeking to live life on a deeper level, as we've been discussing throughout this book?

Aim toward the greatest good of using your talents to love others and turn this planet into a paradise. I promise you one thing—developing virtuous character will lead you to living the most powerful and impactful life possible.

What Stands in the Way of Virtuous Character?

Three things tend to crush one's capacity to develop a virtuous character: (1) the false impression that virtuous character is outdated, (2) an imbalance of modern-day values over divine virtues, and (3) an unintentional preoccupation with vices and bad habits.

Is Virtue Outdated?

The term "virtuous character" often is not seen as sexy. Developing a virtuous character doesn't mean being a goody-two-shoes, emotionally rigid, or puritanical. Aristotle believed that virtuous people were the only people who were truly happy and fulfilled and experienced the Greek term *eudemonia*, or human flourishing.[21] Living with the highest level of character produces the pleasurable yet long-term feeling we get when we give or receive unexpected acts of kindness or compassion, when we finish a tough workout we didn't think we could do, when we're overcome with gratitude, or when we complete a difficult assignment. It feels like the best kind of hug.

These emotions are quite a contrast to the short-term gratification and the unpleasantness we experience from excessive drinking (and the hangover the next day), indulging in the burgers and fries for the third time this week (and the bloating and brain fog aftermath), or betting it all (and losing it again) in a poker game.

Being virtuous comes with myriad benefits. One study compared virtuous CEOs (the business leaders who were scored the highest in character by their employees, who stood up for what's right, had concern for the good of all team members, let go of mistakes, and demonstrated compassion) to self-focused CEOs (the lowest-scoring business leaders who were described as twisting the truth for personal advancement and putting themselves ahead of their employees in their finances, vacation time, and work ethic). The virtuous CEOs had five times more financial profitability than the CEOs with low character marks.[22] Imagine that! A five-times greater financial return over colleagues who had poor character. Now that doesn't seem boring or old-fashioned!

Confusing Values with Virtues

Today, modern *values* are emphasized over *virtues*. These two words might seem similar at first, but they are quite different. Values garner more praise on social media than virtues—you could even think of them as motivational goals based on personal, cultural, or societal beliefs. Examples of modern-day values include self-love, inclusion, self-expression, and ambition. Individualistic values are good for you personally, and maybe even those around you, but virtues are good for everyone and have a more lasting impact.

While both virtues and values are vital for guiding behavior and leading a meaningful life, virtues carry more weight than values. Virtues are fundamental to your character and serve as the foundation upon which values are built. In and of themselves, and used in conjunction with virtues, values can indeed better your life, but when you emphasize modern-day values over, or without, virtue, you end up with a lopsided perspective—which doesn't serve the best interests of everyone and the greatest good.

For instance, empathy without justice and compassion is not wholly effective. Paul Bloom, a Yale University professor of cognitive science and psychology, found that empathy may cloud good judgment.[23] In his clinical research, he found that empathy alone is like a spotlight that highlights an issue but doesn't do anything to help solve or repair the problem. What it can do, however, is become a tool to motivate someone to do something. This is where virtues like justice and compassion—defined as "understanding what another is feeling" and "the willingness to act to alleviate suffering for another," respectively[24]—can lock arms for a purpose. For values to have positive impact, they must be built upon virtues.

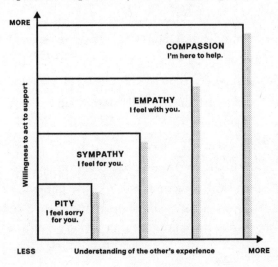

Self-love is another example. We cannot truly love others unless we love ourselves. However, self-love should be balanced with the virtue of self-discipline. If you struggle with overeating or procrastination, you ought to still love yourself, but you cannot reach your full potential without self-control and discipline. Also, too much self-love can cause you to approve of your own bad habits and lead to narcissism. The same truth applies to other values, including tolerance, inclusion, diversity, environmentalism, and patriotism. All these values must be tempered and supported by virtues such as wisdom (if they are to be truly good).

Lastly, values do not lead to internal transformation. Instead, they easily can become an external facade, the part of ourselves we parade before the world to get approval. Virtues, on the other hand, are qualities that are developed in our character and meant to change us from the inside out, which is the only kind of transformation that works and lasts.

The Seven Vices

While values have their place in proper balance with virtue, vices, on the other hand, are virtue's archenemy. Vices are any destructive habits that weaken a person's character and stand in the way of virtuous character development. Billy Graham said, "When wealth is lost, nothing is lost; when health is lost, something is lost; when character is lost, all is lost."[25]

There are seven capital vices—pride, envy, wrath, greed, lust, gluttony, and sloth—which give rise to other vices, or ways to "miss the mark" in life.

The Seven Vices

PRIDE: the belief in and love of one's own superiority. *I am better than everyone.* Pride caps growth. If you believe you know it all and you are the best at everything, you have no capacity to develop. Pride leads to ingratitude and to never being content. It can manifest as jealousy, self-worship, narcissism, and entitlement.

ENVY: wanting and thinking you are entitled to what someone else has. *I deserve that marriage/house/job.* Envy leads to anger, hatred, and personal unhappiness. It can manifest as jealousy, being unhappy or disappointed at the success of others, judgment, and self-aggrandizing behavior.

WRATH: wishing harm on someone. *I hope that person doesn't get the promotion.* Wrath moves in the opposite direction of love and diminishes your capacity to experience positive emotions. Wrath manifests as rage, feeling out of control, being physically or verbally abusive, and aggressive behavior.

GREED: wanting ever more of something or someone, like drugs, shopping, sex, alcohol, or food. *More is always better.* Greed limits the positive impact you can have on other people and will leave you constantly unsatisfied. It manifests as an unhealthy attachment, need for recognition, manipulation, scarcity mentality, and lack of empathy.

LUST: a destructive and excessive sexual desire outside of marriage. *I want you, and I will do what it takes to have you.* Lust will cost you more than you want to spend, whether in the form of a relationship, time, money, or your self-worth. Lust manifests as promiscuity, pornography, living in a fantasy world, shallow relationships, and covetousness.

GLUTTONY: overindulgence in food and drink and other behaviors. *I'm going to have one glass of wine, and then, within the hour, the whole bottle.* Gluttony often pairs with addiction and is time- and mind-consuming. It manifests as idolatry, poor stewardship, lack of self-control, and disrespect for oneself.

SLOTH: laziness, the desire to avoid pain at all costs because you lack purpose. *I know there are problems I can help solve, but I just don't care.* Sloth leads to a meaningless life. It manifests as carelessness, unwillingness to act in the best interests of others, apathy, and self-absorption.

Vices have an interesting relationship with virtues. Operating in too little or too much of a particular virtue can lead to a vice. Aristotle viewed virtues as a "golden mean," the intermediate between excess and deficiency. For example, courage is a virtue. Too little of it leads to cowardice, and too much of it leads to rashness; both can be considered a vice.

THE GOLDEN MEAN

FOOLISHNESS	WISDOM	ARROGANCE
CORRUPTION	JUSTICE	DICTATORSHIP
COWARDICE	COURAGE	RASHNESS
SELFISHNESS	LOVE	ENABLEMENT
SELF-DEGRADATION	HUMILITY	PRIDE

Let's compare the three Vs—virtues, values, and vices—to a tree: The leaves and branches, which can be seen with the naked eye, represent your skills, talents, and accomplishments. The trunk is analogous to habits or the actions you take. The hidden roots, invisible at first glance, represent your identity, values, virtues, and purpose. When the storms of life come, it is much easier for the tree to topple over if it is top-heavy and the roots are shallow. Look at celebrities, politicians, and athletes, among other influencers, who are gifted with incredible skill yet lack integrity. If you want a fruitful tree, focus on growing deep roots and removing vices, which act like boulders that stunt growth. Grab hold of your vices and destroy them.

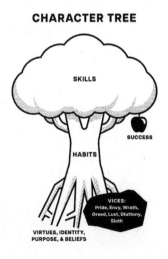

CHARACTER TREE

SKILLS

SUCCESS

HABITS

VICES:
Pride, Envy, Wrath, Greed, Lust, Gluttony, Sloth

VIRTUES, IDENTITY,
PURPOSE, & BELIEFS

The simplest way to do this is to attach as much pain as possible to your vices. First, visualize what will happen if you don't give up this destructive habit. Then take an opposing virtue and attach pleasure to it in visualizing your future. Keep doing this until it becomes habitual and a part of your identity.

Striving for moral and human excellence takes good aim, the opposite of "missing the mark," which in turn takes practice. As Will Durant paraphrased Aristotle, "We are what we repeatedly do."[26]

Practice the Virtues to Become Virtuous

Virtues, much like character, are not things we are born with. We become virtuous by practicing the virtues—and not only once or twice. We must cultivate them daily, over time, as we wrestle with a variety of struggles, challenges, and changes. It's not unlike how we might practice the violin or tennis.

Virtues are not feelings; they are choices. We attain courage by choosing to do something courageous today. And again tomorrow. And again the next day.

Try these two ways to start activating virtues in your life: (1) trade virtue *signaling* for virtue *solutions* and (2) start a virtue *habit*.

Trade virtue *signaling* for virtue *solutions*. Virtue signaling has become so popular in today's culture that it now appears in the *Cambridge Dictionary*. It is defined as "an attempt to show other people that you are a good person, for example by expressing opinions that will be acceptable to them, especially on social media. Virtue signaling is the modern habit of indicating that one has virtue merely by expressing disgust or favor for certain political ideas or cultural happenings."[27] In practical terms, it means doing something virtuous that everyone else is doing and making sure everyone else sees you doing it.

Virtue signaling is not only unvirtuous, but it is actually the vices of falseness, laziness, and cowardice. It is what the NBA did when they touted themselves as the reigning kings of social justice while ignoring human rights violations in China. It is when billionaires lecture the public about saving the environment, then fly in private jets, which give off massive amounts of carbon.

Virtue signaling certainly is not the best way to alleviate a problem. Rather than just posting a blank screen, a hashtag, or a quote from an iconic civil rights leader to prove that you are on the virtuous side of the court, why not come up with a plan to help solve a problem through virtue solutions?

When a social justice movement once was at the peak of publicity, Jordan Rubin and I had serious talks about what we could do for our local Black community. We didn't want to just put out platitudes on social media. We felt the pressure to speak out, with all the virtue signaling that was going on online, but what could we *do*, practically, to help in a real way?

Our team sought the advice of a local Black pastor with excellent, trustworthy character. He told us that the most meaningful thing we could do would be to help provide education for Black young people who lived in poverty. Our company president Colt, Jordan, and I went to work with our leadership team and came up with a plan to provide scholarships to children in the local Black community. Even the smallest solution is better than empty words.

Do something tangible by coming up with concrete solutions: ideas to be generous or spread kindness. The easiest and most efficient way to do this is to simply ask. Inquire what a house of worship, charity, family, or organization needs most desperately. How can you best help your neighbor? Your coworker? Your local animal shelter? What can you do for families in your community who are food insecure? Spread the love another way and spend time guiding/mentoring someone else. These virtue solutions can be custom designed to your talents, resources, and time.

Stop *talking* about it and start *doing* something about it.

Jimmy Donaldson (also known as "MrBeast"), one of the most subscribed-to YouTubers, is known not only for expensive stunts and crazy competitions but for his benevolence. As his brand has evolved over the years, so has his charitable giving. In the beginning of 2023, he paid for the eye surgeries of a thousand blind people so they finally could see.[28] And that's just his most recent act of generosity. Over the years he has donated to and raised millions of dollars for various causes, including global humanitarian aid, homeless shelters, clean water for villages in West Africa, and food insecurity in impoverished US communities.[29] This kind of altruism takes a considerable amount of sacrifice, self-control, and selflessness—qualities of a true hero. I love the fact that MrBeast doesn't merely talk about issues but puts his money where his mouth is.

Start a virtue *habit*. When I was in graduate school, I read *Today Matters* by John Maxwell. In it Maxwell encouraged readers to write down three of their greatest character strengths along with their three greatest character weaknesses. Then out of the three character weaknesses, he suggested readers focus on one to improve each month.

I decided I needed to work on encouraging others, which is a form of the virtue of love. At the time, I wasn't the most generous in my praise of people. I remember thinking of my grandfather. He always had something uplifting to say to those around him, whether it was an encouraging word or a lavish compliment. I wanted to be like that.

I began by typing out the word *encouragement* on one side of an index card. On the other, I added inspiring quotes, questions, and scriptures. This card helped remind me anytime I was in a conversation with someone to say something positive to or about them.

I'll admit that, at first, it was uncomfortable; saying encouraging words didn't come naturally to me. But nonetheless, I did it. I told people things like, "That was a great idea," "I love what you did with your hair," "I appreciate what an empathetic person you are. It's such a gift!" And it wasn't just lip service; I made sure my words were honest and sincere. I challenged myself to look for the best in people rather than focus on their faults.

Over time, it became a natural part of who I was, and I didn't need a card to remind me to do it. A few months later, several different people made a point of telling me that I seemed like a different person. When you make a virtue a habit, it is *impossible* not to become virtuous. Don't just *try* to be virtuous; *train* to be virtuous.

Need help getting started? Take a quick break and visit leaders.com/virtuecards for FREE downloadable/ printable virtue cards to get you started.

Here are other ideas to turn the seven divine virtues into habits.

Seven Divine Virtues

WISDOM: Read books written by the wise, then put their principles into practice. Watch movies and shows that will not only entertain you but also educate you. Seek out truth rather than believing everything you hear and read.

JUSTICE: Make a habit of telling the truth with love, even if it's hard. Make decisions based on what is right rather than on how you feel. Take ownership instead of playing the victim. Fight for the oppressed.

SELF-CONTROL: Think before you speak. Listen more than you talk. Think of others more than yourself. Practice self-discipline and give your best effort in everything.

COURAGE: Do the right thing, even if you feel afraid. Embrace the unknown. Do something that takes you out of your regular routine. Discover inner and outer demons and destroy them.

FAITH: Meditate. Pray. Read spiritual books. Spend time with a community of worship. Take bold steps toward your purpose. Pursue a connection with God.

HOPE: Show optimism in the face of negative circumstances. Hang out with hopeful people. Go out of your way to encourage others. Be grateful in all circumstances.

LOVE: Ask yourself, What is the most loving thing I can do for the person in front of me? and act on the answer. Give up your preferences for someone else's. Be generous with your time, talents, and money (for example, donate your money or volunteer for a local organization).

What virtues have you noticed in your life, or in the lives of people you admire, that have promoted excellence in relationships or developed great purpose? Are you aware of the vices that keep your potential at bay? Which ones need your attention?

Need help uncovering your vices and strengthening your virtues? Visit joshaxe.com/thinkthis and dive into a free exercise that will support you in improving your aim and hitting the mark.

Set "Your Best You" Free

Against all odds, Michelangelo lived until he was eighty-eight years old. During the Renaissance, life expectancy wasn't long, forty or fifty years at best.[30] When he was seventy-one, he believed his life was over and that it was time for him to retire and die.[31] But the tide turned when he was asked to take on a new and unexpected project: to be the chief architect of the largest construction site in the world at the time, St. Peter's Basilica. He said yes.

Sadly, the artist knew that building the structure would take longer than he had to live. In fact, the basilica ended up taking a total of 150 years to complete. But in the eighteen years that Michelangelo was in charge, he made sure the foundation, the framework, and the design were arranged with perfection and excellence so that after he died, no changes needed to be made. This Renaissance master understood that the best way to live was to keep creating masterpieces and keep the wheels of virtue in motion.

Michelangelo once made the comment, "Every block of stone has a statue inside it and it is the task of the sculptor to discover it. I saw the angel in the marble and carved until I set him free."[32]

Your job as a human being is to create masterpieces not only by creating something beautiful but also by removing whatever keeps you from that beauty. If you live with your vices and do nothing about them, your potential will be stuck in stone. So start tapping and chipping away at whatever is stopping you from doing the greatest good in your family, your community, and this world.

Develop your virtues. Make them habits. Realize the potential you have and keep carving away at the parts that keep you from being the person you were born to be. In you there is a masterpiece of a better spouse, a better parent, a better manager, a better friend, a better artist, a better innovator, a better leader.

The philosopher and activist Rabbi Abraham Joshua Heschel shared the following words of wisdom with young people before he died: "Let them be sure that every little deed counts, that every word has power, and that we can do, everyone, our share to redeem the world. . . . And above all, remember that the meaning of life is to live life as if it were a work of art."[33]

It's time to set yourself free.

MINDSHIFT 8:

Bust vices by building virtues.

Vices → Virtues

TURN OFF OPINIONS AND TURN ON PRINCIPLES

When I embarked on my quest to open a functional medicine clinic, I needed some guidance. I began to ask everyone I knew, from local doctors to relatives, for their advice. Numerous ideas and opinions surfaced, many of which were conflicting. Some people supported the idea of starting my own business, while others suggested I work for someone else because 90 percent of small businesses fail. Some people recommended I open an office in the most prestigious area of town, while others said to keep overhead as low as possible; I found it wasn't possible to do either. One doctor told me I would need to work eighty hours a week to survive for my first few years as an entrepreneur or I'd likely fail, while another colleague said it was important to maintain a work-life balance.

With all these conflicting opinions, how was I to know what to do?

To help me wade through all these views, I went to a trusted mentor and asked him how I should discern the truth. He looked me in the eyes and said, "Josh, you need to stop listening to everyone's opinions and follow principles. There are certain principles you can follow in how you should run your practice, and I am going to share with you how to discover what they are. The first and most important principle is to look at the doctors who are getting the best results and running the most successful clinics, and to model their thinking and actions."

This doctor's wise words radically changed my life. I followed his advice and started ignoring opinions and making all my decisions based on principles.

Because of this newfound wisdom, my clinic and influence grew astronomically. I was able to help more people heal than I ever thought possible. Once I learned what principles actually were and how they led to truth and best practices, I started to apply them in every area of my life, including spiritual, family, and business. Later in this chapter, I'll share them with you.

In 2018, I spoke on a panel at the SXSW Conference titled "Food Is Information" along with four other medical experts. Someone in the audience asked, "When it comes to diets, foods, and supplements, how do you know what to believe is true when there is so much conflicting information?"

One doctor on the panel answered, "Follow the latest science. Do whatever the current research and your doctor says to do."

I thought about my colleague's response for a moment. Then I turned to him and offered my feedback. "I respect your opinion, but I wholeheartedly disagree. I believe the way we discover the truth is via principles, studying what's been true throughout existence, understanding those patterns, and applying those evident truths today."

I elaborated further and explained the importance of principles, which are defined as "a foundational law or truth from which others are derived."[1] To review, values are personal and changeable and need virtues to prop them up; virtues are unchanging and form the highest level of character; and principles are systems of beliefs and practical ways to live out virtues. The problem with relying solely on pharmaceutical research is that it can be biased and become outdated, whereas principles never fade away.

Spiritual principles are the foundations of religions such as Taoism (Daoism), Judaism, and Christianity. The Ten Commandments in the book of Exodus[2] and the Sermon on the Mount in the book of Matthew[3] offer timeless principles to live the best life possible. The laws of Karma, a philosophy stating the cycle of cause and effect, is another set of principles.

The Tao (or Dao) in Asian philosophy means "the way," which indicates the path that leads to the best way of being and living.

If you're unsure what principles guide your relationships, marriage, parenting, career, finances, and health, keep reading. We're going to discuss how to *think* principled, *live* principled, and *become* principled.

> **THINK THIS:** Principles lead to successful choices.
> **NOT THAT:** Others' opinions inform my decisions.

The Unprincipled Path to Nowhere

I once heard a story about two unhoused men sitting on a bench. One asked the other, "How did you end up here?"

The man replied, "I didn't listen to anybody. What about you?"

"I listened to everybody," he answered.

Listening both to everybody and to nobody will lead you down the wrong path. The secret is to listen and follow wise leaders who have had the best results in their businesses, their finances, and their relationships.

As John Maxwell stated, a leader is someone who "knows the way, goes the way, and shows the way."[4] The success of great leaders is guided by principles. Often, these truths are paradoxical or confusing at first glance. Have you ever heard the saying "The greatest of all is the servant of all"?[5] That doesn't make any sense. Who wants to be a servant? Yet history proves that the people who lived out that principle of servanthood have had the greatest impact on the world. Think of Nelson Mandela, Mother Teresa, and William Wilberforce.

Choosing the principled path can be difficult because nearly everyone is trying to sell you a path. *Buy this product. Use that method. Follow*

THINK THIS, NOT THAT

this guideline. Try that pill. Author Napoleon Hill wrote, "Opinions are the cheapest commodities on earth. Everyone has a flock of opinions ready to be wished upon anyone who will accept them. If you are influenced by 'opinions' when you reach decisions, you will not succeed in any undertaking."[6]

We are constantly bombarded with messages from every direction—from friends to media to the government to social media communities to our dear aunt Ruth—about what is right or wrong, what is best or worst. This makes it hard to weed out what is right and true. If you want to enjoy success in your relationships, career, and health, choose a path that is lined with principles. Instead of following the latest fad diet endorsed by a famous influencer, eat real food. Rather than taking on debt to level up your lifestyle and showcase it on social media (like many do), spend less than you make.

An unprincipled person is like a captain trying to steer a ship without navigation, lost at sea. Without any truth or standards to guide them, they lack wisdom. Without wisdom, they make poor choices. Making poor choices reinforces poor character. Consider how you might end up living if you have no code of honor. Without abiding by the principle of the Golden Rule, for instance, what standard would you follow? Would you treat people according to how you feel on any given day? Would this change depending on whether you've had your coffee that morning? Unprincipled living results in unpredictable behavior. Unprincipled people are untrustworthy.

It's a troubling reality that many people lack guiding principles in their lives. I believe the two predominant reasons for this are unhealthy family dynamics and educational institutions. Many parents have assigned the responsibility of educating their children to schools and social media. Parents should be teaching their kids life skills, moral wisdom, principles of success, and how to think for themselves, but too few of them are doing that. As a result, young children through college students are indoctrinated with morally void political ideologies and taught to memorize often useless information.

According to an article in the *New York Times*, "The American education model . . . was actually copied from the 18th-century Prussian model designed to create docile subjects and factory workers."[7] John D. Rockefeller was an advocate of this model and said, "I don't want a nation of thinkers, I want a nation of workers."[8] This is in direct opposition to the wisest people in history, including philosophers, rabbis, theologians, doctors, and scientists like Albert Einstein, who believed that education isn't about learning facts but training the mind to think.[9]

I learned calculus in high school and college, but I've never used it since then. A survey by H&R Block found that only 37 percent of the information learned in high school is used postgraduation. Most people surveyed said they wish they would have learned more life skills.[10] What if, instead of being forced to take calculus, we were taught money management? Or how about classes in nutrition, ethics, or the basics of cultivating healthy relationships? I wish I would have learned these things earlier in life. You may agree.

Deep thinking doesn't come from memorizing formulas or regurgitating facts. It comes from knowing how to think for yourself and applying that knowledge to your life. The great sages of the ancient world knew this well. To uncover wisdom in the modern world, look back into the wisdom of the past.

Principled Thinking

Known as the father of Western thought, the Greek philosopher Socrates mentored students including Plato and Xenophon. Socrates didn't inundate the minds of his students with facts and figures; he believed that the way for them to gather information and come to conclusions was by asking thoughtful questions. This is known as the Socratic method. It involves six levels of questions designed to understand, challenge assumptions, examine evidence, consider alternative perspectives, consider consequences, and question the question.[11]

The Socratic method is an example of principled thinking. It allows you to discover the truth about a problem and provide an effective solution.

There are many modern practices or tools of principled thinking to help us think deeply, discover the truth, and come up with innovative ideas. I'd like to introduce to you the three tools of principled thinking I use to come to wise conclusions:

- 5 Whys
- First Principles Thinking
- Iceberg Thinking

These different methods will help you apply principled thinking to different scenarios and root out truth where you need it.

The 5 Whys

When I practiced medicine, I saw thousands of patients who repeated medical myths like "Diets don't matter," "I'll have to live with this for the rest of my life," and "Diabetes cannot be reversed." The truth is, type 2 diabetes is almost always reversible. I know this because I helped hundreds of patients reverse it. My method of practicing medicine was driven by principled thinking. I offered my patients principles that taught them how to think for themselves and taught them that food, lifestyle, and mindset all can be used as medicine.

When a patient presented to me with a diagnosis, I first analyzed the entire situation to get to the root of the problem. Early in my practice, I adopted the "5 Whys" approach. This technique boils things down to a simple question: Why? The more you ask this question, the closer you get to the root of the problem. Sakichi Toyoda of Toyota Industries created this technique decades ago, but the exercise is grounded in the Socratic method.[12]

Here's how to do it:

1. Determine the present problem. Maybe you're wondering why you

suddenly can't sleep at night or why assistants keep quitting on you. Why?

2. For each answer you get, ask, Why? at least four more times. When you determine the root cause, there's no need to go further. With this knowledge in hand, you can proceed to solve the problem.

Here is what this looks like with a diagnosis of diabetes:

PROBLEM: Type 2 diabetes

WHY: Blood sugar is high.

WHY: The pancreas isn't producing enough insulin.

WHY: Too much sugar has damaged their insulin receptors.

WHY: The patient's diet contains too many carbohydrates.

WHY: The patient doesn't know what to eat or has a sugar addiction.

SOLUTION: Educate the patient on the benefits of a low-glycemic diet high in protein, healthy fats, fiber, and nutrients, and monitor their progress.

OUTCOME: A1C levels normalized and type 2 diabetes was reversed.

Look at what a physician with a common half-truth, medical myth-driven approach typically uses for reasoning:

PROBLEM: Type 2 diabetes

SOLUTION: Prescribe drug.

The difference between these two methods can literally be a matter of life and death.

First Principles Thinking

Back in 2002, Elon Musk had a bold and audacious goal in mind—he wanted to land a rocket on Mars. One of the main obstacles preventing him from achieving this goal was the price tag. Buying a rocket could end up costing as much as $65 million, an astronomical amount. But the high cost didn't dissuade Musk from pursuing his dream. Instead, he began using "First Principles Thinking" to analyze the problem.

Using this type of critical thinking, Musk refused to accept that rockets had to be so expensive. He broke down a typical rocket into its components and materials. He looked at commodity prices to compare. From there, he was able to determine that he could build his own rocket for only 10 percent of the quoted price.[13] SpaceX was created soon afterward.

First Principles is often used in physics to examine the world. Musk described it this way: "You boil things down to the most fundamental truths and ask, 'What are we sure is true?' and then reason up from there."[14] Here's how to do it:

1. **Have a basic understanding of what you're questioning.** This will enable you to ask the right questions that will help you break down things to their core truths. Elon Musk might not be a rocket scientist, but he does know basic construction, technology, and materials. That's what allowed him to ask the right questions to find the essential elements and the constraints to solve a complex problem.

2. **Remove all assumptions.** With a basic knowledge of the topic, you can then cast aside common assumptions and embrace more innovative thinking. This isn't always easy to do. All too often we think our assumptions are an absolute reality. Returning to the rocket example, it would have been easy to assume that building a rocket was incredibly expensive. What Elon Musk did was eliminate that assumption by removing biases. You can follow the same principle by removing your biases and opinions related to industry norms, politics, traditions, and modern culture.

3. **Get to the basic principle.** After removing assumptions, you can proceed to break things down into the basic principle or truth. Here you separate what's fact from fiction. This is where the term First Principles Thinking comes from.[15] A first principle is the

basic element of something. Uncovering these elements requires careful questioning, more specifically asking why. You can do this by following the 5 Whys technique.

4. **Be detailed with your thinking.** First Principles thinkers work in details. People like leadership alchemist Shadé Zahrai, C. S. Lewis, and Jordan Peterson are great examples. These highly detailed thinkers carefully choose their words, are specific in expressing thoughts and ideas, and build on them in a unique way.

   Also, think of what makes a good book. For me, the *Lord of the Rings* (surprise, surprise) trilogy presents writing in its most creative and inspirational form. When I look at not just the books but individual words, sentences, and paragraphs, I can feel the details come to life. All those details add up to interesting characters, a great storyline, meaningful themes, and ultimately a masterpiece. The same holds true for First Principles Thinking. Focus on individual parts. Get down into the smallest details. Expand your understanding of those details. As you engage in more detailed thinking, you'll be able to express core truths and build on them in unique ways.

5. **Keep the bigger picture in mind**. When focusing on the details, you must not lose sight of the bigger picture. Always keep your vision and note the potential trade-offs and outcomes so you can be prepared. When keeping the bigger vision in mind, think of how successful Marvel has been with the Marvel Cinematic Universe. While you can point to plenty of factors for the continuing success of the franchise, one of the main reasons is how everything in that universe is connected. Every movie, television show, and even short film plays into the bigger picture. Even so, the individual components that make up the whole are done well too.

First Principles Thinking can be applied to every area of your life. If you're writing your first book, ask yourself what makes a great book. Research the elements that the greatest writers use and then create your own book based on that wisdom. From that, you can come up with an innovative idea to make your goal a reality.

Here is an example of what sketching that out might look like.

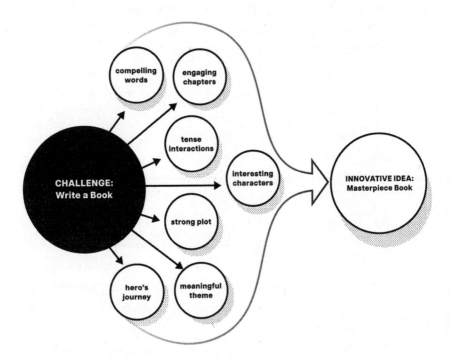

Iceberg Thinking

This is a simple and effective tool to help ascertain what lies beneath the surface. Ask and answer the following four questions.

1. *What* happened? (I'm always getting sick.)
2. *How* did it happen, and what were the patterns that caused it? (I get sick when I don't get enough sleep.)
3. *Who* caused it, and what habits reinforce the pattern? (I always stay up late working, and because I'm so busy, I end up eating fast food all the time.)
4. *Why*? What limiting beliefs and ideas led to these habits? (My identity is tied to my job, and I don't value my body and my health enough to practice better habits.)

ICEBERG THINKING

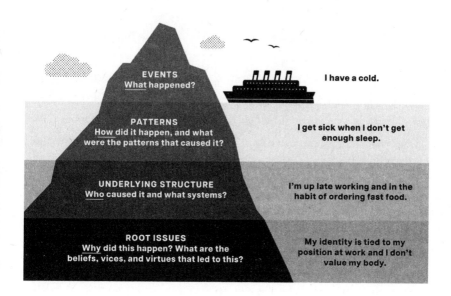

EVENTS How<u>What</u> happened?	I have a cold.
PATTERNS <u>How</u> did it happen, and what were the patterns that caused it?	I get sick when I don't get enough sleep.
UNDERLYING STRUCTURE <u>Who</u> caused it and what systems?	I'm up late working and in the habit of ordering fast food.
ROOT ISSUES <u>Why</u> did this happen? What are the beliefs, vices, and virtues that led to this?	My identity is tied to my position at work and I don't value my body.

Iceberg Thinking is a good tool to use when you need to determine the truth of the daily news and not fall prey to propaganda. Most people focus on the surface of a problem rather than think through to the root cause. Take homelessness, for instance. A cursory glance at the issue might conclude that a lack of housing is the problem, yet there are bigger concerns. The underpinning of homelessness is a combination of lack of purpose, education, and opportunity in addition to mental health challenges.[16] Giving a person who is homeless housing without resources such as substance abuse recovery, job placement services, and life skills sets them up for failure. When people who are housing-insecure are invested in, given opportunities, and shown their true potential, they are able to provide and sustain a better living environment for themselves.

Whatever approach you use, thinking with principles will keep you from believing whatever you hear, or using the "I don't know" excuse for staying stuck without clarity and direction. This type of deep thinking will propel you into a new world of choosing a wise next step or making an informed decision.

Principled Living

While there is much to glean from Socrates and the Greek thinkers, the ancient Hebraic rabbis and philosophers lived at another level.

Like Socrates, the Torah (which means "instruction" or "to take aim"[17]) encourages asking questions to gain deeper understanding. The Jewish people have an obligation to teach their progeny to do more than blindly follow a religion; they ought to be curious and inquisitive.[18]

Mentorship, too, is essential. The Hebrew word *talmid* is synonymous with "disciple."[19] It means more than just learning what is being taught by the rabbi; the objective of being a *talmid* is to emulate the rabbi. Don't just absorb what he says; do as he does. Follow in his footsteps. The correct path here is to do (become a master) and then teach others. There is much value in learning from a person rather than just learning a task.

I experienced this very principle from the same mentor I mentioned in the beginning of this chapter who spoke into my life and helped me find truth in a fog of opinions. Years before I opened my own practice, I had the opportunity to shadow him in his practice. I even lived with him and his family for three months. This personal experience gave me a clear picture of what he was like at work and at home. From my observations, it quickly became obvious that my mentor was principled in both thinking and living.

I watched him get up early, pray, exercise, and spend time with his family. He taught me the principle of rhythm: "Win the morning, win the day." I watched him treat the employees in his office with respect and serve his patients with great care. I learned more from observing him in action and modeling his behavior than I ever could from reading a book or taking a course.

Principles are a map to truth and success. They guide you in the highest level of conduct, character, and choice. When you live with principles, you approach people, ideas, opinions, and beliefs with a new lens. You take advice not from just anybody but from people who have yielded great results. You ask questions rather than blindly follow. You fine-tune your thinking to understand, not just accept.

When you become principled, you also acquire the gift of foresight. You see what others don't see. You often perceive what's going to happen before it happens because you observe patterns at play and know how the dominos will fall. This is how investors such as Michael Burry anticipated and thrived through the 2008 housing and stock market crash. He, along with others like Ray Dalio, recognized that healthy economic principles, such as giving loans to those who are credit worthy, were being broken. Burry was able to grow his personal wealth by $100 million and his investors' by $700 million when most others were losing all their wealth.[20] Knowing principles and following principled people can be a matter of losing it all or tripling your net worth.

Warren Buffett, known as the Oracle of Omaha and as the most successful investor of the past century, has a net worth of more than $100 billion and ranks number five on the *Forbes* billionaires list.[21] Buffett sets the gold standard of solid investment decisions. The secret to his success? Ignoring opinions, trends, and media hype and investing in businesses with great people, great products, and great potential for profit.[22] These simple principles have allowed him to thrive.

And principles can work for you, too, in whatever area you want to thrive in.

It's time to look at some fundamental principles that will help you become a better leader, spouse, parent, or contributing member of society.

> **THINK THIS:** I think in principles.
> **NOT THAT:** I believe what's popular.

Life Principles for Greater Living

I uncovered the power of financial principles after an unwise investment I made cost me every penny of savings (more on that in the next chapter). At the time, I had started my own business and was beginning to bring home income. I knew a lot about health and functional medicine but little about how I should save and invest my money. I thought my idea of risking it all on the success of one business venture was a good one, but I hadn't done the work of researching investment options. After it failed, I had to start saving up again. It was a humbling lesson, but I knew I wouldn't make the same mistake twice.

My second round of financial planning started with more foresight. I thought about the most successful people I knew who were financially wise and flourishing. I wrote down the names of people I personally knew, like Jordan Rubin and Dave Ramsey. Then I jotted down the names of the people I esteemed from afar, like Warren Buffett, Ray Dalio, Elon Musk, Robert Kiyosaki, Cathie Wood, and Mark Cuban.

I met with the two individuals I personally knew and asked them for their best advice on how to build wealth. Rubin and Ramsey gave me similar advice: get out of debt, charitably give 10 percent of your income after taxes, invest in your personal and business development, and invest 10 percent of your income into real estate or the stock market after you pay off your debts. Additionally, these men of great character taught me to invest my time, talent, and treasures into my family.

Next, I dove into the mindsets of the other financial giants I mentioned and studied the principles they put into practice. I learned the fundamentals like buying when the market is down and selling high and investing in what you understand, not just what everyone else is investing in.

Over the years, through life experience and being a disciple under many wise mentors, I've collected a variety of principles that I live by. I want to offer you the top ten that have added the most value to my life. If you study and apply them to your life, I can guarantee that you will see a positive change in yourself and your outcomes.

1. Recognize the wise by their results.
2. Model those who are wise and virtuous.
3. You reap what you sow.[23]
4. The word is mightier than the sword.[24]

5. The greatest of all is the servant of all.[25]
6. Find *the* truth.
7. Iron sharpens iron.[26]
8. We are what we repeatedly do; therefore, virtue is a habit.
9. Be the change.
10. Love (*agape*) wins.

1. **Recognize the wise by their results**. How do you determine who to believe or whose advice is right? One of the best ways is to observe the results in their own life. I can trust the financial advice of Warren Buffett because, over the past five decades, he has gotten consistently great results from his investments. Think of people as fruit trees. Good trees produce good fruit. Rotten trees produce rotten fruit. An apple may look good on the outside but still be rotten on the inside. At one time, I considered a particular leader to be a potential mentor—but then he chose to leave his wife and break his family apart for a significantly younger woman. I didn't want that type of fruit in my life. That same individual also had recommended that I not donate to charitable causes early on in my practice. I knew from speaking with others I trusted and from my faith that giving generously is an essential part of flourishing in life. This rotten fruit spoke volumes about this individual's lack of wisdom.

2. **Model those who are wise and virtuous**. As we've discussed in previous chapters, this is essential. Look for people with strong character you can imitate, knowing that not everyone is going to get it right in every area of their life. Steve Jobs, for example, was an excellent innovator but could have used some help in the parenting department. Others might shine in the financial arena but struggle in their marriage. Find mentors—in person, in books, and online—who can teach you principled thinking and living in the most important areas of your life. Stick with their direction and ignore the opinions of the unprincipled.

3. **You reap what you sow.** This is both a karmic and biblical principle. If you don't invest time, energy, and care into building relationships, you are not going to have any friends. The same principle holds true for your marriage, health, and wealth. When it comes to finances, most people focus on spending and saving their money. But the key principle I've learned is to do neither and instead focus on sowing, which is synonymous with investing. I am always looking for opportunities to invest in companies and people I believe in. When investing in a business, the number-one thing I look for is strong leadership. This is akin to another principle: when you sow seeds, make sure those seeds fall on good soil. Sowing good seeds on sand, rock, or weeds won't yield much fruit.[27] Don't sow into people who aren't hungry for growth; you'll just be giving something valuable to someone who is going to waste it.[28] When you sow your seeds (time, talents, and treasure) on good soil (hardworking people), you can reap a big harvest in your faith, fitness, family, finances/work, and free time.

4. **The word is mightier than the sword.** *Word* and *sword* are only one letter apart. Both are symbolic of their power to influence, yet words reign supreme. We saw the power of this in Dr. Martin Luther King Jr.'s "I Have a Dream" speech, which was more powerful than violence. Motivational speaker Brian Tracy estimated that "85% of your success in life is determined by your ability to communicate."[29] The best tool for navigating conflict, strengthening partnerships, and effectively sharing thoughts, ideas, and feelings is good communication. Words carry so much weight that ancient proverbs say they even hold the power of life and death.[30] Words have fueled world wars and declared the independence of nations. Just think of words that have encouraged you to rise to the occasion or broken your heart. Be mindful of what you say. Consider words a sword of truth. Use your words wisely, and wisely choose which ones you listen to.

5. **The greatest of all is the servant of all.** Making success and achievement primarily about yourself is the fastest way to become a

failure. This principle centers on how best you can serve your family, friends, and clients or customers. I think of how well Amazon, at its prime, put its customers at the forefront of its vision and service. This successful company aims to have the largest assortment of products at the cheapest price delivered in the shortest amount of time to those it serves. This vision speaks volumes. Consider this principle activated in marriage. Contrary to popular opinion, the primary goal is not for your spouse to make you happy but for each of you to serve the other.

6. **Find *the* truth.** To summarize Nietzsche, the measure of a man is determined by how much truth he can tolerate.[31] Truth can be hard to handle, sometimes so hard that people take the easier route of failing to accept it and going along with a lie. This happens because of pride (they don't want to be wrong), fear (they don't want to be canceled or ostracized), or laziness (it's easier to follow than think for yourself). To further complicate things, *the* truth, objective truth, has been replaced with *my/your* truth. This kind of language simply masks an opinion or lie. There are significant differences between *my/your* truth and *the* truth. *My truth* will make you as comfortable as possible. *The truth* will force you to change. *My truth* is dependent on what will make me feel good right now. *The truth* leads to a better outcome in the long run. It takes wisdom and courage to find and fight for the truth. Don't seek to discover *your* truth; act with wisdom and courage to uncover *the* truth, which leads to life.

7. **Iron sharpens iron.** Serena Williams and Venus Williams are two of the best tennis players of all time, ranking number one in both singles and doubles. They have a long-standing rivalry on the court, but they also support and inspire each other. When you grow in a community of greatness, you spur each other toward success and excellence. Not only is there shared encouragement, but there is also space for hard truth-telling to bring out the best in the other. The company you keep directly impacts the person

you become. Surround yourself with people who make you better, raise your standards, and help you transform into the person you were created to be.

8. **We are what we repeatedly do; therefore, virtue is a habit.**[32] If you want to become a person of virtue, you need to create habits that cultivate character. Want to be more generous? Practice generosity. Tip an extra 5 percent. Donate your time and services on the weekends. And do those things often. Before you know it, these habits will become a part of who you are. If you want to be more loving, start a love habit. Need more compassion? Start a compassion habit. You become the virtue that you practice consistently.

9. **Be the change.** As Mahatma Gandhi modeled a century ago through ethics and intelligence, we must first change in ourselves the things we wish would change in other people and the world. When we don't make a difference in our own life, we can't expect anything to change. Rather than judging others, we need to listen and learn and do things virtuously as we lead our families and teams. If we want others to be kinder, we become kind to others. If we wish for better environmental practices in our communities, we use less plastic, conserve water, and are mindful of what businesses we support through our purchases.

10. **Love (*agape*) wins.** In the classic tale *Beauty and the Beast*, heroine Belle loves a monster back into a human being. We deal with this real-life scenario almost every day when we come across people who are annoying, villainous, and even beastly. Most of us find it hard to respond like Belle did; it's tempting to be beastly back. The principle *love wins* means that, no matter what the situation, acting with love is the best response. As we discussed earlier, this love (*agape*) is not a romantic love but a sacrificial love in which you fight for and *will* the good of another. You do everything in your power to help the person succeed by sacrificing and sowing your effort, time, and resources. It's a picture of a parent sacrificing their money to save up for their child's college fund, forgiving

someone who has wronged you, or giving a loving response to a troll on social media. Practice the principle of *agape*, knowing that it conquers all.

To close this section, I'll share a few more key principles I aim to follow in specific life areas.

PRINCIPLES

Health Principles

1. Food, movement, and mindset are medicine.
2. Treat the root cause, not the symptoms.
3. First, do no harm.
4. Aim for eight hours of sleep.
5. Optimize nutrients and reduce toxicity.
6. The body heals itself.
7. Get outside for sun and circulation.
8. Eat real food (ideally, local and organic).

Career Principles

1. Aim for excellence in everything.
2. Virtuous leadership is essential.
3. MVP: Create the most valuable product possible.
4. Start with *why* and *who* before *how*.
5. Play to your strengths.
6. Have audacious goals and a detailed strategy, then execute and improve.

7. Be committed to constant growth.

8. Innovate in untapped markets and increase value.

Marriage and Family Principles

1. Be present and prioritize your family (your time should show it).

2. Teach your children principles and virtues.

3. Love and be gracious to one another.

4. A date night a week will keep the marriage sweet.

5. Communication is crucial.

6. Don't keep score. Out-serve one another instead.

7. Live out family values, purpose, and principles.

8. Honor and respect one another in tone and in all things.

If you run into a couple who have been married for forty or more years and still hold hands, chances are that one of the first questions you will ask them is, "What's the secret to a happy marriage?" If you're wise, you'll listen up because this couple will likely share some great principles to make love last. You may even learn more in a thirty-minute conversation with them than from reading a marriage self-help book.

While Chelsea and I haven't been married for decades, we've followed key principles (like the eight listed above) that have helped ward off some arguments and allowed our marriage to flourish. The two big principles we aim to live are (1) to honor each other (especially in our tone) and (2) to out-serve each other.

The first principle has guided the way we talk to each other, helping us maintain a respectful tone, particularly when it comes to conflict. I don't know about you, but when I get frustrated about a situation, a tempting response can be to raise my voice or have an unkind tone. Tone is a nonverbal cue that often speaks louder than words. Chelsea and I have learned to be intentional with how we carry our voices. Our tone is always loving and respectful, even when we disagree on things.

The second principle about out-serving each other prevents us from keeping score of who has done more for the other. We are a team, and we try to focus on ways we can give support and make each other's days better. Chelsea may do this by giving me an encouraging word, and I may do this by watching our daughter while Chelsea gets in a Peloton ride.

We've seen good fruit in our lives when we've practiced these principles.

What are the guiding principles of your life? If you don't have any, you're likely riding the current of the crowd, your feelings, or careless whims instead of intentionally rising above the status quo. Principles will always lead you to a higher level of being.

When you choose the path of principled thinking and living, you become more than your words; you become your actions. It is only when actions speak louder than words that true transformation at the optimum level can begin to unfold.

Turn off opinions and turn on principles.

Opinions → Principles

FLIP THE FEAR TO TURN ON THE GROWTH

Soon after my wife, Chelsea, and I got married in 2012, we began to talk about our future. We'd sit down in the morning with coffee or green tea in hand and share our life dreams. One day I told her that even though I liked being in clinical practice, I loved educating people in health and leadership even more and would love to do that full-time one day. Not long after, an opportunity arose to help start a company where I got to do just that. My clinic was doing well, but I felt ready to take the leap.

Chelsea encouraged me to pursue my dreams. We invested everything we had into the new business and moved from Nashville to South Florida. I was certain this venture would be a success. For the next few years, I traveled all over the country, sacrificing comfort, sleep, and time with my new bride to make the business succeed.

But to our dismay, the business never took off—it failed. Not only had Chelsea and I not earned a dime, but we also had lost all the money we poured into it.

I'll never forget looking at our bank account balance one day and realizing we had only enough to pay expenses for two more months. Without any income coming in, Chelsea and I realized we couldn't pay our upcoming bills and would need to make a change. I exited the business and moved back to Nashville. Shortly afterward I saw a sign in one of my favorite coffee shops that read, "When you're in trouble, get on your knees and pray, then get on your feet and work." And that's exactly what Chelsea and I did.

The following week I sought counsel from wise, trusted friends and mentors. One of the best pieces of advice I received was to focus wholeheartedly on the single most important thing I wanted to do. At the time, it was to create the number-one natural health website in the world, which was in line with my dream to educate people in health and leadership. Shortly thereafter, I attended a workshop that taught me how to create online courses and build an online business. Ten weeks later, I launched an online health course, which exploded with immediate success and brought in profit quicker than I could have possibly imagined. Over the course of the next few years, the website grew into the largest natural health website and later birthed Ancient Nutrition, one of the most successful supplement companies in the world.

After that original venture failed, I stood at a crossroads in my life. I had an important choice to make: I could fixate on the pain of the loss, give up on my dreams, and even return to my old job. Or I could accept responsibility for the mistakes made, learn from those mistakes, and start over in a different way.

That opportunity-turned-failure was one of my greatest teachers. It exposed the weaknesses I needed to work on. It taught me how to make wise investments and build the right team. It helped me understand the value of making data-driven decisions and so many other things that I since have put into practice. Above all, I learned the essential business principle of failing forward, or learning from your mistakes instead of hiding from them or giving up.

The truth is that most people let a fear-based mindset cripple their progress. This mindset causes you to exist in a self-protective state in which you are fearful of what others think about you. Instead of focusing on personal growth, progress, and self-development, you become fixated on maintaining the right self-image and appearing smart, talented, and successful. The only way out is by facing and embracing your failures head-on and understanding that they always pave the way to a flourishing future. That is, if you let them.

> **THINK THIS:** Failure can lead to flourishing.
> **NOT THAT:** I must avoid failure at all costs.

A Fear-Based Mindset

Do any of these statements sound familiar?

"If I don't get this promotion, my career is over."

"There is no room for mistakes. I must be perfect."

If you've used any type of this "all or nothing" language, aloud or in your head, these words reveal a fear-based mindset. Other symptoms include *either/or* thinking. ("If I don't win, I lose.") These all, of course, are limiting beliefs.

When you are locked within this headspace, you live in fear because you've tied an event (or series of events) to your identity. If you receive a bad performance review or don't get a job offer, you deem yourself a failure. Because you are so invested in maintaining this idea of perfection and setting unrealistic expectations for yourself, you'll do anything to protect your self-image, including keeping up the lie at whatever cost. You won't be honest with yourself or others. You'll never grow beyond superficial status because the goal isn't to develop your character and skills but to achieve, accomplish, and arrive—at least in the eyes of others.

Researchers, however, have proven that process trumps performance. Psychologist Carol Dweck at Stanford University published a study, with Claudia Mueller, that showed the benefits of a growth (flourishing) mindset versus a fixed (fear-based) mindset. Fifth graders were tested on a series of math problems and were praised over the course of these tests either for being smart (their natural intelligence) or for their effort (drive and hard work).[1]

The children who were praised for how intelligent they were cared more about their performance rather than what they were learning. After experiencing failure, these same children struggled with self-doubt and negative feelings and had poorer performance.

On the contrary, children who were praised for their efforts understood that the process of learning is important and that reward is found in hard work and growth. These fifth graders even used their failure to motivate them when they were given more difficult math problems to work on.

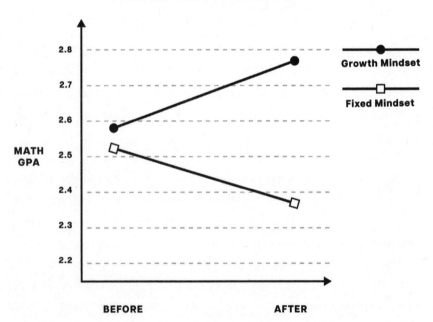

Math Grades Before & After Intervention

When we challenge ourselves in new ways and try to learn new things, we become empowered, self-confident, resilient, and heathier, and live a more meaningful existence.[2] Success isn't bred from the A you earned in a class for knowledge that you've never used since that final exam; it flows from a genuine curiosity and effort put forth in learning something new.

Often when children who are praised for the traits they are born with (such as intelligence, artistic talent, athletic ability) become adults, they internalize this kind of thinking and develop a fear-based mindset. It threatens their very identity, paralyzes them, and thereby limits their potential. This leads to a depressing, demotivating, and draining existence. Who they are is tied to an outcome rather than to their own virtue, growth trajectory, and divine identity.

The following graphic outlines some of the helpful insights found in Carol Dweck's landmark book *Mindset*.[3]

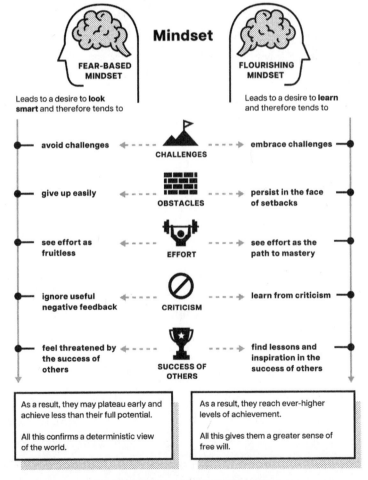

Summary of insights from Carol Dweck's The Growth Mindset

In medicine, doctors correlate a fear-based mindset with a fight-or-flight response. Fear is a normal response to stress or a dangerous situation. This hardwired reaction is a built-in survival response. Here is what happens when the fight-or-flight response is activated:

- Your brain registers a threat, whether it's emotional, mental, or physical.
- The adrenal medulla in the brain releases cortisol and adrenaline hormones to help you react to the threat (the fight-or-flight response), rushing blood to the brain, eyes, heart, and muscles.
- The adrenal cortex then releases corticosteroids to dampen processes like digestion, immune response, creative thinking, and other functions not necessary for immediate survival.[4]

This survival mechanism is helpful when we are legitimately threatened, like sensing an imminent attack from a bad guy or a snarling dog, but it takes a toll on the body when it is repeatedly activated. Fear becomes less of an alarm signal and more of a disproportionate reaction to difficult circumstances, like a perfectionist existing in constant fear of failure.

That said, a little stress is good. Muscles cannot grow without tension. When you lift weights, you cause tiny tears in your muscles, which eventually heal, and the muscles get bigger. In essence, you must break down muscles to build them back up. Certain life stresses—like having to meet tight deadlines, manage difficult relationships, and navigate challenges—strengthen our identity and character. It's only when stress is activated to an unreasonable degree that we find ourselves living in a constant fight-or-flight state, and we begin to freeze and stay stuck.

Studies show that 75 to 90 percent of all doctor's office visits have to do with complaints and ailments related to stress.[5] Headaches, sleeping problems, digestive issues—these external issues often stem from internal concerns like fear, worry, and anxiety. Living in a fearful state not only disrupts your health but causes you to be less creative. It also lessens your ability to think with principles, so you are more likely to act as a blind follower instead of a leader.

When you attack stress at the source by consciously and deliberately quieting your fear, you activate the parasympathetic nervous system, a.k.a. the "rest and digest" system, which lowers cortisol levels, reduces blood pressure, and directs blood back to your organs and digestive tract. In this lower state of stress, you age more slowly. It's the zone that allows for peaceful contentment, joyful connection with your loved ones, and cultivation of wisdom or positive learning from your not-so-great experiences.

A fear-based mindset will lock you in a state of worry (constantly afraid of being not good enough and jealous of the achievements and progress of others) and in paralysis (huddled in a corner and shut down like a victim). The alternative is embracing the flourishing mindset of heroes and guides, prioritizing progress over perfection, and focusing on growing instead of maintaining the status quo.

THE MINDSET SPECTRUM

(Protection)	(Stress)	(Growth)
FREEZE - - - - - - - - - - - - -	**FEAR** - - - - - - - - - - - - -	**FLOURISH**
(Shut Down)	(Fight or Flight)	(Rest & Digest)
Depression	Worry	Creativity
Shame/Guilt	Anxiety	Peace
Helplessness	Anger	Compassion
Hopelessness	Uncertainty	Hope

A Flourishing Mindset

Think about the statements we looked at earlier that come from a fear-based echo chamber: "If I don't get this promotion, my career is over," and "There is no room for mistakes. I must be perfect."

THINK THIS, NOT THAT

A flourishing mindset, on the other hand, sounds like this:
"I can learn from my mistakes."
"I am successful if I get better every day."
"I will work hard to develop my character and my skills."

The word *flourishing* has ancient roots in Greek and Hebrew thought and paints a word picture of a tree with thick roots and lush leaves, abundant with fruit. Psychologists define it as living in the "optimal range of human functioning,"[6] one that connotes "goodness, generativity, growth, and resilience."[7] When you flourish, you have such an abundance of combined character and skill that you are constantly adding value to the lives of others. Sadly, according to studies, only 18.1 percent of Americans are flourishing today.[8]

When fear leaves your headspace, your ability to flourish unlocks. You increase your capacity to solve problems and think clearly. You expand your creativity. Your character deepens and grows.

The key to a flourishing mindset is to focus on improving, not maintaining perfection. It's not about comparing yourself to others but comparing yourself to how far you've come from the day before.

FEAR-BASED MINDSET	FLOURISHING MINDSET
Disregards constructive feedback	Accepts useful feedback
Feels threatened by the success of others	Encourages and is inspired/ motivated by the success of others
Hides/ignores flaws	Works on weaknesses
Afraid of challenges because of potential for failure	Embraces challenges because of opportunity to learn and grow
Looking smart is more important than learning	Learning is more important than looking smart
Sticks to what they know and/ or what comes easy	Not afraid to learn new things or new ways of doing things
Failure is the end of the story	Failure is just the beginning

Each one of us holds an incredible capacity to grow and transform. There are four keys to overcoming fear and beginning to live with a flourishing mindset:

1. Think of failure as a guide.
2. Embrace your fear.
3. Optimize your skills.
4. Raise your standards.

Think of Failure as a Guide

Often we see failure as something to avoid at all costs. It's embarrassing. It's hard to accept. It can be demoralizing. If you tie failure to your identity, you will allow it to reflect poorly on your self-image and keep you from trying again. Maybe you vow you'll never find yourself behind a podium because of the speech you bombed at graduation. Or you keep your creative ideas under lock and key because your boss berated one of your brainstorms in front of the team.

A fear of failure can come from anywhere. Maybe you have a tendency toward perfectionism, or your parents had high and unrealistic expectations of you as a child. Whatever the source of the fear of failure, the consequences of avoiding failure at all costs will keep you from realizing your full potential. You'll stop trying and stop growing. I want you to look at failure in a new light.

Failure isn't a vicious and scary villain, out to dominate and decimate your dreams and goals. Nor is failure a victim, something destined to keep you cowering in a corner, unable to take the next step.

Failure can be one of your greatest guides. Just ask Sara Blakely.

Blakely, a former door-to-door fax machine salesperson, created an immensely successful billion-dollar company by solving a real-life problem. Before her product came on the market, she noticed that women were wrestling with how to create a seamless, smooth body shape underneath their clothing. Blakely was one of these women. She created a simple solution, a one-of-a-kind idea that worked. After a year of finessing the prototype, SPANX, a company worth $1.2 billion today, was born.[9] Today, Blakely's undergarments are staples in female wardrobes all over the world.

From a young age, the entrepreneur learned that failure is nothing to be afraid of. Growing up, she got a weekly lesson in failing from her father. She said,

> He used to ask my brother and me what we had failed at the dinner table, which was so interesting. And he'd celebrate it. He'd actually be disappointed if I didn't have something I failed at that week. I remember saying, "Dad! Dad! I tried out for this and I was horrible!" and he would actually high-five me and say, "Congratulations, way to go!" What it did was reframe my definition of failure. Failure for me became not trying versus the outcome.[10]

By embracing the idea of failing forward, Blakely has become one of the most successful businesswomen in the world.

Failure has been touted as an essential ingredient to success by icons including Walt Disney, Steve Jobs, and Dave Ramsey. These groundbreaking entrepreneurs used their lessons of failure to create incredibly successful ventures.

When you stop looking at failure as a villain or a victim, your relationship with it changes. You begin to approach mistakes with a learning lens, asking more questions about what you could do better next time instead of berating yourself for what you did wrong this time. Failure becomes an opportunity for growth rather than a shame-inducing memory.

If you need to improve your relationship with failure, here are three steps you can start taking today:

1. **Keep your eye on the prize.** Don't be discouraged by your misstep; look at the bigger picture. What is the ultimate goal? What are you trying to achieve? If you want to create a fantastic marriage and feel terrible that you spoke harshly to your spouse yesterday, then today direct your energies toward serving your spouse to create a marriage that flourishes.

2. **Take smart risks.** When I started my own practice, I knew it was a

risk, but I also knew people who had gone into business for themselves and had succeeded. I was realistic and counted the cost. With my own practice, I could impact more lives, use my skills at another level, and earn multiple times more income. At the same time, I risked not making money for years and even losing it all. I decided to accept a risk of failure because it was less painful than living with the regret of not trying to reach a worthwhile goal.

3. **Adopt a third-person perspective.** Think of the Batman Effect you learned about in mindshift 3. Just as the exercise of viewing yourself as your possible or future self can build momentum for change, self-distancing from your mistakes can also help you navigate tough emotions and course correct from a different lens.[11] Instead of asking yourself, What did I do wrong? try asking, What did [insert your name] do wrong, and what can he/she do better next time?

> **THINK THIS:** Failure is essential to becoming successful.
> **NOT THAT:** Failing means I am a failure.

Embrace Your Fear

You don't have to *feel* courageous to *be* courageous. Heroes don't earn a hero badge just because they do heroic things, but because they do them despite their fears. You may think that avoiding fears is the way to overcome them, but that couldn't be further from the truth. Facing your fears is courage in action.

Survival expert and fate defier Bear Grylls has thrilled and shocked millions of viewers around the world with his hit TV shows like *Man vs. Wild*, *Running Wild with Bear Grylls*, and *Get Out Alive with Bear Grylls*. Grylls is known for eating wild snakes and scorpions, wrestling alligators, crossing the North Atlantic Ocean in an inflatable boat, and being the youngest Brit to climb Mount Everest—which he did only two years after a freefall skydive broke his back in three places.[12] Grylls has accumulated more near-death experiences than most people want to imagine.

Still, this revered adventurer and survivalist has admitted to being afraid of many things.[13] He has struggled with self-doubt and confidence issues and, since getting severely injured, is still terrified of jumping out of airplanes. Through continuing to take risks and push limits, Grylls has taught himself to face fears head-on.

"I've learned that if I do the things I'm scared of and I do them often enough, I become good at managing fear," he said. "It's like a muscle, and it gives me an edge."[14]

You can train your brain to believe it doesn't have to be afraid of something by confronting that fear.[15] When you purposely put yourself in a situation or face what causes fear to rise up in you, you send a message to your brain that there is nothing to be alarmed about. Do this frequently, and you will rewire your brain to not be afraid. Studies show facing your fears actually heals your brain.[16]

Psychologists call this method *exposure therapy*, and it is known as the gold standard for fear management. Stanford neuroscientist Philippe Goldin calls exposure therapy "hands down the most successful way to deal with phobias, anxiety disorders, and everyday fears of any sort."[17] In this treatment, psychologists create an environment that is safe for the individual and monitor them as, over a period of time, they gradually are exposed to what makes them afraid (e.g., public speaking, strangers, being out in public). In most situations, the fear and anxiety are dramatically reduced.

If the fear of public speaking is keeping you limited in the opportunities you reach for at work, there's only one way to overcome this obstacle: speak in front of others. I've been there. When I started out, I was terrified of speaking in public. I was most afraid of other people hearing my voice shake as I spoke, a dead giveaway for fear. Despite getting nervous before any lecture I gave, I continued to embrace my fear, and it dwindled.

If you share my pain, here's some advice. Start small. Take a course or workshop. Give a talk in front of a couple of your closest friends. Gain courage by taking one step forward, then the next one after that. You may still get butterflies the first time you have to give a presentation, but each time will get easier and easier if you just have the courage to keep doing it.

What are you afraid of? What is keeping your mind and your life from flourishing? It doesn't have to be a fear of failure. You might fear becoming successful. Maybe you're afraid of the accompanying stress and new responsibilities a higher level of achievement will bring. In the words of Grylls, "If you really want to live empowered, you've got to face those fears."[18]

Need help facing your fears? Start by admitting the thing you are afraid of. You can't fix what you're unaware of. Denying the sight of a black, hairy spider climbing up your leg isn't the formula to make it go away. Are you a people pleaser and worried that the person you say no to will stop giving you their approval? Sit with yourself, alone, and determine the fears that keep you from flourishing.

Don't forget: heroes don't become transformative and self-sacrificial overnight. In keeping with the above people-pleasing example, take baby steps: practice saying no, or even "Not at this time; maybe next time."

Celebrate little victories along the way. Progress, not perfection, is key. If you said no to adding a fourth activity this week that would only add stress, reward yourself with a latte or say something positive to yourself. Focus on your efforts, and your achievements will follow.

Optimize Your Skills

Along with gaining from failure and facing your fear, flourishing requires taking your skills and abilities to the highest level possible. Think of Michelangelo as an artist, Lincoln as a president, Shakespeare as a writer, and Taylor Swift as an entertainer. None of these people became extraordinary in their craft without taking the time to work on it. You are uniquely designed with talents that no one else has. Want to become your greatest self? Sharpen your skills daily. Your aim should be to become one of the best in your field.

Write down the talents in which you have the greatest potential to grow. Then schedule time to practice and improve these skills (take classes, get a coach, read a book) and create daily habits to optimize those things. Become aware of where you are and aim to continually get better.

A trio of professors once studied the behavior of experts such as surgeons, athletes, musicians, and chess players. What set these individuals apart from others was their willingness to put their skills into "deliberate practice," or "a sustained focus."[19] It's more than repeating the same skill over and over; it's a detailed effort of mastering a skill and improving on it daily.[20] Be willing to do more than anyone else is willing to do.

As you practice, think about the smaller skills that make up your skill and how you can optimize those subsets. If you want to master the public-speaking game, consider the subskills that make up the big picture and train them separately. For example, consider working on eliminating pauses, being more engaging with the audience, and telling powerful stories. Work on those individual subskills and watch how much you improve.

Invite experienced peers into the process and create a feedback loop. Think of one or two people who can offer constructive feedback on what you are doing right and what you need to improve. Using their feedback, adjust accordingly. Then, ask for feedback again. Adjust on the second round of feedback. Repeat the process.

Once you've developed your approach to practicing effectively, create consistent habits. One strategy I've implemented for years now is what I call "habit synergizing." The idea is to combine two activities that, individually, help you grow and achieve your goals. Here's how I synergize health habits with spiritual growth ones. I begin my day with a gratitude practice or prayer while I make a superfood smoothie. Next, I get in a forty-five-minute workout while listening to a book or podcast on spiritual or personal growth. Finally, while I am doing a cool-down stretch or a ten-minute yoga practice to finish, I will meditate on what I just learned. Habit synergizing has compounded my growth!

Try creating your own system of habits for exponential growth. For instance, you can read one leadership book a month and highlight and take notes while you read. Then put those notes into a PowerPoint and teach on the topic once a month to a mentee, to someone in your business, or even on your own YouTube channel. Refine that system as you progress.

Raise Your Standards

One of the fastest ways to grow is to set higher standards for yourself today than you did yesterday. When I first opened my practice, I wanted to educate people on the principle of food as medicine. Doing this via YouTube videos was the way to go. When I launched the channel, my standard was what today I call D Level. I talked about something and posted a video.

The goal was to get started rather than to excel in my performance on camera. But I wanted to get better at it too. I wasn't a great communicator when I started out and recognized I had to practice and master the skill.

I began to increase my standards and set new ones for myself, reaching to take my videos to a C Level. This included being more consistent in uploading videos and engaging more with my audience. Then I leveled up to B by adding props and anecdotes or personal stories to my videos. Eventually, I worked up to a Level A standard by spending more time researching my topic and adding a higher level of production value. All the while, I was working behind the scenes on becoming a better speaker by reading books and listening to podcasts by renowned public speakers, practicing in front of a mirror, and getting tips from mentors.

You must constantly raise your standard to get closer to the top of the mountain.

STANDARDS OF EXCELLENCE

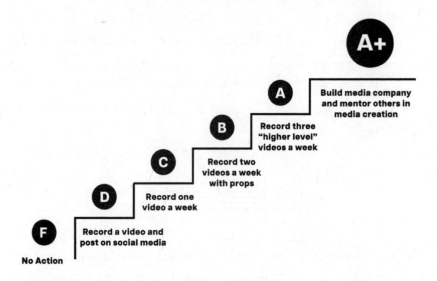

A+

A — Build media company and mentor others in media creation

B — Record three "higher level" videos a week

C — Record two videos a week with props

D — Record one video a week

F — Record a video and post on social media

No Action

Striving to flourish is a continual effort to better oneself. If you worked up to ten pushups yesterday, try twelve today. If you want to become more charitable and have already begun donating your time to an organization, take it up a notch by contributing your money—then donate anonymously. If you get 1 percent better at something today and continue the effort for several weeks, you are going to notice a significant difference six months from now.

Begin the process of increasing your standards by assessing what your standards are right now. Consider the areas in which you need improvement. Do you want to write a book but have trouble being consistent? Set a standard for writing a certain number of words each day. Do this consistently over time. Then climb the next step and set a higher standard. Focus on writing with a specific goal in mind. What's your storyline? Do you have a theme? Begin honing that skill and standard, and in time climb another step.

Aim high, but continue to grade yourself and adjust as needed before you upgrade to the next standard. Compare your progress to how far you've come rather than to the standard of an established writer. If you

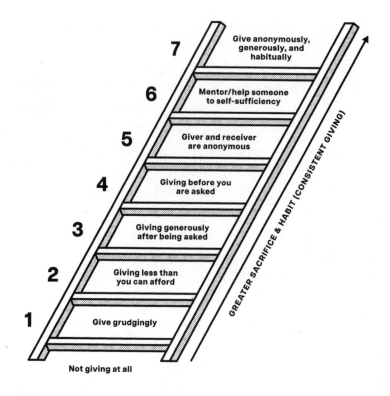

just started out and are equating your headway, or lack thereof, to the fact that Stephen King can pump out three books a year, you'll likely feel deflated. When you compare yourself to where you were a day, a week, or six months ago, however, you will be more encouraged, and that momentum will push you to keep moving forward.

Remember, the goal is excellence, not perfection. Excellence is aiming for the bull's-eye and getting closer and closer to it. It is continually raising your bar over time. Perfection is impossible. Holding yourself to an impossible standard typically leads to burnout and hinders creativity. Perfection is not crucial to success; high standards are.

> **THINK THIS:** Progress is about setting and maintaining a higher standard of excellence.
> **NOT THAT:** Progress = perfection.

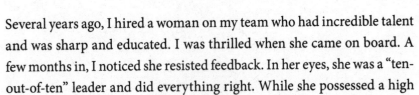

Several years ago, I hired a woman on my team who had incredible talent and was sharp and educated. I was thrilled when she came on board. A few months in, I noticed she resisted feedback. In her eyes, she was a "ten-out-of-ten" leader and did everything right. While she possessed a high intellect, her growth potential was limited as a result of this blind spot.

I mentioned this to her one day. After praising her work and efforts, I gave her an example of how she could further flourish by being open to mentorship and improving in how she dealt with the team.

She was utterly opposed to entertaining it. She liked her leadership skills just as they were, and that was that. It still pains me that she put a cap on her potential because she wouldn't receive constructive feedback. After a period of time, her self-protection mindset became toxic, and we decided to part ways.

If you choose to face your fears and see failing as an essential ingredient to success, you plant yourself in a place where you can flourish like a fruitful tree. Don't let ego, pride, and fear of failure stand in the way of growing to new heights. Embrace the flourishing mindset so you can operate with excellence and expand your skills for the good of the world.

Flip the fear to turn on the growth.

Fear → Flourishing

VISUALIZE TO REALIZE

After Chelsea and I got married, we took a short honeymoon in a cluster of beach towns known as 30A, Florida. One day, we rented beach cruiser bikes and explored the quaint towns. While riding through a neighborhood called Watercolor, we fell in love with the area. Lakefront homes dotted the tranquil coast. Trails wound through scrub-oak groves. It was a small-town vibe with natural preserves that could be discovered on foot or on bike. I turned to my wife at one point and said, "I would love to have a house here one day." She agreed.

When I went back home, I looked up houses in that area, finding hundreds of beautiful homes. I chose one at random and posted it on my vision board that I update annually and keep in my office.

Chelsea and I also began to strategize. What did we need to do to make our dream a reality? We discussed this with her parents, who agreed to combine forces with us to make an offer for a joint purchase. Over a few days, we reviewed our budget and calculated the expenses we needed to eliminate and the amount of money we needed to save. We strategized, set goals, and enacted our plan.

Six years later, Chelsea and I took a trip down to 30A with her parents. My wife and I were riding beach cruisers in the same area we had explored years earlier and happened to see a lot for sale on a lake that connected to the ocean. This was the moment we had been preparing and saving for. After negotiations with the real estate company, we purchased the lot and began plans to start building.

Then came the spectacular moment.

I was recording a webinar in my office one day when I glanced at my vision board. My eyes fell on the picture of the house I had posted a few years back. Something was vaguely familiar about it. I walked over to the vision board to get a closer look, and it hit me. The lot Chelsea and I bought was part of the picture! It was next door to the house in it. While the house in the vision board wasn't the one that we had purchased, we were building one that we were even more excited about on the lot next door to it.

This confirmed in me the power of visualizing and strategizing. Visualizing helps you paint a clear picture of your ideal future. Strategizing gives you the plan to make that dream a reality.

What can you envision that you don't have right now? A thriving marriage? A flourishing business? A job in which you can both support your family and spend time with them? Filling a need in your community that seems impossible to meet? It's not about having a second home or making more money; it's about living in alignment with and fulfilling your purpose in life.

I've found that most people never fulfill their dreams and live a life of ultimate significance because they lack clarity on what they want—and because they're too busy. Today, busyness is a pandemic. It is often equated with significance, which is a lie. If you are busy with tasks that offer little value, you will start to feel overwhelmed and unfulfilled. Busyness not only sabotages our capacity for self-awareness but can prevent us from dreaming big, setting goals, and experiencing the manifestation of those things.

In 1967, Charles Hummel published a small book called *Tyranny of the Urgent*, which has sold more than one million copies. He wrote,

We live in constant tension between the urgent and the important. The problem is that many important tasks need not be done today, or even this week. . . . The appeal of these demands seems irresistible, and they devour our energy. But in the light of eternity their momentary prominence fades. With a sense of loss we recall the important tasks that have been shunted aside. We realize that we've become slaves to the tyranny of the urgent.[1]

Think about the tyrants in your day. Packed schedules. Saying yes to countless activities. Checking messages. Unfinished projects. Putting out metaphoric fires at work. Keeping up on social media. Appointments. Meetings. The list is endless.

Busyness has become a way for us to validate that we matter, that we are useful, or that we are in demand. Yet being busy does not equal being productive or significant. According to studies, people spend 62 percent of their workday focused on mundane tasks.[2] Another study shows that only 10 percent of a workday is spent doing useful work like strategic planning.[3]

It is impossible to live the best life possible without a plan. A wise proverb says it best: "By failing to prepare, you are preparing to fail."[4]

Without making changes, nothing changes. You can achieve your goals only when you set a sequence of events in place to make them happen. And until you do that, you will keep doing the same things and walking the same path and using busyness as an excuse.

It just might be time for you to hero up, own your busyness, and do something about it. I'm going to show you how with a five-step process:

1. Prioritize.
2. Visualize.
3. Strategize.
4. Systematize.
5. Realize.

> **THINK THIS:** I can dream big and make things happen when I set the right steps in motion. **NOT THAT:** I have too much going on to dream big.

Prioritize

Reality TV stars and home renovation icons Chip and Joanna Gaines have expanded their design empire into real estate, a quarterly magazine, home decor, and their own television network. Balancing their robust professional lives and their family, including five children, is not for the faint of heart.

Their successful entrepreneurship and its accompanying demands and expectations exposed Joanna's obsession with perfectionism. Slowly, over time, it began to suffocate her. The talented designer has admitted to saying yes more often than she ought to have and succumbing to the pressure to appear perfect. In the process, even amid the myriad accomplishments, she found herself feeling anxious and empty.[5]

Joanna wrote in her book *The Stories We Tell*, "If we don't choose for ourselves where we show up and lean in and get close, other people will. And if we don't choose to be present for the moments we truly care about, our lives could spin on distractions and interruptions till the day we die."[6]

To help her focus on living a life of purpose, Joanne has learned to make her family her top priority.[7] Together, she and Chip put first things first, and their business has continued to flourish in the process.

Like the Gaines family, my family and my faith sit at the top of my priority list. I love this quote by Andy Stanley: "Your greatest accomplishment may not be something you do, but someone you raise."[8] I believe this to be true and have adjusted my schedule to reflect this principle. Once Chelsea and I had our first child, I chose to commit to fewer speaking engagements. I used to speak at twenty-five events a year, but

VISUALIZE TO REALIZE

after baby Arwyn came along, I attend no more than ten. I try to schedule more virtual speaking engagements and even turn the off-site events into family trips to optimize my time.

The schedules of the most successful people in the world reflect their truest priorities. As the German philosopher Johann Wolfgang von Goethe is often quoted, "The things that matter most must never be at the mercy of the things that matter least."[9] Many of us allow menial tasks, errands, or mindless entertainment to overrun our lives. The average person spends at least two hours per day on social media[10] and two and a half hours per day watching television.[11] Think about who you could become and what goals are possible if you spent those hours with things that matter most to you, like playing a pickup game of basketball with your son or daughter or reading a book or learning a new skill for work. Imagine the difference in outcome!

> **THINK THIS:** I can prioritize what matters most.
> **NOT THAT:** I am at the mercy of all of life's demands, distractions, and responsibilities.

Prioritizing requires some sacrifice. To gain something of value, you must give something up. You have to give up even the good to spend time on the great. The principle of sacrifice says the only way to experience long-term success is to sacrifice short-term comfort. And—as long as your sacrifice aligns with your priorities and builds toward the greatest good—the greater the sacrifice, the greater the reward.

Ask yourself the following questions:

- Can I say no to something now so I can say yes to what I really want later?
- What am I willing to give up to see my vision board come to life? Will I choose nights of reading or studying over Netflix binges? Should I eat in instead of dining out to trim my expenses?

You must sacrifice who you are today to become who you are meant to be.

Over the years, I've learned to say no much more than I say yes. I prioritize five areas in my life: faith, family, fitness, finances/work/career, and free time. I eliminate anything that conflicts with those things.

On the target below, think of where you are now versus where you want to be.

PRIORITIES TARGET

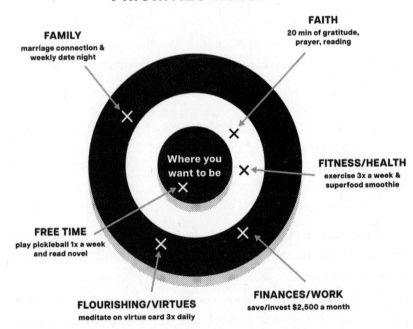

Prioritizing is simple. Create a schedule so your day looks proportional to your priorities. Here's how to start:

1. Pay attention to how you currently spend your time each day. Make a list of what you do when you've got some free time: reading, watching TV, browsing the web, scrolling through social

media, working, exercising, and so on. Write these activities down
and estimate how much time they take.

2. Write down a list of the top five things that are most important
    to you. How do your two lists compare? What are you spending
    time focusing on that isn't serving your priorities? Which things
    have you been neglecting?

3. Eliminate wasteful activities and block off dedicated time for what
    will serve you best.

Visualize

Visualization is defined as "the act of visualizing something or someone
(forming a picture of it in your mind)."[12] It is a tool meant to enhance
practice, performance, and outcome. It increases self-confidence and
improves the likelihood of you achieving your goals. Visualization positions you to focus on the strategies and systems required to succeed.
Think of it as a mode to connect with your future self.

The ritual of visualization is a common practice among elite athletes
such as Michael Jordan, Wayne Gretzky, Tiger Woods, Lindsey Vonn, and
Michael Phelps. Golfing legend Jack Nicklaus said, "I never hit a single
shot, not even in practice, without having a very sharp, in-focus picture
of it in my head."[13]

A study published in *Neuropsychologia* concluded that imagining
moving parts of your body can be as effective as physically training
them.[14] In 1967, Alan Richardson, an Australian psychologist, chose
a group of student basketball players and divided them into three
groups. Group 1 practiced free throws for twenty minutes a few days
a week for four weeks. Group 2 was told not to practice and not even
to think about basketball. Group 3 visualized shooting free throws
without physically touching the ball for the same amount of time as
Group 1. At the end of the study, Richardson measured each group's
progress. Group 1 had improved 24 percent. Group 2, as one might

expect, showed no improvement. Most impressive, however, was the result of Group 3. These students had improved 23 percent, almost as much as Group 1, and all without even practicing a single shot.[15] Imagine that! Mental rehearsals are just as important as the physical performance.

Visualization starts with painting a clear mental picture of something you are passionate about. It is more than mental imagery; it involves capturing the feelings, the smells, even the taste of what you are visualizing. This tool requires connecting all your senses to your mind picture and, therefore, must be emotionally captivating.

If you want to improve your relationship with your teenage child, sit in a quiet space and see yourself at the breakfast table with them and encouraging them before they leave for the day. Imagine the sun on your face as you take a walk in the evening and share advice about what college to choose or how to navigate boyfriend/girlfriend issues. What does it feel like when your teenager squeezes your shoulders in a warm hug and says, "I love you," and means it?

Visualization is not a form of voodoo or magic or manifestation. It's a practical way to set your feet in the direction of where you intend to go. The Torah records an instance when God promised Abraham, who had no children, that he one day would have countless children. God told him to look up at the night sky and "look attentively" at the vast number of stars as the number of descendants he would have.[16] Abraham believed God, and this vision eventually came to pass.

Generations later, when Israel was enslaved by Egypt, God promised them that, through Moses, they would receive a land of their own one day. This promised land would "flow with milk and honey."[17] Consider the visual significance of that phrase. The word *Egypt* in Hebrew is *mitzrayim*, which means "narrow places."[18] The land God promised them that would flow with milk and honey had to be spacious, fertile, and abundant, a far cry from the harsh reality they were experiencing. I imagine many of them held on to this robust picture as they toiled in captivity, longing for freedom.

What Do You Want?

The first step in visualization is deciding what you truly want. You should wisely think through your ideal outcome and make sure it aligns with your purpose and priorities.

Here's how to do it:

1. Get in a quiet place free of distractions. No phones. No kids. No notifications.
2. Think of your life in the following areas: faith, fitness, finances/work, family, and free time.
3. Sit in a comfortable position and close your eyes. Create a mental picture of what you would like your future to look like in each of the five categories. Don't just see it in your mind; imagine what it feels like. Let the image stir your emotions. To do this, you must evoke all your senses. In this mental picture, is it hot or cold? Can you smell anything? Who is around you? Now visualize the process and outcome in continued vivid detail. In the career category of my life, I've visualized my patients and followers hugging me at a live event because their lives were transformed by the advice I shared or by finding my products in stores like Whole Foods and Target. For my family and faith, I've visualized going on mission trips with my family and making meaningful memories together at a lake house.
4. Write down the vision that you see. Is it an image of you and your spouse celebrating your fiftieth wedding anniversary? The opening of a second location of your business? A curriculum you designed that has been implemented in your local school? These are the goals you will strategize to realize. When I look back at the visions I've written down over the years, I am blown away by the similarities with later realities. The manifestation of those mental pictures was spot-on—or above and beyond what I had imagined. Writing down goals builds faith, hope, and confidence and gets you on the right track to goal-setting.

Do this visualization exercise for a few minutes every day, either before you start your day or before you go to bed. Setting aside time each day to close your eyes and turn your attention inward is critical for staying focused.

Billionaire entrepreneur Sara Blakely credits her visualization practice as a top determining factor of SPANX's success. During her fax-machine-selling days, she began developing a clear picture of the life she wanted. Visualizing her hopes helped her start setting goals in that direction.[19]

"I had a very clear vision of what my life was going to be like. . . . My vision was to: be self-employed, invent a product that I could sell to lots of people . . . and create a business for myself that would continue to fund itself if I wasn't present," she said during a speech.[20]

For Blakely, the key to visualization was specificity. When imagining her future business and life, she spared no details. For example, she even visualized being on Oprah's show, which later happened and was a complete career changer. Blakely is proof that practicing visualization yields fruitful results.

Vision Boards

I want to circle back to how I began this chapter. Making a vision board and refining it every year has had a profound impact on my life. Because it's something that's so critical to success, I want to share with you exactly how to create a vision board that works. Don't think of this creative idea as an arts-and-crafts project involving glue sticks, scissors, magazine cutouts, and printed pictures. A vision board is so much more. It's a visual representation of the life you want to have. It showcases what you desire to do with your time on this earth.

When you write down your goals (in words and/or in pictures) in a way that allows you to see them, such as with a vision board, they'll stick in your memory. Studies show that simply displaying goals increases recall by up to 80 percent in three hours and 65 percent after three days.[21] Like visualization, thinking of your goals each day will naturally force you to align your actions and decisions in a way that supports them. And when your daily actions and decisions align with your stated goals, your chances of achieving them increase tremendously.

Here are some tips for creating your vision board:

1. **Make it personal**. Arrange pictures that represent your vision on a posterboard or a corkboard. You can also arrange them in a collage or a digital vision board. The pictures must be specific and relevant to what *you* want. Meditate on it. Pray over it. Make it motivating.

2. **Make it visible**. Unwritten and unseen goals tend to never materialize or hold anyone accountable. Place your vision board somewhere you will see it every day. You want to be reminded of your goals daily so that your actions and habits always support them.

3. **Update it**. What you want out of life can change, and that's okay. Maybe you've discovered a new passion or interest you'd like to explore. If you need to change out pictures, set new specific goals, or update your strategy, be sure to do so.

Visit joshaxe.com/thinkthis for more FREE tips and to see my vision boards over the years.

Strategize

Strategizing is the process of taking your vision and goals out of the abstract dream space and directing them toward actionable steps that will make them a reality. When you plan out the best approach to achieve an optimal result, you engage a strategic mindset.

Stanford psychologists once conducted a study showing that people who have a strategic mindset were more creative and successful in their professional, educational, health, and fitness lives compared to people who do not.[22] In multiple experiments, students were divided into two groups and asked to diagnose a problem, find the solution, and then execute the task. The students who had a strategic mindset performed 24 to 29 percent better than the others. The primary difference between the two groups was that the strategic thinkers asked themselves questions during the problem-solving experiment, such as "Is there a different way to do this?" "Is there a way to do this even better?" and "What are things I can do to make myself better at this?" If you are going to be successful at nearly anything in life, you need to develop a strategic mindset.

Strategizing is a great partner to visualization. Once you have visualized the areas of your life you want to focus on, write down the specific actions you need to take to achieve them. What are the daily, weekly, and monthly steps needed to get the house of your dreams? Or to become a leader in your field? Or to get out of debt and experience financial freedom? For example, if you wanted to become a CEO, you could start studying the traits and habits of top executives and CEOs.

Start with the end in mind. Pinpoint a specific goal and think through the best step-by-step process to get you from point A to point B. When I started my health website, my goal was for it to become the number-one resource for people looking to use food as medicine. I researched the top website at the time and analyzed what they were doing. Then I set a plan in motion to take it one step further. For example, if they were publishing twenty articles a week, I aimed to publish twenty-five.

Strategy-wise, I needed to figure out the *who* and then *how*. Who were the best people I could hire? How many writers and editors would I need to produce twenty-five amazing articles a week? As time went on, I reevaluated the goal and continuously refined and improved the strategy. It was because of a strategic mindset that, several years later, my health website experienced the success it did.

Most people spend more time planning out a trip than they do planning out their lives. I've found that everything in life turns out better when you embrace a strategic mindset.

A surefire way to keep your priorities in their proper place is to create a strategic game plan for every one of them. Because family is important to me, I researched the key elements that build a great family life. I zeroed in on the core components of regular family dinners, one-on-one time with your spouse, modeling and teaching your kids great character, attending religious services, being connected to other on-purpose couples and families, and sharing meaningful traditions. Then I started to strategize what each component would look like and created a schedule for each, which I'll get into next.

A natural progression of strategy is to create rhythms that maintain your strategies in motion.

Systematize

So far, you have prioritized, visualized, and strategized to meet your goals. Now comes the most important part—putting them into consistent action. A *system* is a collection of actions, rituals, or habits that work together to achieve a common purpose. It's answering the question, What must I consistently do in order to accomplish my goals? A great system is constructed of good habits that propel your strategies forward.

Hollywood icon Mark Wahlberg credits his career success to being disciplined in his habits. He consistently wakes up around four every morning, works out, and spends time in prayer and gratitude.[23] He also prioritizes his wife and four children by scheduling time with them rather than giving his loved ones the leftovers of his day.[24] These habits build on one another and create a system that nurtures his health, his faith, and his family—as well as a solid foundation from which he pursues his professional success.

Another icon known not only for her vocals but for her healthy habits is Carrie Underwood. While Carrie's routine differs when she's at home versus when she's on tour, she generally wakes up at 7:00 a.m. to read her Bible with a cup of coffee in hand. When she's not on tour, she helps her two boys get ready for school. Then Carrie jumps into her daily one-hour workout. She makes lunch from the food she grows in her backyard, which includes a garden, greenhouse, and chicken coop. In the afternoon, she focuses on her work, and in the evening she spends time with her husband, Mike, and their children.[25]

While Mark Wahlberg and Carrie Underwood have different lives, you can see the overlap in their habits of investing in their faith, family, and fitness nearly every single day. They've developed systems that help them maintain the habits that move them toward their goals. Legendary basketball coach John Wooden once said, "Make each day your master-piece."[26] Habits will do just that.

Here are some ways you can do the same.

1. **Master your time.** Time is our most valuable commodity. If I don't schedule my days in advance, my time will get dominated by meetings, appointments, or other things that don't ultimately serve my purpose. I call this my weekly war plan, which is based on time-boxing. According to a study, time-boxing was the most productive time management technique compared to one hundred other methods.[27]

It's simple. Pick your top three priorities for the day. Put each task in a virtual box. Allot a fixed amount of time to work on one task without any distractions. Let's say you want to write an eight-hundred-word blog post once a week. Mark a two-hour box on your calendar every week and devote that time to getting it done.

Time-boxing improves productivity by instilling a sense of urgency and focus. When you know that you have a limited amount of time to complete a task, you are less likely to get distracted or lose focus.

WEEKLY WAR PLAN

Below is Josh's weekly war plan example:

Monday
6:30a-8a Time with God and leadership reading
8a-9a Workout
9:30a-12p Writing and Emails
12p-12:45p Lunch
1p-5p Meetings
6p-7p Dinner
7p-10p Family Time
10p Sleep

Tuesday
6:30a-8a Spiritual Triathlon (Gratitude,
Read Bible, Prayer)
8a-9a Workout
9a-12p Business planning
12p-1p Lunch
1p-5p Ancient Nutrition Podcasts and Videos
5:30p Guys Night or Game Night with Friends
10p Sleep

Wednesday
6:30a-7:30a Time with God and
personal growth
8a-9a Workout
9:30a-12p Create content
12p-1p Lunch
1p-5p Meetings or filming/videos
5p-6p Family dinner
6p-9:30p Family time
9:30p-10p Get in bed and listen to Bible audio

Thursday
6:30a-7:30a Spiritual Triathlon
8a-9a Workout
9:30a-12a Create Content
12p-1p Lunch
1p-5p Leadership content or leadership group
5:30p-9p Josh and Chelsea Date Night

Friday
6:30a-7:30a Spiritual Triathlon
8a-9a Workout with friends
9a-10a Breakfast with friends
10a-12a Emails and meetings
12p Lunch
1p-5p Brainstorm and creative work
6p-10p Dinner and Fun Time

Saturday/Sabbath
8a-10a Read and morning coffee talk with Chelsea
10a-12a Josh and Chelsea Workout
12p-1p Family Brunch
1p-10p Time with Friends and Family

Sunday
7a-8a Spiritual triathlon
10a-11:30a Church
12p-1p Family Brunch
1p-10p Time with Friends and Family

2. Plan for growth. Pick one or two areas you desire to grow in (examples: leadership, character, time management, self-confidence, spirituality). Write down how many hours a week you can devote to this goal (minimum two hours). List the resources (books, podcasts, conferences, growth groups) and people who can help you flourish in this area. Box time in your schedule each week to cultivate growth and watch as your skill and wisdom expand.

Albert Einstein is often quoted as referring to compounding interest as the eighth wonder of the world. "Those who understand it, earn it," he said. "And those who don't, will pay it." The same principle applies to our habits.

When we make the same positive choices over and over, we compound interest in our self-development. You may notice only a small difference in yourself within the first three months, but if you continue the same habits for six months, one year, five years, and beyond, your growth will surpass your expectations.

Over time, investments produce a significant change. This is the key that turns visualizations into reality.

3. Stop, start, keep. This is one of my favorite systems to help me prioritize and maximize my time and life. It also helps me visualize what to do next to achieve growth. Think of those five areas of your life in which you have visualized and written down your goals (faith, fitness, finances/ work, family, and free time). For each category, write down:

1. the behaviors, actions, and habits that have not worked and need to be stopped;
2. whatever is missing in your habits and systems that will help you grow and improve toward your purpose; and
3. your successes. Evaluate what has worked well and what you should keep doing.

Below is one example to give you a sense of what this can look like. Visit joshaxe.com/thinkthis for more FREE exercises, quizzes, ideas, and downloadable PDFs to help you grow.

Family:

1. Stop: giving kids iPads when they are bored; saying no to everything they ask for; prioritizing social media time over one-on-one time with spouse
2. Start: playing outside with kids; complimenting spouse once a day

3. Keep: weekly date night routine; reading books to children before bed

What systems, or chain of habits, do you need to set to stimulate progress? Find what works for you and refine the system as you grow.

Realize

When you prioritize the things that matter most, create a compelling vision, and use the right strategies and systems to make them a reality, you can make your life a masterpiece.

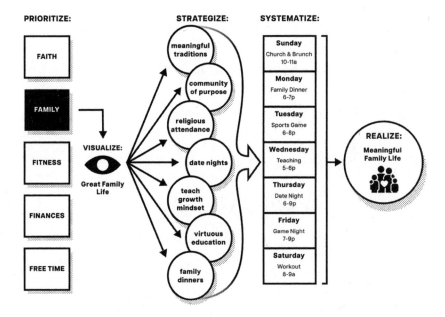

Eighteen years ago, I heard John Maxwell speak on leadership. I took copious notes and soaked in everything he said. As he talked, I remember at one point saying to myself, *I'd like to become more like him one day.* It was as if Maxwell was reading my mind. Moments later, he said in his

speech that he is often approached by people who want to do what he does. He said he always asks them, "Are you sure?" because most people don't realize how much work it takes. While people may be capable, Maxwell said, most of them are not committed.

That's true about many interests. We all have things we'd "like" to do and be. But if you are going to realize your goals, you must possess both intention and commitment. Commitment is what drives the entire process from visualization to realization.

It's easy to pause your intentions because things get hard—unmet expectations, unexpected illness or injury, a job transition—but keeping your eye on the prize is what will fuel the momentum to keep going. The next and final mindshift is based on the biggest challenge I had while writing this book and will serve to refuel your energy and recharge your focus when you hit hard times.

All the tools and techniques in this chapter are meant to be used multiple times over the years. Every three to twelve months, set aside time to self-evaluate, adjust your plan, and reset your course. If you're having trouble accomplishing tasks you have deemed important, be honest about why. What's getting in the way? Maybe it's poor prioritizing, lack of delegation, too much wasted time, too many interruptions, or a need to rethink your goals.

Also, always remember to celebrate the wins. Revisit your schedule periodically, every day/week/month/year, and pick one thing that you can be proud of.

For your dreams to become a reality, a few other key ingredients are necessary. The final mindshift will teach you how to overcome the impossible by focusing on what is possible.

Visualize
to
realize.

Unplanned → Strategic

POWER UP YOUR POTENTIAL WITH POSITIVE PERSEVERANCE

When I started writing this book, I was in the best shape of my life. I enjoyed a regular exercise routine of swimming, running, and lifting weights. But a previous back injury I had sustained seven years earlier still nagged at me. I decided to undergo a simple and natural procedure to fix my back issue once and for all by putting stem cells into my disc. Unfortunately, an unforeseen side effect occurred that wasn't diagnosed until months later. The pain was worse than it was before. Over the next four months, the pain went from nagging to outright agony.

One day I woke up and I couldn't walk. We ended up calling an ambulance to bring me in for an MRI. Chelsea and Arwyn, tears in her eyes and gripping tight to her mother's hand, watched anxiously as the paramedics pulled me away on a stretcher. After undergoing a slew of tests, I was diagnosed with a spinal infection that had seeped into my disc and vertebrae, causing osteomyelitis, a condition in which infection eats away at the bone.

My prognosis was anything but optimistic. "You may or may not experience a full recovery," the doctor told me, "and you will likely experience pain for the rest of your life." At one point, he even told me that I could be permanently disabled or even die.

I decided to do everything in my power to help my body heal. I took numerous supplements, ate a strict anti-inflammatory diet, did daily nutrient IVs, and received multiple natural and conventional therapies. For months, nothing worked, and the pain became so severe I couldn't move and was confined to bed. I felt like I was a prisoner trapped in my body.

While I generally have a positive mindset, there were a few days when I was engulfed in a dark feeling of despair. I was used to playing with my daughter, tossing her up in the air and crawling through forts we built. But the pain became so bad I couldn't even hold her. Not being able to engage my wife and two-year-old was gut-wrenching. The sense of loss overwhelmed me; I felt like I was missing out on the most precious moments of her life and my life. I didn't know how or when I would begin to physically feel better, but one thing was certain: the emotion of despair was not moving me forward in my recovery or helping me love my family.

One day I made a choice. I was going to endure with hope. Even if I wasn't able to toss my daughter up in the air, I still could watch TV with her, tickle her, join her in playing with her toys, and tell her that I loved her. I would have meaningful conversations with my wife and plan our bright future. I would allow the suffering to refine me, help me prioritize, and help me grow in character. I would write this book in order to help others experience the mindshifts that transformed my life. Instead of feeling pity for myself, I strove to rise above my feelings and pursue a mindshift of hope, grit, and gratitude.

Finally, after six months of suffering and losing forty pounds, I noticed a positive shift. Little by little, I began to improve. It was a slow and arduous process, but every week my mobility advanced, ever so slightly. As months passed, I was able to roll over, which, eventually, led to being able to crawl. As a former triathlete, I didn't find it easy to remain encouraged as I experienced such slow physical progress, but every day I made the choice. One day, I was able to shuffle along a hallway with a walker. Days later, I got into a pool.

It took me an entire year before I could walk on my own, which included daily physical therapy and other treatments.

It wasn't until about a year after the procedure that I could walk without any assistance.

I can say with much gratitude that, as I turned this manuscript over to my publisher for the editing process, I'd experienced tremendous strides in healing. Today, I am walking on my own, and I'm back to working out. I can say with hope that soon I will get back into shape physically—even better shape than I've ever been in. In a few weeks, I will be officiating my sister-in-law's wedding. Best of all, we just found out my wife is pregnant with our second child!

We all face seasons of suffering, but if we embrace our challenges with positive perseverance, just as the heroes before us have, we can stand victorious in the end.

We are surrounded by a continuous loop of negative information, though—from the media to our friends and coworkers to our own self-talk. We can always find a reason to be pessimistic or disillusioned. But focusing on the negative will only create a negative life.

When was the last time you experienced a positive outcome from a season of complaining, feeling sorry for yourself, or indulging a bitter attitude? Granted, we've all done it. It's natural to feel out of sorts or overwhelmed at times; we all experience an array of negative emotions every day. The key is to recognize the ones that are most likely to trip you up—and face them. The longer negative emotions linger, the more likely they are to become toxic.

Confronting negativity can be challenging. Let's look at why many people struggle to maintain optimistic attitudes when shadows loom.

> **THINK THIS:** I have the power to choose positivity.
> **NOT THAT:** I am at the mercy of whatever life throws my way.

Negative Undercurrents

Staying informed with what's happening in the world today is generally a positive thing, until it isn't. It doesn't take much for media consumption to turn dark, especially when today's fear-based journalism practices are synced with the decades-old mantra "If it bleeds, it leads."

I admit, I was glued to the national headlines around the 2020 US presidential election. After a few months, I realized it was affecting my sleep and putting me more on edge. Research indicates that when we are constantly exposed to negative news, our stress levels increase. We get anxious and depressed. In some cases—and this is quite alarming—people may even show signs of post-traumatic stress disorder.[1] It's no wonder we can't find peaceful equilibrium in our daily routine when one minute we're reading about the aftermath of a devasting earthquake that has killed tens of thousands of people and the next we're hearing about the ethical failings of another political leader or rising gas prices—and all this in less than five minutes.

It's not just the news that blasts negativity in our faces all day; the entertainment we are exposed to on a regular basis—music, television shows, movies, video games—is replete with casual incidences of dark themes and gratuitous sex and violence. Instead of turning off this negative noise, most people are tuning in.

Have you ever gotten sucked into doomscrolling? This is the phenomenon of diving down a deep, dark rabbit hole of depressing content (things like researching worst-case scenarios of your stomach pain or bingeing on negative news). Spending an hour consuming material about diseases, divorces, and deaths will only leave you feeling overwhelmed, depressed, and hopeless.

There's a name for a human being's bent toward the dark and twisted. Known as the negativity bias, or positive-negative asymmetry, this tendency means we are wired to "attend to, learn from, and use negative information far more than positive information."[2]

Negativity bias is why you may be more apt to

- remember critique rather than praise;
- focus more quickly on negative events than positive ones; and
- have a stronger emotional and mental response to negative stimuli than positive.

Catch a glimpse of negativity bias in subconscious action by answering a few questions. Do you tend to remember the rude comment someone wrote on your social media account more than the kind word someone said about you last week? Do you harp on the fact that your steak wasn't seasoned perfectly more than the deliciousness of the entire meal? Are you more likely to share bad news with a friend than a positive story or event? Answering yes to at least one of these questions shows the power of negativity bias.

This psychological phenomenon isn't all bad. It's what kept our ancestors alive as they remained constantly on high alert to threats and dangers.[3] The problem is, negativity bias doesn't actual prepare you for anything useful. In reality, it keeps you locked in a state of stress, unhappiness, and selfishness, and causes you to age more quickly.[4]

The opposite of negativity bias is, naturally, positivity bias, or optimism bias. Before I address optimism bias, I want to share the danger in taking a positive attitude to an extreme. Toxic positivity happens when you allow good feelings and thinking to fog or distort reality, or when you deny what is a truly negative experience or event. Some signs include:

- Responding to high-stress events with cheap and trite platitudes like "Everything will be okay," or "Everything happens for a reason."
- Dismissing or avoiding real emotions like grief or anger when a loved one dies or you lose your job.
- Pretending problems aren't there instead of facing them (like ignoring unpaid bills).

Living in a dream world and wearing a hat that reads "Good vibes only" isn't the fix for consuming dark content and fostering a negative mindset. It's unrealistic and naive. There is a better way.

Optimism bias (as opposed to toxic positivity) nurtures a positive expectation about the future. Tali Sharot, a neuroscientist and a professor at University College London, has researched optimism using a combination of neuroimaging and behavioral science. "Although the belief in a better future is often an illusion, optimism has clear benefits in the present," she wrote. "Hope keeps our minds at ease, lowers stress, and improves physical health. This is probably the most surprising benefit of optimism. All else being equal, optimists are healthier and live longer. It is not just that healthy people are more optimistic, but optimism can enhance health. Expecting our future to be good reduces stress and anxiety, which is good for our health."[5]

Optimism is indispensable, but when I was lying in bed battling despair, I needed more than positive thinking to anchor my perspective in the right place. I discovered what worked was a fusion of hope, grit, and gratitude, or what I call *positive perseverance*.

Positive Perseverance: Hope, Grit, and Gratitude

Let's take a look at this powerful combination of enduring positivity and how it kicks optimism into its highest gear.

Hope

Hope is defined as "a desire accompanied by expectation of or belief in fulfillment."[6] It's choosing to think and act in a way that is contrary to the negativity of our present experience. Hope sticks around long after setbacks come and go. As Martin Luther King Jr. said, "We must accept finite disappointment, and yet cling to the infinite hope."[7] This is a virtue we need to keep a tight grip on as we navigate a dark world.

Known as the father of the hope theory, positive psychologist Charles Snyder argued that hope is more than a feeling or the act of repeating a mantra (like "I am going to be great!") until it sticks. Snyder referred to it as a cognitive process that encompasses three components:

1. goals (thinking with purpose, priorities, and vision),
2. pathways (developing strategies and systems to reach goals), and
3. agency (taking responsibility and believing in the expected change).[8]

According to Snyder's research, people who have more hope have better outcomes in their mental and physical health, academics, and athletics. They also possess higher self-esteem.[9] In other studies, hope is shown to be a deterrent against anxiety.[10]

When I was hit with that moment of despair I mentioned earlier, the choice was clear: either download despair, or haul in hope. I decided to stop entertaining questions like *What if I can't ever participate in a triathlon again?* or *What if I never get well?* and started believing and visualizing that I would run again. I set goals, stayed consistent with the work involved in the goals, and continued to tune into a hopeful perspective of getting my body back to full strength.

Hope is more than optimistic thinking; it is optimism in action.

When I was learning to walk again, I never would have imagined how painful the experience would be. My tendons and ligaments were shortened and weak and required intense rehab and therapies to regain strength. Day after day, I winced through what seemed to be the easiest of exercises. It wasn't fun. But it was necessary, and I resolved with fierce determination to work through the pain and believe in a better outcome.

Grit

After studying the virtue of *grit* for more than fifteen years, psychologist Angela Duckworth defined it as "passion and perseverance for long-term goals."[11] She also described it as "having stamina . . . living life like it's a marathon, not a sprint."[12] Grit is being all in to create your *future self.* It is enduring through challenges and obstacles, no matter the pain involved.

Duckworth once observed more than a thousand young cadets from

West Point in their first year, otherwise known as "beast barracks."[13] She and her team studied participants during this mentally and physically grueling experience in which cadets trained for seventeen hours a day. Duckworth found that the students who succeeded in the program shared one thing in common: they had grit. It was found to be a greater indicator of success than IQ (brains) or physical ability (brawn).[14] In her years studying grit, Duckworth proved this trait to be essential for achievement and overcoming obstacles not only in military students but in entrepreneurs, artists, college students at top schools, and kids in disadvantaged schools.

Grit doesn't mean the absence of failure or feeling dispirited in times of resistance. Even Duckworth admitted, "I do get discouraged. I'm no stranger to doubt. And yet eventually, I get up again. I fall seven [times] and rise eight."[15]

When you approach life with grit, you commit to staying in the game and persevering with passion and positivity.

Gratitude

Living with a spirit of gratitude is more than being thankful for obvious blessings. It is an attitude that changes your perspective, strengthens your relationships with others, and taps into the abundance of the little things. It's what I learned to do when I found myself shaken because I couldn't play with Arwyn when I was incapacitated. Instead of wallowing in self-pity because I couldn't lift and throw my little girl up in the air when we were in the pool together, I was grateful to share smiles and giggles with her as we cuddled in bed and watched *Peppa Pig* and *VeggieTales* together.

A growing body of scientific evidence suggests that gratitude supports greater physical and psychological health, increases life satisfaction, and helps people adopt healthier habits.[16] One study conducted by the University of California San Diego observed 185 patients who had heart failure. Patients who had an attitude of gratitude reported less fatigue, better sleep, and a lower level of cellular inflammation compared with patients who did not have this disposition.[17]

Further studies in cardiac patients researched the effect of gratitude journal writing in conjunction with their usual medical care. The patients who daily wrote down what they were grateful for showed higher levels of physical improvement than the patients who received medical care alone.[18]

Another study set out to measure the effects of gratitude on the brain through MRI. Participants were shown documentaries of Holocaust survivors who shared stories of how they survived or were helped through acts of kindness and provisions.[19] After viewing these videos, participants were asked how they would feel if they were in the same situations. As they reflected, scientists imaged the participants' brains. Then participants were asked to rate their level of gratitude. The study concluded that gratitude lowered stress and increased moral awareness.

We often can find ourselves swept up in financial worries, a struggling relationship, or a health concern, but when we make a point to reflect on what we do have, we reap the many mood-lifting benefits of gratitude.

> **THINK THIS:** When I cultivate hope, grit, and gratitude, I build up resilience to thrive through hard things.
> **NOT THAT:** Wishful thinking or ignoring stress will make hard things go away.

"Prime Time" Positivity

You may not be able to control what happens to you, but you have power over how you choose to endure through it. When I think of positive perseverance, I think of two-time Super Bowl champion Deion "Prime Time" Sanders.

Prime Time's parents got divorced when he was two. His biological father was a drug addict, and his stepfather, who came into the picture later, was an alcoholic.[20] In spite of his difficult upbringing, Sanders went on to become one of the greatest athletes of all time, playing fourteen NFL seasons and nine seasons in MLB. Sanders is the only athlete to hit an MLB home run and score an NFL touchdown in the same week. The charismatic athlete is a pop culture icon, having appeared in many TV commercials and music videos, and even released his own rap album featuring a hit song.

The Hall of Famer's career accomplishments and flashy lifestyle may have prompted awe and admiration, but they also contributed to his character downfall. The title of the book he released in 1999 said it all: *Power, Money, and Sex: How Success Almost Ruined My Life*. Sanders admitted that his party habits, philandering, and wild life on and off the field weren't all they were cracked up to be.[21] In 1997, the stress caused Sanders to attempt suicide.

"I was going through the trials and tribulations of life," he said. "I was empty, no peace, no joy. Losing hope with the progression of everything."[22] He survived, turned to God, and used that miracle to change his life.

When the football legend's professional playing career and then his stretch as an NFL analyst ended, Sanders chose a different calling, one that helped bring the lessons he learned from his negative experiences into a positive light. He began to coach football, first on a high school level, then at Jackson State, and currently at the University of Colorado. His focus today is to help young men develop not only their skill as football players but their character. Sanders instills in the young men he coaches the virtues of honor, respect, personal responsibility, integrity, and hard work.

I love what Sanders said in a team meeting about his players. "These young men are going to be on campus respectful and considerate and kind; opening doors for you . . . . They're going to say, 'Yes, sir, no sir and yes ma'am, no ma'am' or they're going to have to deal with me. That's just the way I fathered, the way I parent, the way I coach. . . . You send us a boy, we'll send you back a man."[23]

Part of his coaching style is calling out the grit in his players. "You all want to be the man until it's time to be the man. The man, sooner or later, is going to have to prove he can fight. You're going to have your back up against the wall. You have to come out fighting. And I want to make sure you have that in you."[24]

Fighting in this sense is grit, the determination to give it your all and live with excellence every day. It's about fighting against your challenges, your painful experiences, your setbacks, and whatever obstacle is keeping you from fulfilling your greatest potential and coming out stronger and better for it.

Recently, Sanders suffered from multiple blood clots in his leg, which led to blood flow being cut off to his left foot. At first, doctors recommended amputation from the knee down, but miraculously, they were able to save everything but two toes.

Prime Time was honest about his recovery. "I never gave up hope and I never questioned God, but I'd never been down like that."[25] Still, the man continues to exude positive perseverance, positioning himself in a constant space of gratitude for his life and every blessing that comes his way. "God is so good. My life is so good and purposeful."[26]

When you face a challenge, you can let it cripple you or refine you. You have a choice to use your pain for good or evil. I admire men and women who have gone through difficult times and have come out the other side with a higher level of character, new wisdom, and a grateful spirit.

You can't stay in that place while you're bugging out over the latest negative news cycle or pretending what hurts doesn't exist. Hope, grit, and gratitude are choices you make every day. No one can do it for you; only you can choose it.

Positive Words and Perspective

Let's look at two practical ways you can live out positive perseverance today: choosing positive words and choosing a positive perspective.

Positive Words

Think back to the first chapter and the story I told about my teachers, Mrs. Nobel and Mrs. Williams. Mrs. Nobel shut down my potential with her words of discouragement; Mrs. Williams unlocked a realm of possibility with her words of praise. Both teachers had a profound effect on my life through their speeches, but only one made a positive difference.

Researchers estimate that both males and females speak about sixteen thousand words per day.[27] How much of what you say is empowering, uplifting, and optimistic? Scientists have measured the brain's response to both positive and negative words. Negative words activate certain areas in the brain that increase stress levels.[28] On the flip side, according to researchers like neuroscientist Dr. Andrew Newberg, the use of consistent positive language can create a new reality.[29]

Becoming aware of self-talk matters because thoughts become your reality, for good or bad. As the proverb says, "As he thinketh in his heart, so is he."[30] Negative words will keep you stuck, whereas positive words help you progress and open new possibilities. Do your words, thoughts, and self-talk have a negative or a positive bent?

One study claims that up to 80 percent of our daily thoughts are negative.[31] Here's a quick and easy exercise to see if that's true for you. At any point during the day, give yourself a ten-minute window and record the words you say to yourself in your head. Don't judge them, just write them down. After the ten minutes, calculate the difference between the positive thoughts and the negative ones. Is there room for improvement?

When you build up muscle for the mindshift of positive perseverance with positive words, according to the Mayo Clinic[32] you're moving toward:

- a longer life span
- less depression
- lower levels of pain
- greater resistance to illnesses
- better psychological and physical well-being

Begin right now to cultivate more positive speech, to others and to yourself. One caveat: remember the dangers of toxic positivity. Express honest feelings rather than drown them in trite (and false) words.

When I was in the initial stage of recovery and progress felt stagnant, I was cautious in how I responded when people asked how I was. On one hand, I didn't want to pretend everything was great. On the other hand, I understood the power of my words. I chose *honest optimism*. I'd say something like "I'm not improving as fast as I'd like, but I will be soon." Following are some ways to increase your positive vocabulary.

Use empowering language. Using phrases and statements that encourage hope stimulates internal energy, which drives your behavior to respond in the same way. This includes not just saying positive words but rephrasing statements in a more positive way.

SAY THIS (EMPOWERING)	NOT THAT (DISEMPOWERING)
"I am able to"	"I can't"
"I get to"	"I have/need to"
"I'll think of a better way"	"Yeah, but"
"I am starting to"	"I should"
"I like/love/prefer"	"I can't stand"

Don't say anything to yourself that you wouldn't say to anyone else. If you wouldn't say the words you tell yourself to your best friend, shut down that negative self-talk immediately.

Don't say anything to others that you wouldn't want anyone saying to your child (or other loved one). Are you tempted to call out a negative trait in someone else out of anger or frustration? If you wouldn't want someone saying those same things to your child, don't say anything at all.

Positive Perspective

The day Chelsea and I got married, it rained. Did I mention we had an outside wedding? While this is a nightmare for most brides, my wife-to-be responded brilliantly. Chelsea didn't show an ounce of stress. In fact, I remember her saying something like "It would be awesome to get wedding pictures in the rain! It'll be so fun and different!" You can see why I chose to commit to her and partner with her for life. Chelsea's response to what could have been a devastating outcome to our big day made a significant impact on the energy and outcome of our wedding. While the rain did let up thirty minutes before we said "I do," even if it hadn't, our wedding still would have been wonderful.

Alia Crum, a Stanford University psychology professor, conducted a study showing the power of perspective on physiological fullness and satisfaction. Participants drank a 380-calorie milkshake but were led to believe it was either a 620-calorie indulgence or a 140-calorie sensible choice. Despite the identical calorie content, those who believed it was high-calorie experienced a significant decline in ghrelin, the hunger hormone. The other group's ghrelin response remained unchanged. Crum concluded that our beliefs about the satisfying and nourishing nature of food affect our hormonal responses, emphasizing the role of beliefs in shaping our physiology and reality.[33]

As you intentionally maintain a positive perspective, there are a couple of things you should keep in mind: positive stress and positive reframing.

Consider "positive" stress. While a high-stress lifestyle has been shown to have detrimental effects physically and mentally, we often don't consider the positive side to stress. *Physiological thriving* is a term scientists use for how stress hormones can improve the body and make it better than it was before. When you have a positive view of stress, you will perform better and have fewer stress-induced symptoms.[34]

Think of it this way: exercise in the right proportions strengthens your muscles and cardiovascular system. Navigating relational conflict can help you get better at it. Challenges can help you achieve your goal, improve your confidence, and strengthen your character.

The bottom line is, growth happens when you do hard things.

Try positive reframing. Activate the mindshift of self-awareness and then step outside of yourself. Look at your perspective from a different angle.

I've always been convicted by the Persian proverb "I cried because I had no shoes until I met a man who had no feet." I did not enjoy being confined to my bed. I was frustrated I wasn't healing faster. And at the same time, I forced myself to remember that, although my circumstances were difficult, numerous people have endured far worse situations and overcome them.

Suffering is difficult, but when we accompany it with hope, grit, and gratefulness, it can refine us. When you are going through a challenging season, ask, How can I grow from this and use it for good?

Intentional gratitude is essential, even if you're not feeling it. Gratitude makes you more resilient and gives you your greatest chance of getting through challenges. When I was going through my health battle, I had three low points, and during each of those days I saw a rainbow out of a small window in the bedroom I was confined to. For some people, seeing a rainbow could have been a coincidence, but for me, it was a sign and reminder that God is good and I would be made well.

Your perspective can be either *Nothing is a miracle* or *Everything is a miracle.* Begin your day by being thankful. Find beauty in unexpected places. Position your mind so the things that normally may seem like coincidences or no big deal have the potential to fill you with awe, wonder, and gratitude.

Your best life or your worst life is determined by how virtuously you walk through the valleys, deserts, and fires.

Input = Output

If you are going to grow into your highest possible self, you must be aware of the principle "You become what you consume."

When I was growing up, my parents might have been considered strict in keeping a close eye on what I watched and listened to. At one point, they even found my contraband stash of rap and rock CDs and wasted no time tossing them in the trash. They enforced restrictions on television programming as well. While shows like *The Simpsons* were a no-go, Friday nights were devoted to ABC's TGIF (Thank God It's Friday) programming, which featured hit shows like *Family Matters, Full House, Step by Step*, and my wife's favorite, *Boy Meets World*.

When I was a teenager, my parents maintained a tight grip on not only my entertainment selections but also who I hung out with. Instead of allowing children to dictate the rules, which we see in many homes today, my parents created rules in order to maximize who I could become. Looking back, they did the right thing.

TGIF didn't sizzle with the dark and corruptive content of much of today's television programming, and I learned a moral lesson in less than thirty minutes. I enjoyed the comedy, great acting, and even went to bed with some guidance. At times I was frustrated with my parents for their rules, but they knew something I didn't—what we consume has a significant influence over what we think and how we act.

This boils down to the simple equation:

Input (what you take in) = Output (who you become)

It's akin to the principle "You are what you eat." Consume natural, whole foods, take the right supplements, and exercise, and you'll reap the benefits of optimal health. Drink soda all day, count the walk from the sofa to the fridge as exercise, and rarely see a fruit or vegetable on your plate, and your health will inevitably suffer. The concept of input = output holds true for nearly everything.

The social media, news, entertainment, and conversations you consume matter. To ensure positive input and keep the negative to a minimum, ask yourself if what you are reading, watching, or listening to is adding value to yourself or to others. If it isn't, eliminate it. Go through your social media accounts and make a list of the toxic content you are exposing yourself to (i.e., negative news feeds, followers/influencers whose identities are based on looks, fame, and money or who create unnecessary drama).

Next, make some swaps to positive exposure (influencers/followers who motivate and challenge you to make better choices). If you are a parent, do the same for your kids. Review what they are listening to and watching. Swap out the negative content with voices and subjects that are uplifting.

Embracing a mindshift of positive perseverance is a choice. The Greek philosopher Heraclitus said, "Day by day, what you choose, what you think, and what you do is who you become." Be wisely selective about what you listen to, what you watch, and what you allow to influence your thoughts, actions, and behaviors.

In *Man's Search for Meaning*, Viktor Frankl tells a story of watching a fellow female prisoner in a concentration camp who knew she was going to die in a few days. He was amazed that despite the inevitable tragedy, the woman's attitude remained cheerful. Frankl wrote how she often looked out a tiny window and stared at a tree branch with two blossoms on it. The tree was her only friend, she told Frankl, and it spoke to her. Frankl wondered if the woman was perhaps hallucinating.

Then she told him what the tree said. "I am here—I am here—I am life, eternal life."[35] In a world of darkness and suffering, the woman gripped onto hope in the form of the one living thing she could see: a tree.

How does one acquire such hope when oppression, suffering, and evil reign? By accepting the power to choose belief in a greater goodness and to not allow the darkness to take center stage.

A mindshift of positive perseverance is not about masking reality with toxic positivity but zeroing in with intention and precision on what is virtuous, carries meaning, and has eternal significance. In the words of rabbi, theologian, and philosopher Abraham Joshua Heschel, "Our goal should be to live life in radical amazement, to get up in the morning and look at the world in a way that takes nothing for granted. Everything is phenomenal; everything is incredible; never treat life casually."[36]

Choose to find something every day that amazes you—a loved one, the way the sun warms your skin, a good story, a completed deadline, even a tree branch with two blossoms.

Every day we can choose to believe the worst or the best about ourselves, about others, and about the world. I faced my limiting beliefs of not being smart and my debilitating health condition with hope, gratitude, and grit. The same is possible for you, whether you are struggling with a financial or health crisis, navigating relationship chaos, losing the battle between vices and virtues, or trying to build an unshakable sense of self in an unsteady world.

The battle starts and is won in the same place: your mind. Often, we perceive an obstacle that looms before us to be a mountain blocking our ability to change. But if we elevate our thinking, that mountain becomes a step that leads us to a higher level of living.

With every mindshift you make, you move one step closer to becoming the leader, friend, parent, and spouse you were born to be. I can't wait to see who you will become.

MINDSHIFT 12:

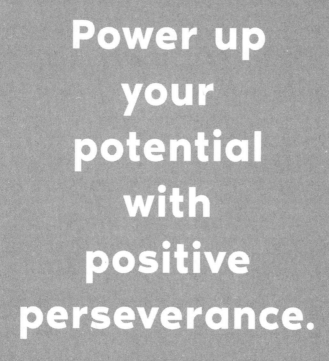

Power up your potential with positive perseverance.

Negative → Positive

CONCLUSION

My grandfather Howard was a man of adventure. He wrote a life story that inspired many people, including me, to serve others, take chances, and become more. Upon graduating high school in 1940, he yearned to explore the United States. He and a friend hitchhiked from his hometown of Lima, Ohio, all the way to Yellowstone National Park, making stops in Lexington, Kentucky; Nashville, Tennessee; and the Grand Canyon. When he returned from his expedition, he started working for Bell Telephone. Grandfather Howard's plans drastically changed when Pearl Harbor was attacked in 1941, and he immediately enlisted in the Navy and fought in one of the largest naval battles of World War II. When his service was over, he returned to his job at Bell Telephone.

My grandfather Howard had a strong identity and was incredibly loyal, patriotic, committed, and resilient, always putting duty before pleasure. His generation was known for their selflessness in serving their family and their country but also tended to lean on traditional job stability before following their passions.

At the age of forty-four, my grandfather decided he wanted to work with people, not telephone poles, and do something to fulfill his purpose to love others, honor God, and make earth a heavenly place. He envisioned building a place where families could have fun and make meaningful memories.

One day my grandmother was reading the paper and noticed an ad selling sixty acres of land with a lake. After encouraging her husband to take the leap and purchase the property, she and my grandfather invested their life savings into building Winona Lake Water Park and Campground, the very one I shared about in the beginning of this book. Some people told my grandfather he was crazy, but he persisted in following his passion, setting in place a strategic plan, and ultimately realizing his dream.

Grandfather Howard may have had his own limiting beliefs about quitting a stable job, but he was willing to sacrifice comfort for calling. As a result, he multiplied his talents during the fifty years he ran that camp and became a man of great character who was honored by all when he passed away at age ninety-six.

By taking this leap of faith and becoming an outlier of his day, my grandfather unlocked greater potential than he thought was possible. He became a positive influence on every person who stepped onto his park and campground. He inspired *me* to find the courage to make my own life-changing shifts in my career, and that has led me to where I am today. I'm continually inspired to think like him, and I see the results.

When we choose to break through our limiting beliefs and pick the path of purpose and perseverance, we leave behind a ripple effect of positive influence, just as my grandpa Howard did.

It's your turn to make your life into a masterpiece and help others do the same. Your mindset about yourself and your circumstances has the power to change your destiny. When you become self-aware and align your priorities with your purpose, you can begin to optimize your skill and character and become the best version of yourself. Not only will it require kicking your limiting beliefs and vices to the curb, but you'll also need to surround yourself with the best people who can help you grow and set a higher standard for yourself.

When storms rage and doubt shows up uninvited, remember who you are—a world changer, a purpose builder, a person created to turn this planet into heaven on earth. When culture tries to sell you a limiting narrative of what's possible, tune into your divine identity. Make choices today in line with who you want to be tomorrow.

Grandfather Howard embarked on his purpose-fueled quest to bring people together with his swim park and campground and, in the process, impact lives. What about you? What's your swim park? What can you start building today that will lead you to optimize your potential and bring value to others? Your swim park could be a flourishing marriage, starting your own business, or developing a healthy body, an enlightened mind, or a not-for-profit organization. Disrupt your mental narrative, and embrace beliefs that will cause you to flourish.

It's time to shift your mindset, rewrite your story, and become who you were born to be!

The fortune is in the follow-through. You've seen the below link and QR code throughout the book.

Click on joshaxe.com/thinkthis to discover thousands of dollars of FREE extra content to take your growth to the next level!

NOTES

Mindshift 1: Create a Breakthrough by Unlimiting Your Beliefs

1. Britannica Dictionary, s.v. "belief," accessed August 11, 2023, https://www
.britannica.com/dictionary/belief.
2. Lauren Venticinque, "Social Proof Examples: How 11 Brands Wield This Marketing
Superpower," The Bazaar Voice, May 23, 2022, https://www.bazaarvoice.com/blog/
social-proof-examples/.
3. Alissa Finerman, "The Impact of Limiting Beliefs," *Wharton Magazine*,
November 19, 2019, https://magazine.wharton.upenn.edu/digital/the-impact
-of-limiting-beliefs/.
4. Fyodor Dostoevsky, *The Brothers Karamazov* (New York: Farrar, Straus and
Giroux, 1990), 44.
5. Jonathan Jarry, MSc, "The Legend of the Wartime Placebo," McGill Office for
Science and Society, February 11, 2022, https://www.mcgill.ca/oss/article/critical
-thinking-health-and-nutrition-history/legend-wartime-placebo.
6. John Kelley, cited in Serusha Govender, "Is the Nocebo Effect Hurting Your
Health," WebMD, accessed April 6, 2023, https://www.webmd.com/balance
/features/is-the-nocebo-effect-hurting-your-health.
7. "13 More Things: The Nocebo Effect," New Scientist, September 2, 2009, https://
www.newscientist.com/article/mg20327247-100–13-more-things-the-nocebo-effect/.
8. Tony Robbins (@TonyRobbins), Twitter, January 19, 2017, https://twitter.com
/TonyRobbins/status/822152960927010816?lang=en.
9. Sanne Feenstra et al., "Contextualizing the Impostor 'Syndrome,'" *Frontiers in
Psychology* 11 (November 13, 2020), https://www.frontiersin.org/articles/10.3389
/fpsyg.2020.575024/full; Corner Office, "Good C.E.Os Are Insecure (and Know
It)," *New York Times*, October 9, 2010, https://www.nytimes.com/2010/10/10
/business/10corner.html?_r=1.
10. Feenstra, "Contextualizing the Impostor 'Syndrome.'"
11. "CBT and the ABCDE Model," Counseling Tutor, accessed August 12, 2023,
https://counsellingtutor.com/cbt-abcde-model/.

12. Kendra Cherry, MSEd, "What Is Rational Emotive Behavior Therapy (REBT)?", VeryWell Mind, February 9, 2023, https://www.verywellmind.com/rational -emotive-behavior-therapy-2796000.
13. American Psychological Association, s.v. "pleasure principle," accessed August 12, 2023, https://dictionary.apa.org/pleasure-principle.
14. *Canandaigua Daily Messenger*, Words of Wisdom (freestanding quotation credited to Frank Outlaw), October 31, 1977: 4 (Canandaigua, New York, newspaper archive).
15. Jamie Kern Lima, *Believe IT: How to Go from Underestimated to Unstoppable* (New York: Gallery Books, 2021), 20, Kindle edition.
16. Lima, 7.
17. Lima, 7.
18. Lima, 8.
19. Lima, x.
20. Lima, 267–68.
21. Jade Scipioni, "IT Cosmetics Jamie Kern Lima: 'I Lived Completely Burnt Out for Almost a Decade,'" CNBC, updated May 20, 2021, https://www.cnbc.com/2021 /03/09/it-cosmetics-jamie-kern-lima-on-building-a-billion-dollar-company.html.
22. Profile, "Jamie Kern Lima," *Forbes*, accessed August 12, 2023, https://www.forbes .com/profile/jamie-kern-lima/?sh=7a30b87466c1.

Mindshift 2: Redefine Success by *Becoming*, Not *Accomplishing*

1. Tom Van Riper, "The Most Influential Athletes," *Forbes*, April 21, 2010, https:// www.forbes.com/2010/04/21/lance-armstrong-endorsements-business-sports -influential-athletes_slide.html?sh=708a810540de.
2. Brent Schrotenboer, "Lance Armstrong ESPN Documentary Details Forgery, Grudges and 10,000 Lies," *USA Today*, May 21, 2020, https://www.usatoday.com /story/sports/2020/05/21/lance-armstrong-espn-documentary-details-forgery -grudges-and-lies/5226636002/.
3. John Maxwell, *Talent Is Never Enough* (Nashville: Thomas Nelson, 2007).
4. "How Most of Steve Jobs' $10 Billion Net Worth Had Nothing to Do with Apple When He Died," Worthly, accessed August 12, 2023, https://worthly.com/richest /steve-jobs-net-worth/.
5. Walter Isaacson, *Steve Jobs* (New York: Simon & Schuster, 2011), 556, Kindle edition.
6. See Matthew 16:26.
7. ABC News, "Looks, Money, Fame Don't Bring Happiness," ABC News, May 22, 2009, https://abcnews.go.com/Health/Healthday/story?id=7658253&page=1.
8. "Death of a Genius: His Fourth Dimension, Time, Overtakes Einstein," subsection: "Old Man's Advice to Youth: 'Never Lose a Holy Curiosity'" by William Miller, ed., *LIFE* magazine, May 2, 1955, 64. https://books.google.com /books?id=dlYEAAAAMBAJ&q=%22man+of+value%22#v=snippet&q=%22 man%20of%20value%22&f=false.
9. Tamara Khader, "The Story Behind Five Daughters Bakery Is as Sweet as Its Doughnuts," *Atlanta*, July 6, 2018, https://www.atlantamagazine.com/dining -news/story-behind-five-daughters-bakery-sweet-as-doughnuts/.

10. Neil Patel, "90% of Startups Fail: Here's What You Need to Know About the 10%," *Forbes*, January 16, 2015, https://www.forbes.com/sites/neilpatel/2015/01/16/90-of -startups-will-fail-heres-what-you-need-to-know-about-the-10/?sh=2d3956506679.

11. John Maxwell, "Character: Who We Are on the Inside," *John C. Maxwell* (blog), April 23, 2013, https://www.johnmaxwell.com/blog/character-who-we-are-on-the -inside/; John C. Maxwell, *The 15 Invaluable Laws of Growth* (New York: Center Street, 2012), https://www.google.com/books/edition/The_15_Invaluable_Laws _of_Growth/p_Qe4Svj0jsC?hl=en&gbpv=1&dq=%22Character+is+a+quality+that +embodies+many+important+traits,+such+as+integrity,+courage,+perseverance, +confidence+and+wisdom.+Unlike%22&pg=PT147&printsec=frontcover.

12. Bobby Allyn, "Top Reason for CEO Departures Among Largest Companies Is Now Misconduct, Study Finds," NPR, May 20, 2019, https://www.npr.org/2019 /05/20/725108825/top-reason-for-ceo-departures-among-largest-companies-is -now-misconduct-study-fi.

13. Jennifer Liu, "78% of Job Seekers Lie During the Hiring Process—Here's What Happened to 4 of Them," Make It, February 20, 2020, https://www.cnbc.com /2020/02/19/how-many-job-seekers-lie-on-their-job-application.html.

14. Jared Lindzon, "What the Lies We All Tell at Work Say About Us," *Fast Company*, August 6, 2019, https://www.fastcompany.com/90380520/what-the-lies-we-tell -at-work-say-about-us.

15. Lindzon, "What the Lies We All Tell at Work Say About Us."

16. Josh Barro, "People Who Claim to Work 75-Hour Weeks Usually Only Work About 50 Hours," *New York Magazine*, April 25, 2019, https://nymag.com /intelligencer/2019/04/people-who-claim-to-work-75-hour-weeks-are-lying.html.

17. "Did Lincoln Ever Walk Miles to Return Change to a Store Customer?," The Lincoln Connection, accessed August 12, 2023, https://www.lincolncollection .org/discover/ask-an-expert/qa-archive/did-lincoln-ever-walk-miles-to-return -change-to-a-store-customer/.

18. Gordon Leidner, "Lincoln's Honesty," Great American History, accessed August 12, 2023, https://greatamericanhistory.net/honesty.htm.

19. Proverbs 22:1.

20. Dorota Weziak-Bialowolska et al., "Prospective Associations Between Strengths of Moral Character and Health: Longitudinal Evidence from Survey and Insurance Claims Data," *Social Psychiatry and Psychiatric Epidemiology* 58 (2022): 163–76, https://link.springer.com/article/10.1007/s00127–022–02344–5; Clea Simon, "Being Good for Goodness' Sake—and Your Own," *The Harvard Gazette*, August 30, 2022, https://news.harvard.edu/gazette/story/2022/08/the -health-benefits-of-character/; Maayan Boiman-Meshita and Hadassah Littman-Ovadia, "Is It Me or You? An Actor-Partner Examination of the Relationship Between Partners' Character Strengths and Marital Quality," *Journal of Happiness Studies* 23 (2022): 195–210, https://link.springer.com/article/10.1007 /s10902–021–00394–1; "Character Strengths and Positive Relationships," Institute on Character, updated August 2022, https://www.viacharacter.org/research /findings/character-strengths-and-positive-relationships.

21. "Transcript: Lance Armstrong Admits to Doping and Bullying," bikebiz, accessed August 12, 2023, https://bikebiz.com/transcript-lance-armstrong-admits-to-doping-and-bullying/amp/.

22. Dr. Myles Munroe, *Discover the Hidden You: The Secret to Living the Good Life* (Shippensburg, PA: Destiny Image Publishers, Inc., 2021), 198–99, Kindle edition.

23. Hazel Markus and Paula Nurius, "Possible Selves," *American Psychologist* (September 1986), https://web.stanford.edu/~hazelm/publications/1986_Markus%20&%20Nurius_PossibleSelves.pdf.

24. Markus and Nurius, "Possible Selves."

25. See Proverbs 23:7.

26. Melissa Dahl, "It's Time to Get Acquainted with Your Future Self," The Cut, January 14, 2015, https://www.thecut.com/2015/01/time-to-get-acquainted-with-future-you.html.

27. David Robson, "How Thinking About 'Future You' Can Build a Happier Life," BBC, February 1, 2022, https://www.bbc.com/worklife/article/20220201-how-thinking-about-future-you-can-build-a-happier-life.

28. "This Problem for Future Homer," YouTube, accessed August 14, 2023, https://www.youtube.com/watch?v=mS9LCR5P5wI.

29. Dahl, "It's Time to Get Acquainted."

Mindshift 3: Become Self-Aware to Get Where You Need to Go

1. Kendra Cherry, MSEd, "Emotional Intelligence: How We Perceive, Evaluate, Express, and Control Emotions," VeryWell Mind, May 2, 2023, https://www.verywellmind.com/what-is-emotional-intelligence-2795423.

2. Daniel Goleman, *Emotional Intelligence* (New York: Random House, 2005), 41, Kindle edition.

3. Rhett Power, "Work on Your Business, Not in Your Business," *Inc.*, April 6, 2015, https://www.inc.com/rhett-power/work-on-your-business-not-in-your-business.html.

4. Tasha Eurich, "What Self-Awareness Really Is (and How to Cultivate It)," *Harvard Business Review*, January 4, 2018, https://hbr.org/2018/01/what-self-awareness-really-is-and-how-to-cultivate-it.

5. Dana Talesnik, "Eurich Explores Why Self-Awareness Matters," National Institutes of Health, vol. LXXI, no. 13 (June 28, 2019), https://nihrecord.nih.gov/2019/06/28/eurich-explores-why-self-awareness-matters.

6. Eurich, "What Self-Awareness Really Is"; Anna Sutton, "Measuring the Effects of Self-Awareness: Construction of the Self-Awareness Outcomes Questionnaire," *European Journal of Psychology* 12, no. 4 (November 2016): 645–58, https://www.ncbi.nlm.nih.gov/pmc/articles/PMC5114878.

7. Eurich, "What Self-Awareness Really Is"; Anna Sutton et al., "A Longitudinal, Mixed Method Evaluation of Self-Awareness Training in the Workplace," *European Journal of Training and Development* 39, no. 7 (August 3, 2015): 610–27, https://www.emerald.com/insight/content/doi/10.1108/EJTD-04-2015-0031/full/html.

8. Rachel E. White et al., "The 'Batman Effect': Improving Perseverance in Young

Children," *Child Development* 88, no. 5 (September/October 2017): 1563–71, https://srcd.onlinelibrary.wiley.com/doi/epdf/10.1111/cdev.12695.

9. "Measuring the Return on Character," *Harvard Business Review*, April 2015, https://hbr.org/2015/04/measuring-the-return-on-character.

10. Eurich, "What Self-Awareness Really Is."

11. Wikipedia, s.v. "Shoshin," accessed August 14, 2023, https://en.wikipedia.org /wiki/Shoshin.

12. "Jordan Peterson—Rules for Life," Strategies for Influence, accessed August 12, 2023, https://strategiesforinfluence.com/jordan-peterson-rules-for-life/.

13. Katie Young, "6 in 10 Are Social Networking for Entertainment," GWI, August 11, 2016, https://blog.gwi.com/chart-of-the-day/6-in-10-are-social-networking-for -entertainment/.

14. Susan S. Lang, "Study of German Children Living Near Airports Shows Jet Aircraft Noise Impairs Long-term Memory and Reading Ability," *Cornell Chronicle*, October 7, 2002, https://news.cornell.edu/stories/2002/10/airport-noise-impairs -long-term-memory-and-reading.

15. Stephanie Dutchen, "Noise and Health," *Harvard Medicine* (magazine), Spring 2022, https://hms.harvard.edu/magazine/viral-world/effects-noise-health.

16. Imke Kirste et al., "Is Silence Golden? Effects of Auditory Stimuli and Their Absence on Adult Hippocampal Neurogenesis," *Brain Structure and Function* 220, no. 2 (2015): 1221–28, https://www.ncbi.nlm.nih.gov/pmc/articles/PMC4087081/.

17. Deborah Siegel-Acevedo, "Writing Can Help Us Heal from Trauma," *Harvard Business Review*, July 1, 2021, https://hbr.org/2021/07/writing-can-help-us-heal-from-trauma.

18. Lee Colan, "What Science Says About Mastering Your Emotions," *Inc.*, July 31, 2019, https://www.inc.com/lee-colan/what-science-says-about-mastering-your -emotions.html.

19. Hannah Ritchie and Max Roser, "Access to Energy," Our World in Data, accessed August 14, 2023, https://ourworldindata.org/energy-access.

20. Hanna Kang, "2.2 Million People in American Live Without Access to Running Water and Basic Plumbing: Report," Insider, June 28, 2022, https://www.business insider.com/clean-water-access-plumbing-digdeep-2022–6.

21. See Plato's Dialogue, Apology (38a).

22. Erwin McManus, *Uprising* (Nashville, TN: Thomas Nelson, 2006), 47.

Mindshift 4: Find a Why or Risk Wasting It All

1. Dictionary.com, s.v. "purpose," accessed August 14, 2023, https://www.dictionary .com/browse/purpose.

2. John Nemo, "What a NASA Janitor Can Teach Us About Living a Bigger Life," *The Business Journals*, December 23, 2014, https://www.bizjournals.com/bizjournals /how-to/growth-strategies/2014/12/what-a-nasa-janitor-can-teach-us.html.

3. Jeffrey Gaines, "The Philosophy of Ikigai: 3 Examples About Finding Purpose," Positive Psychology, November 17, 2020, https://positivepsychology.com/ikigai /#perspective.

4. Dhruv Khullar, "Finding Purpose for a Good Life. But Also a Healthy One," *New York Times*, January 1, 2018, https://www.nytimes.com/2018/01/01/upshot/finding -purpose-for-a-good-life-but-also-a-healthy-one.html.
5. Khullar, "Finding Purpose for a Good Life."
6. Pia Hedberg et al., "Depression in Relation to Purpose in Life Among a Very Old Population: A Five-Year Follow-up Study," *Aging and Mental Health* 14, no. 6 (2010): 757–63, https://doi.org/10.1080/13607861003713216.
7. Arlener D. Turner, Christine E. Smith, and Jason C. Ong, "Is Purpose in Life Associated with Less Sleep Disturbance in Older Adults?," *Sleep Science and Practice* 1, no. 14 (2017), https://sleep.biomedcentral.com/articles/10.1186 /s41606-017-0015-6.
8. Aliya Alimujiang et al., "Association Between Life Purpose and Mortality Among US Adults Older Than 50 Years," *JAMA Network Open* 2, no. 5 (2019), https://doi .org/10.1001/jamanetworkopen.2019.4270.
9. Alimujiang, "Association Between Life Purpose and Mortality."
10. Brett Q. Ford et al., "Desperately Seeking Happiness: Valuing Happiness Is Associated with Symptoms and Diagnosis of Depression," *Journal of Social and Clinical Psychology* 33, no. 10 (2014): 890–905, https://www.ncbi.nlm.nih.gov /pmc/articles/PMC4321693/.
11. Viktor E. Frankl, *Man's Search for Meaning* (Boston: Beacon Press, 2014), 67, Kindle edition.
12. Frankl, *Man's Search for Meaning*, 74.
13. Jessica Morgan and Tom Farsides, "Measuring Meaning in Life," *Journal of Happiness Studies* 10 (2009): 197–214, https://link.springer.com/article/10.1007 /s10902-007-9075-0.
14. Paraphrased, Friedrich Nietzsche, *Twilight of the Idols and The Anti-Christ* (translated by Thomas Common with introductions by Willard Huntington Wright), Digireads.com Publishing, Kindle edition.
15. P. L. Hill et al., "Collegiate Purpose Orientations and Well-being in Early and Middle Adulthood," *Journal of Applied Developmental Psychology* 31, no. 2 (March–April 2010): 173–79, https://doi.org/10.1016/j.appdev.2009.12.001.
16. Jennifer Crocker et al., "Interpersonal Goals and Change in Anxiety and Dysphoria in First-Semester College Students," *Journal of Personality and Social Psychology* 98, no. 6 (June 2010): 1,009–24, https://www.ncbi.nlm.nih.gov/pmc /articles/PMC2966869/.
17. "The Purpose of Life Is Not to Be Happy but to Matter," Quote Investigator, November 29, 2014, https://quoteinvestigator.com/2014/11/29/purpose/#f+10187+1+1.
18. James Baraz and Shoshana Alexander, "The Helper's High," *Greater Good*, February 1, 2010, https://greatergood.berkeley.edu/article/item/the_helpers_high.
19. Baraz and Alexander, "The Helper's High."
20. Genesis 2.
21. Revelation 21 and 22.
22. Alice Klein, "First Farm to Grow Veg in a Desert Using Only Sun and

Seawater," New Scientist, October 6, 2016, https://www.newscientist.com/article/2108296-first-farm-to-grow-veg-in-a-desert-using-only-sun-and-seawater/.

23. Chris Skinner, "Using Regenerative Agriculture to Combat Climate Change," University of Vermont, June 22, 2022, https://www.uvm.edu/news/cals/using-regenerative-agriculture-combat-climate-change.

24. Bethany Biron, "The Rise of Patagonia: How Rock Climber and Activist Yvon Chouinard Created One of the World's Biggest Outdoor Brands from the Trunk of His Car," Insider, September 17, 2022, https://www.businessinsider.com/rise-patagonia-yvon-chouinard-history-photos-2022-9#ready-for-a-new-adventure-in-1965-chouinard-teamed-up-with-tom-frost-to-create-chouinard-equipment-with-a-focus-on-redesigning-climbing-tools-to-make-them-stronger-lighter-simpler-and-more-functional-7.

25. Jeff Beer, "Exclusive: 'Patagonia Is in Business to Save Our Home Planet,'" *Fast Company*, December 13, 2018, https://www.fastcompany.com/90280950/exclusive-patagonia-is-in-business-to-save-our-home-planet.

26. Yvon Chouinard, "Earth Is Now Our Only Shareholder," Patagonia, accessed August 14, 2023, https://www.patagonia.com/ownership/.

27. Chouinard, "Earth Is Now Our Only Shareholder."

28. David Green, "My Decision to Give Away Ownership of Hobby Lobby: I Chose God," Fox News, October 21, 2022, https://www.foxnews.com/opinion/decision-to-give-away-ownership-hobby-lobby-chose-god.

29. Green, "My Decision to Give Away Ownership."

30. Arlener D. Turner, Christine E. Smith, and Jason C. Ong, "Is Purpose in Life Associated with Less Sleep Disturbance in Older Adults?" *Sleep Science and Practice* 1, no. 14 (2017), https://sleep.biomedcentral.com/articles/10.1186/s41606-017-0015-6.

31. Alimujiang, "Association Between Life Purpose and Mortality."

32. Alimujiang, "Association Between Life Purpose and Mortality."

33. Fei Li et al., "The Role of Stress Management in the Relationship between Purpose in Life and Self-Rated Health in Teachers: A Mediation Analysis," *International Journal of Environmental Research and Public Health* 13, no. 7 (2016): 719, https://www.ncbi.nlm.nih.gov/pmc/articles/PMC4962260/.

34. Alimujiang, "Association Between Life Purpose and Mortality."

Mindshift 5: Rewrite Your Role in the Story

1. Donald Miller, *Hero on a Mission* (New York: HarperCollins Leadership, 2022), 56, Kindle edition.

2. "Holocaust Misconceptions," Illinois Holocaust Museum and Education Center, accessed August 14, 2023, https://www.ilholocaustmuseum.org/holocaust-misconceptions/.

3. History.com Editors, "Joseph Stalin," History.com, April 25, 2023, https://www.history.com/topics/russia/joseph-stalin.

4. History.com Editors, "Harriet Tubman," History.com, March 29, 2023, https://

www.history.com/topics/black-history/harriet-tubman#escape-from-slavery; "Did Harriet Tubman Have Epilepsy?" epsyhealth.com, February 10, 2021, https://www.epsyhealth.com/seizure-epilepsy-blog/did-harriet-tubman-have-epilepsy#:~:text=Auburn%2C%20New%20York.-,Why%20did%20Harriet%20Tubman%20have%20seizures%3F,slave%2C%20accidentally%20striking%20Harriet%20instead.; "1863: Harriet Tubman—Covert Spy Behind Enemy Lines," Intel.gov, accessed August 14, 2023, https://www.intelligence.gov/people/barrier-breakers-in-history/454-harriet-tubman.

5. Jocko Willink and Leif Babin, *Extreme Ownership* (St. New York: Martin's Publishing Group, 2017), 29, Kindle edition.

Mindshift 6: Assemble a Team to Fulfill Your Dreams

1. "Low on Self-Control? Surrounding Yourself with Strong-Willed Friends May Help," Association for Psychological Science, April 9, 2013, https://www.psychologicalscience.org/news/releases/low-on-self-control-surrounding-yourself-with-strong-willed-friends-may-help.html.
2. "Dunbar's Number: Why We Can Only Maintain 150 Relationships," BBC, accessed August 14, 2023, https://www.bbc.com/future/article/20191001-dunbars-number-why-we-can-only-maintain-150-relationships.
3. Brené Brown, *The Gifts of Imperfection*, 10th Anniversary Edition (Center City, MN: Hazelden Publishing, 2020), 30.
4. Sebastian Ocklenburg, "The World's Biggest Study on Loneliness," Psychology Today, June 9, 2020, https://www.psychologytoday.com/us/blog/the-asymmetric-brain/202006/the-world-s-biggest-study-loneliness.
5. Dhruv Khullar, "How Social Isolation Is Killing Us," *New York Times*, December 22, 2016, https://www.nytimes.com/2016/12/22/upshot/how-social-isolation-is-killing-us.html.
6. Matthew Pittman and Brandon Reich, "Social Media and Loneliness: Why an Instagram Picture May Be Worth More Than a Thousand Twitter Words," *Computers in Human Behavior* 62 (September 2016): 115–67, https://www.sciencedirect.com/science/article/abs/pii/S0747563216302552.
7. Reviewed by Dan Brennan, "What to Know About Emotional Health," WebMD, October 25, 2021, https://www.webmd.com/balance/news/20180504/loneliness-rivals-obesity-smoking-as-health-risk.
8. Brennan, "What to Know About Emotional Health."
9. Vivek Murthy, "Work and the Loneliness Epidemic," *Harvard Business Review*, September 26, 2017, https://hbr.org/2017/09/work-and-the-loneliness-epidemic.
10. Proverbs 27:17.
11. "Tzedakah—Charity in the Jewish Tradition," BJE.org, accessed August 14, 2023, https://bje.org.au/knowledge-centre/jewish-ethics/tzedakah/.
12. Chaya Shuchat, "Eight Degrees of Giving," Chabad.org, accessed August 14, 2023, https://www.chabad.org/library/article_cdo/aid/256321/jewish/Eight-Degrees-of-Giving.htm.

13. Christine Comaford, "76% of People Think Mentors Are Important, but Only 37% Have One," *Forbes*, July 3, 2019, https://www.forbes.com/sites/christinecomaford/2019/07/03/new-study-76-of-people-think-mentors-are-important-but-only-37-have-one/?sh=1edb95043297.
14. "Why Mentoring: What the Stats Say," McCarthy Mentoring, May 2017, https://mccarthymentoring.com/why-mentoring-what-the-stats-say/.
15. "Why Mentoring: What the Stats Say."
16. "The Learning Pyramid," Education Corner, accessed August 14, 2023, https://www.educationcorner.com/the-learning-pyramid.html.

Mindshift 7: Build an Unshakable Identity So No One Else Does It for You

1. "Be Like Mike Gatorade Commercial," YouTube, accessed August 14, 2023, https://www.youtube.com/watch?v=b0AGiq9j_Ak.
2. Charles Taylor, *Sources of the Self: The Making of the Modern Identity* (Cambridge, MA: Harvard University Press, 1989).
3. "Let It Go," performed by Idina Menzel, *Frozen*, produced by Tom MacDougall et al., https://genius.com/Idina-menzel-let-it-go-lyrics.
4. Scotty Hendricks, "'God Is Dead': What Nietzsche Really Meant," Big Think, January 29, 2022, https://bigthink.com/thinking/what-nietzsche-really-meant-by-god-is-dead/.
5. Britannica, s.v. "rationalism," accessed August 14, 2023, https://www.britannica.com/topic/rationalism.
6. Dan Gordon, "High Anxiety," UCLA Newsroom, September 19, 2022, https://newsroom.ucla.edu/magazine/anxiety-stress-semel-institute-7-ways-cope.
7. David Brooks, "The Death of Idealism," *New York Times*, September 30, 2016, https://www.nytimes.com/2016/09/30/opinion/the-death-of-idealism.html.
8. "James Earl Jones: Mufasa," *The Lion King*, IMDb, accessed August 14, 2023, https://www.imdb.com/title/tt0110357/characters/nm0000469.
9. C. S. Lewis, *The Weight of Glory* (New York: HarperCollins, 2000), 45–46, https://www.google.com/books/edition/Weight_of_Glory/WNTT_8NW_qwC?hl=en&gbpv=1&bsq=mere%20mortal.
10. Jeffrey M. Jones, "Belief in God in U.S. Dips to 81%, a New Low," Gallup, June 17, 2022, https://news.gallup.com/poll/393737/belief-god-dips-new-low.aspx.
11. "Religion in Everyday Life," Pew Research Center, April 12, 2016, https://www.pewresearch.org/religion/2016/04/12/religion-in-everyday-life/.
12. "Reflections: Living in Hope," C. S. Lewis Institute, December 1, 2006, https://www.cslewisinstitute.org/resources/reflections-december-2006/.
13. Femi Lewis, "5 Men Who Inspired Martin Luther King, Jr. to Be a Leader," ThoughtCo., December 15, 2020, https://www.thoughtco.com/men-who-inspired-martin-luther-king-jr-4019032; "Martin Luther King, Jr.," NAACP, accessed August 14, 2023, https://naacp.org/find-resources/history-explained/civil-rights-leaders/martin-luther-king-jr; "How Gandhi's Philosophy of Nonviolence Influenced MLK," WABE, February 14, 2018, https://mlk.wabe.org/gandhis

-philosophy-nonviolence-influenced-mlk/; Michael Knigge, "How Martin Luther Influenced Martin Luther King Jr.," October 31, 2017, https://www.dw.com/en /how-martin-luther-influenced-martin-luther-king-jr/a-41082670#; Brandon Ambrosino, "How Martin Luther King Jr.'s Faith Drove His Activism," Vox, January 19, 2015, https://www.vox.com/2015/1/19/7852311/martin-luther-king-faith; Rabbi Barry L. Schwartz, "Martin Luther King Jr. and the Hebrew Prophets—a 50th Anniversary Appreciation," January 11, 2018, https://jewishstandard.timesofisrael.com /martin-luther-king-jr-and-the-hebrew-prophets-a-50th-anniversary-appreciation/.

14. Rev. Martin Luther King Jr., "Martin Luther King's Final Speech: 'I've Been to the Mountaintop'—the Full Text," ABC News, April 3, 2013, https://abcnews.go.com /Politics/martin-luther-kings-final-speech-ive-mountaintop-full/story?id=18872817.

15. Ben Johnson, "The Great Fire of London," Historic UK, accessed August 14, 2023, https://www.historic-uk.com/HistoryUK/HistoryofEngland/The-Great-Fire-of -London/.

16. "Origin Story: Parable of the Three Bricklayers," DJ Chuang, November 23, 2021, https://djchuang.com/origin-story-parable-of-the-three-bricklayers/.

17. "Worship Is Good for Your Health: Vanderbilt Study," Vanderbilt Research News, May 31, 2017, https://news.vanderbilt.edu/2017/05/31/worship-is-good-for-your -health-vanderbilt-study/.

18. "James Earl Jones: Mufasa," *The Lion King*, IMDb, accessed August 14, 2023, https://www.imdb.com/title/tt0110357/characters/nm0000469.

Mindshift 8: Bust Vices by Building Virtues

1. Mia Forbes, "The Sistine Chapel: Unfolded and Explained," The Collector, May 10, 2020, https://www.thecollector.com/sistine-chapel/.

2. "Leadership Lessons from Michelangelo," Leadership Ministries, Inc., January 27, 2023, https://leadmin.org/articles/leadership-lessons-from-michelangelo.

3. Jessie Szalay, "Sistine Chapel: Facts, History & Visitor Information," Live Science, October 29, 2013, https://www.livescience.com/40802-sistine-chapel.html.

4. Ken Weliever, "God Will See," The Preachers Word, November 1, 2022, https://the preachersword.com/2022/11/01/god-will-see/.

5. Frances Prather, "How Does Aristotle Believe That Virtue and Excellence Are Related?," Enotes.com, accessed August 14, 2023, https://www.enotes.com/homework -help/how-does-aristotle-believe-that-virtue-and-2044809.

6. Ryan Griffith, "The Seven Heavenly Virtues," Desiring God, November 1, 2021, https://www.desiringgod.org/articles/the-seven-heavenly-virtues.

7. "Aristotle's Doctrine of the Mean," plosin.com, accessed August 14, 2023, http://www.plosin.com/work/AristotleMean.html.

8. "Definition," Torah Resources International, accessed December 6, 2023, https://torahresourcesinternational.com/definition/.

9. Bibleapps.com, s.v. "264. hamartanó," accessed August 14, 2023, https://bibleapps .com/greek/264.htm.

10. Matthew 22:36–40; A. L. Komáromi, "St Augustine on Happiness, Virtue and Love of God and Neighbor," Philosophy Models, September 6, 2019, https://philosophy-models.blog/2019/06/09/st-augustine-on-happiness-virtue-love-of-god/.

11. "Four Kinds of Love in Greek," BAS Library, Fall 2020, https://www.baslibrary.org/biblical-archaeology-review/46/4/28.

12. Rob Stroud, "The Glory of Storge (Love)," Mere Inkling Press, October 11, 2012, https://mereinkling.net/2012/10/11/the-glory-of-storge-love/.

13. "Four Kinds of Love in Greek."

14. Tim Tebow (@TimTebow). 2021. "My life purpose is to fight for those who can't fight for themselves." Twitter, May 8, 2021, 7:34 p.m. https://twitter.com/timtebow/status/1423442335942299650?lang=gl.

15. "Question 20: God's Love," Aquinas 101, accessed August 14, 2023, https://aquinas101.thomisticinstitute.org/st-ia-q-20.

16. James M. Stedman, "Aristotle's Cardinal Virtues: Their Application to Assessment of Psychopathology and Psychotherapy," *Practical Philosophy* (2011), http://www.society-for-philosophy-in-practice.org/journal/pdf/10–1%20057%20Stedman%20-%20Aristotles%20Virtues.pdf.

17. "Thomas Aquinas," Pursuit of Happiness, accessed August 14, 2023, https://www.pursuit-of-happiness.org/history-of-happiness/thomas-aquinas/#:~:text=Furthermore%2C%20God%20in%20his%20grace,as%20we%20begin%20the%20effort.

18. "Night to Shine," Tim Tebow Foundation, accessed December 6, 2023, https://www.timtebowfoundation.org/night-to-shine//.

19. Tim Tebow, *Mission Possible* (New York: Penguin Random House, 2022), 74.

20. Isabel Gonzalez, "LOOK: Tim Tebow Auctions Off His Heisman Trophy Every Year to Raise Money for Charity," CBS News, September 21, 2022, https://www.cbssports.com/college-football/news/look-tim-tebow-auctions-off-his-heisman-trophy-every-year-to-raise-money-for-charity/.

21. Catherine Moore, "What Is Eudaimonia? Aristotle and Eudaimonic Wellbeing," Positive Psychology, April 8, 2019, https://positivepsychology.com/eudaimonia/.

22. "Measuring the Return on Character," *Harvard Business Review*, April 2015, https://hbr.org/2015/04/measuring-the-return-on-character?registration=success.

23. Rasmus Hougaard, Jacqueline Carter, and Marissa Afton, "Connect with Empathy, but Lead with Compassion," *Harvard Business Review*, December 23, 2021, https://hbr.org/2021/12/connect-with-empathy-but-lead-with-compassion.

24. Hougaard, Carter, and Afton, "Connect with Empathy."

25. Debbie Lord, "Billy Graham Quotes: He Made Christian Principles Accessible to Millions," *Atlanta Journal-Constitution*, February 21, 2018, https://www.ajc.com/news/national/billy-graham-quotes-made-christian-principles-accessible-millions/vmeaUI4HGTKhI9kdimpn9J/.

26. Will Durant, *The Story of Philosophy* (Garden City, NY: Dover Publications, 2022), 69.

27. *Cambridge Dictionary*, s.v. "virtue signalling," accessed August 14, 2023, https://dictionary.cambridge.org/dictionary/english/virtue-signalling.

28. Eleanor Pringle, "'I Promise to Give All of My Money Away Before I Die': World's Biggest YouTuber Paid for 1,000 People to Get Eye Surgery but Is Slammed for 'Making Content Out of People Who Can't See,'" *Fortune*, February 2, 2023, https://fortune.com/2023/02/02/world-biggest-youtube-mr-beast-paid-1000 -people-eye-surgery-but-slammed-making-content-people-who-cannot-see/.
29. "Make the World a Better Place," Beast Philanthropy, accessed August 14, 2023, https://www.beastphilanthropy.org.
30. Menachem Wecker, "Michaelangelo's Architecture of Faith," NCR, December 22, 2017, https://www.ncronline.org/culture/michelangelos-architecture-faith.
31. Janelle Zara, "How Michelangelo Spent His Final Years Designing St. Peter's Basilica in Rome," *Architectural Digest*, June 25, 2019, https://www.architecturaldigest.com /story/how-michelangelo-spent-final-years-designing-st-peters-basilica-rome.
32. "David: The Neglected Block of Marble Given to the 26-Year-Old Michelangelo to Complete," Abir Pothi, August 16, 2022, https://abirpothi.com/david-the-neglected -block-of-marble-given-to-the-26-year-old-michelangelo-to-complete/.
33. "Meaning Beyond Tragedy," Carleton, March 26, 2014, https://www.carleton.edu /chaplain/news/meaning-beyond-tragedy/.

Mindshift 9: Turn Off Opinions and Turn On Principles

1. Dictionary.com, s.v. "principle," accessed August 14, 2023, https://www.dictionary .com/browse/principles.
2. Exodus 20:3–17.
3. Matthew 5–7.
4. Mark Cole, "Mark Cole: Five Tools for Communicating Vision," *John C. Maxwell* (blog), November 15, 2019, https://www.johnmaxwell.com/blog/mark-cole-five -tools-for-communicating-vision/.
5. See Matthew 23:11.
6. Napoleon Hill, *Think and Grow Rich!* (Anderson, C: The Mindpower Press, 2015), 150.
7. David Brooks, "The Relationship School," *New York Times*, March 22, 2012, https://www.nytimes.com/2012/03/23/opinion/brooks-the-relationship-school.html.
8. Ken McElroy, "A Nation of Workers: How Public Education Is Dummying Down Our Labor Force," *Jetset Magazine*, August 15, 2016, https://www.jetsetmag.com /exclusive/business/nation-workers-public-education-dummying-labor-force/.
9. "Education Is Not the Learning of Facts, but the Training of the Mind to Think," Quote Investigator, May 28, 2016, https://quoteinvestigator.com/2016/05/28 /not-facts/.
10. "Americans Use Just 37 Percent of Information Learned in School, Survey Finds," CBS News Philadelphia, January 26, 2019, https://www.cbsnews.com/philadelphia /news/americans-use-just-37-percent-of-information-learned-in-school-survey-finds/.
11. "The 6 Types of Socratic Questions," James Bowman, accessed August 14, 2023, http://www.jamesbowman.me/post/socratic-questions-infographic.pdf.
12. Shubhangi Choudhary, "5 Whys—Getting to the Root of a Problem Quickly," Medium, February 16, 2019, 5-whys-getting-to-the-root-of-a-problem-quickly-a779f8ae7e3c.

13. James Clear, "First Principles: Elon Musk on the Power of Thinking for Yourself," James Clear, accessed August 14, 2023, https://jamesclear.com/first-principles.

14. Drake Baer, "Elon Musk Uses This Ancient Critical-Thinking Strategy to Outsmart Everybody Else," Insider, January 5, 2015, https://www.businessinsider.com/elon-musk-first-principles-2015-1.

15. Clear, "First Principles."

16. "Missed Opportunities: Youth Homelessness in America," Voices of Youth Count, November 2017,https://voicesofyouthcount.org/wp-content/uploads/2017/11/ChapinHall_VoYC_1-Pager_Final_111517.pdf.

17. My Jewish Learning, "What Does 'Torah' Mean?," accessed August 14, 2023, https://www.myjewishlearning.com/article/what-does-the-word-torah-mean/.

18. Rabbi Jonathan Sacks, "The Necessity of Asking Questions," Chabad.org, accessed August 14, 2023, https://www.chabad.org/parshah/article_cdo/aid/3574984/jewish/The-Necessity-of-Asking-Questions.htm.

19. "Talmid Definition," That the World May Know, accessed August 14, 2023, https://www.thattheworldmayknow.com/define-talmid.

20. Will Daniel, "Hedge Funder Michael Burry, Made Famous in 'The Big Short,' Warns of an 'Extended Multiyear Recession,'" Yahoo!, November 30, 2022, https://www.yahoo.com/video/hedge-funder-michael-burry-made-185133729.html.

21. "Warren Buffett," Forbes, accessed August 14, 2023, https://www.forbes.com/profile/warren-buffett/?list=billionaires&sh=4c9a51094639.

22. Dan Newman, "Warren Buffett: Ignore Market Predictions," The Motley Fool, March 22, 2014, https://www.fool.com/investing/general/2014/03/22/warren-buffett-ignore-market-predictions.aspx.

23. See Galatians 6:7.

24. Adapted from Sir Edward Bulwer-Lytton, Word Histories, https://wordhistories.net/2020/07/01/pen-mightier-than-sword/.

25. See Matthew 23:11.

26. See Proverbs 27:17.

27. See Matthew 13:1–9.

28. See Matthew 7:6.

29. Marcel Schwantes, "These 3 Billionaires Agree: You Need This Skill to Be Successful," Inc.com, accessed August 14, 2023, https://www.inc.com/marcel-schwantes/these-3-billionaires-agree-you-need-this-1-critical-skill-to-be-successful.html.

30. Proverbs 18:21.

31. Friedrich Nietzsche, Beyond Good and Evil, Classic Illustrated Edition (Heritage Illustrated Publishing), 29, Kindle edition.

32. Paraphrased from Aristotle, Durant, The Story of Philosophy.

Mindshift 10: Flip the Fear to Turn On the Growth

1. Claudia M. Mueller and Carol S. Dweck, "Praise for Intelligence Can Undermine Children's Motivation and Performance," Journal of Personality and Social Psychology 75, no. 1 (1998): 33–52, https://psycnet.apa.org/record/1998-04530-003?doi=1.

2. Tracy Brower, "Learning Is a Sure Path to Happiness: Science Proves It," *Forbes*, October 17, 2021, https://www.forbes.com/sites/tracybrower/2021/10/17/learning -is-a-sure-path-to-happiness-science-proves-it/?sh=5b38eaa6768e.

3. Carol Dweck, *Mindset: The New Psychology of Success* (New York: Random House, 2016).

4. Dr. Josh Axe, "What Is Adrenal Fatigue? Steps to Overcome It Naturally," Dr. Axe, November 14, 2022, https://draxe.com/health/3-steps-to-heal-adrenal-fatigue/.

5. Smitha Bhandari, reviewer, "The Effects of Stress on Your Body," WebMD, December 8, 2021, https://www.webmd.com/balance/stress-management/effects -of-stress-on-your-body.

6. Barbara L. Fredrickson and Marcial F. Losada, "Positive Affect and the Complex Dynamics of Human Flourishing," *American Psychologist* 60, no. 7 (October 2005): 678–86, https://www.ncbi.nlm.nih.gov/pmc/articles/PMC3126111/.

7. Fredrickson and Losada, "Positive Affect."

8. Fredrickson and Losada, "Positive Affect."

9. Steve Dickson, "Oprah and Reese Witherspoon Are New Spanx Investors After Buying in at a $1.2 Billion Valuation," *Fortune*, November 18, 2021, https://fortune .com/2021/11/18/oprah-winfrey-reese-witherspoon-spanx-investors-sara-blakely -blackstone-billion-valuation/.

10. Emma Fierberg and Alana Kakoyiannis, "Learning to Celebrate Failure at a Young Age Led to This Billionaire's Success," Business Insider, June 17, 2018, https://www .businessinsider.com/sara-blakely-spanx-ceo-offersadvice-redefine-failure-retail -2016-7.

11. E. Kross and O. Ayduk, "Chapter Two - Self-Distancing: Theory, Research, and Current Directions," *Advances in Experimental Social Psychology* 55 (2017): 81–136, https://www.sciencedirect.com/science/article/abs/pii/S0065260116300338.

12. Brad Wieners, "The Bear Grylls Survival Manual," Men's Journal, November 18, 2019, https://www.mensjournal.com/adventure/the-bear-grylls-survival-manual-20121012.

13. Sean Coughlan, "What Really Makes Bear Grylls Afraid?," BBC, March 22, 2017, https://www.bbc.com/news/business-39334917.

14. MovieGuide Contributor, "'Storms Make Us Stronger': Bear Brylls Discusses Prayer, Facing Fears, Perseverance," MovieGuide, June 16, 2022, https://www .movieguide.org/news-articles/storms-make-us-stronger-bear-grylls-discusses -prayer-facing-fears-perseverance.html.

15. Susan Biali Haas, MD, "Help for Anxiety: Facing Your Fears Will Heal Your Brain," Psychology Today, August 27, 2018, https://www.psychologytoday.com/us/blog /prescriptions-life/201808/help-anxiety-facing-your-fears-will-heal-your-brain.

16. "What Is Exposure Therapy?," APA Div. 12, Society of Clinical Psychology, 2017, https://www.apa.org/ptsd-guideline/patients-and-families/exposure-therapy.

17. Jaimal Rogis, "Baby Steps: The Best Way to Overcome Your Greatest Fears," Life Hacker, January 8, 2013, https://lifehacker.com/ baby-steps-the-best-way-to-overcome-your-greatest-fear-5973996.

18. Stephanie Larratt, "'It's Scary to Be Vulnerable': Celebritites Talk Conquering

Fear and Finding Success," Today, March 24, 2020, https://www.today.com/tmrw /overcoming-fear-celebs-share-inspiring-stories-about-overcoming-fear-t173976.

19. K. Anders Ericsson, Michael J. Prietula, and Edward T. Cokely, "The Making of an Expert," *Harvard Business Review*, July-August 2007, https://hbr.org/2007/07 /the-making-of-an-expert.

20. Ericsson, Prietula, and Cokely, "The Making of an Expert."

Mindshift 11: Visualize to Realize

1. Charles E. Hummel, *Tyranny of the Urgent* (Downers Grove, IL: InterVarsity Press, 2013), 5–6, Kindle edition.

2. "The Anatomy of Work Global Index," Asana, 2023, https://asana.com/resources /anatomy-of-work.

3. Jennifer Liu, "People Spend More than Half Their Day Doing Busy Work, According to Survey of 10,000-plus Workers," CNBC, April 6, 2022, https://www .cnbc.com/2022/04/06/people-spend-more-than-half-of-the-day-on-busy-work -says-asana-survey.html.

4. *The Biblical World* 53, no. 1, excerpt from "The Group Plan" by Rev. H. K. Williams in the "Young People's Service," (Chicago: University of Chicago Press, 1919), 80–81.

5. Erin Jensen, "Joanna Gaines' Renovated Her Relationship with Perfectionism: 'I Am Enough, Period,'" *USA Today*, updated November 19, 2022, https://www .usatoday.com/story/entertainment/books/2022/11/08/joanna-gaines-interview -memoir-stories-we-tell/8265700001/.

6. Joanna Gaines, *The Stories We Tell* (New York: Harper Select, 2022), 81, Kindle edition.

7. Samantha Bergeson, "Do Chip & Joanna Gaines Ever Need a Break from Each Other? The Couple Says . . . ," E News, July 12, 2021, https://www.eonline.com/news/1288474 /do-chip-joanna-gaines-ever-need-a-break-from-each-other-the-couple-says'.

8. Andy Stanley (@AndyStanley). 2013. "Your greatest contribution to the kingdom of God." Twitter, April 17, 2013, 9:38 p.m. https://twitter.com/AndyStanley/status /324713440541290498.

9. Quoted in Brian Tracy, *Eat That Frog! 21 Great Ways to Stop Procrastinating and Get More Done in Less Time* (Berrett-Koehler Publishers, 2017), https://www .google.com/books/edition/Eat_That_Frog/QG4KDgAAQBAJ?hl=en&gbpv=1 &dq=%C2%A0%22the+things+that+matter+most+must%22+who+said+it&pg =PT43&printsec=frontcover.

10. "Average Daily Time Spent on Social Media (Latest 2023 Data)," Broadband Search, accessed August 15, 2023, https://www.broadbandsearch.net/blog/average -daily-time-on-social-media.

11. Julia Stoll, "Time Spent Watching TV in the United States from 2019 to 2024," Statista, March 15, 2023, https://www.statista.com/statistics/186833/average -television-use-per-person-in-the-us-since-2002/.

12. Cambridge Dictionary, s.v. "visualization," accessed August 15, 2023, https://dictionary.cambridge.org/us/dictionary/english/visualization.

13. Dr. Dan Vosgerichian, "Use Visualization, Imagery Like Many of Golf's Greats," *Golf WRX*, October 13, 2013, https://www.golfwrx.com/140719/use-visualization -imagery-like-many-of-golfs-greats/.
14. Vinoth K. Ranganathan et al., "From Mental Power to Muscle Power—Gaining Strength by Using the Mind," *Neuropsychologia* 42, no. 7 (2004): 944–56, https:// www.sciencedirect.com/science/article/abs/pii/S0028393203003257?via%3Dihub.
15. Alan Richardson, "Mental Practice: A Review and Discussion Part I," *Research Quarterly.* 38, no. 1 (1967): 95–107, 10.1080/10671188.1967.10614808.
16. Genesis 15:5 YLT.
17. Exodus 3:8.
18. "mitzrayim," Balashon—Hebrew Language Detective, March 31, 2009, https://www .balashon.com/2009/03/mitzrayim.html.
19. Hannah L. Miller, "Sara Blakely: 7 Life Lessons from the Founder of SPANX," Leaders.com, November 18, 2021, https://leaders.com/articles/women-in-business /sara-blakely-spanx/.
20. Miller, "Sara Blakely."
21. "Active Learning," Changing Minds, accessed August 15, 2023, http://changingmind s.org/explanations/learning/active_learning.htm.
22. Patricia Chen et al., "A Strategic Mindset: An Orientation Toward Strategic Behavior During Goal Pursuit," *PNAS* vol. 117, no. 25 (June 10, 2020): 14066–72, https://www.pnas.org/doi/10.1073/pnas.2002529117.
23. Lindsay Tigar, "5 Daily Habits to Steal from Mark Wahlberg," Goalcast, accessed August 15, 2023, https://www.goalcast.com/daily-habits-mark-wahlberg/.
24. Brandon Turner, "6 Habits from Mark Wahlberg's Schedule That Can Make You a Success," Bigger Pockets, December 28, 2019, https://www.biggerpockets.com /blog/mark-wahlbergs-schedule.
25. Liv Lane, "Here's Exactly What Carrie Underwood Eats Every Day on Tour," Heavy, February 8, 2023, https://heavy.com/entertainment/american-idol/carrie -underwood-daily-diet-on-tour/ and instagram.
26. Craig Impelman, "Make Each Day Your Masterpiece," The Wooden Effect, January 18, 2017, https://www.thewoodeneffect.com/your-masterpiece/.
27. Marc Zao-Sanders, "How Timeboxing Works and Why It Will Make You More Productive," *Harvard Business Review*, December 12, 2018, https://hbr.org/2018 /12/how-timeboxing-works-and-why-it-will-make-you-more-productive.

Mindshift 12: Power Up Your Potential with Positive Perseverance

1. Robin Blades, "Protecting the Brain Against Bad News," *Canadian Medical Association Journal* 193, no. 12 (March 22, 2021): E428–29, https://www.ncbi.nlm .nih.gov/pmc/articles/PMC8096381/.
2. Catherine Moore, "What Is Negativity Bias and How Can It Be Overcome?," Positive Psychology, December 30, 2019, https://positivepsychology.com/3-steps -negativity-bias/#bias.
3. "Why Does Your Brain Love Negativity? The Negativity Bias," Marbella

International University Centre, February 8, 2017, https://miuc.org/brain-love-negativity-negativity-bias/.

4. "Why Does Your Brain Love Negativity?"

5. Maria Popova, "The Science of Our Optimism Bias and the Life-Cycle of Happiness," The Marginalian, accessed August 15, 2023, https://www.themarginalian.org/2012/12/12/science-of-optimism-sharot/.

6. *Merriam-Webster*, s.v. "hope," accessed August 15, 2023, https://www.merriam-webster.com/dictionary/hope.

7. "Draft of Chapter X, 'Shattered Dreams,'" Stanford, The Martin Luther King, Jr. Research and Education Institute, accessed August 15, 2023, https://kinginstitute.stanford.edu/king-papers/documents/draft-chapter-x-shattered-dreams.

8. Elaine Houston, "What Is Hope in Psychology +7 Exercises & Worksheets," Positive Psychology, August 27, 2019, https://positivepsychology.com/hope-therapy/#hope.

9. C. R. Snyder, "Hope Theory: Rainbows in the Mind," *Psychological Inquiry* 13, no. 4 (2002): 249–75, https://www.jstor.org/stable/1448867.

10. Houston, "What Is Hope in Psychology."

11. "FAQ," Angela Duckworth, accessed August 15, 2023, https://angeladuckworth.com/qa/.

12. Angela Duckworth, "*Grit: The Power of Passion and Perseverance* by Angela Duckworth—Book Summary," *NJ Life Hacks* (blog), December 17, 2021, https://www.njlifehacks.com/grit-angela-duckworth-summary/.

13. Angela Duckworth et al., "Cognitive and Noncognitive Predictors of Success," *PNAS* 116, no. 47 (November 4, 2019): 23499–504, https://www.pnas.org/doi/10.1073/pnas.1910510116.

14. Duckworth, "Cognitive and Noncognitive Predictors of Success."

15. Angela Duckworth, "Even Gritty People Get Discouraged," Ideas.Ted.com, November 2, 2022, https://ideas.ted.com/even-gritty-people-get-discouraged/.

16. Summer Allen, "The Science of Gratitude," Greater Good Science Center, May 2018, https://ggsc.berkeley.edu/images/uploads/GGSC-JTF_White_Paper-Gratitude-FINAL.pdf?_ga=2.51257770.246418475.1638563377–157927757.1638563377.

17. Paul J. Mills et al., "The Role of Gratitude in Spiritual Well-Being in Asymptomatic Heart Failure Patients," *Spirituality in Clinical Practice* 2, no. 1 (2015): 5–17, https://www.apa.org/pubs/journals/releases/scp-0000050.pdf.

18. Paul J. Mills and Laura Redwine, "Can Gratitude Be Good for Your Heart?," *Greater Good*, October 25, 2017, https://greatergood.berkeley.edu/article/item/can_gratitude_be_good_for_your_heart.

19. Glenn R. Fox et al., "Neural Correlates of Gratitude," *Frontiers in Psychology* 6 (2015), https://www.frontiersin.org/articles/10.3389/fpsyg.2015.01491/full.

20. Deion Sanders (@COACHPRIME), Instagram, July 6, 2022, https://www.instagram.com/p/Cfr9PExAtmd/?utm_source=ig_embed&utm_campaign=embed_video_watch_again.

21. "Deion Sanders: I Used Money, Partying and Sex . . . to Mask Real Pain," TMZ, March 27, 2019, https://www.tmz.com/2019/03/27/deion-sanders-rock-bottom/.

22. Kia Morgan-Smith, "Deion Sanders Details Suicide Attempt Ahead of ESPN Story," The Grio, December 24, 2018, https://thegrio.com/2018/12/24/deion -sanders-details-suicide-attempt-ahead-of-espn-story/.
23. Andrew Powell, "'That's Just the Way I Fathered': Deion Sanders Already Setting the Tone for Colorado Players," Daily Caller, January 27, 2023, https://dailycaller .com/2023/01/27/deion-sanders-colorado-buffaloes-ncaa-college-football/.
24. "Watch: Deion Sanders' Speech to Students on Acting Like Men, Being Fighters Is Powerful," Louder with Crowder, March 21, 2023, https://www.louderwithcrowder .com/deion-sanders-man-fighting.
25. Donovan X. Ramsey, "Deion Sanders Enters His Prime," GQ Sports, January 9, 2023, https://www.gq.com/story/deion-sanders-style-hall-of-fame-february-cover.
26. Ramsey, "Deion Sanders Enters His Prime."
27. Matthias R. Mehl et al., "Are Women Really More Talkative Than Men?," Science 317 (August 2007): 82, https://www.researchgate.net/publication/6223260_Are _Women_Really_More_Talkative_Than_Men.
28. Maria Richter et al., "Do Words Hurt? Brain Activation During the Processing of Pain-related Words," PAIN 148, no. 2 (February 2010): 198–205, https://www .sciencedirect.com/science/article/abs/pii/S0304395909004564.
29. Dr. Andrew Newberg, Words Can Change Your Brain (New York: Hudson Street Press, 2012), 33.
30. Proverbs 23:7 KJV.
31. "Self-Talk: By the Numbers," Top Mental Game, November 4, 2019, https://www .topmentalgame.com/blog/self-talk-by-the-numbers.
32. Mayo Clinic Staff, "Positive Thinking: Stop Negative Self-Talk to Reduce Stress," Mayo Clinic, accessed August 15, 2023, https://www.mayoclinic.org/healthy -lifestyle/stress-management/in-depth/positive-thinking/art-20043950.
33. A. J. Crum et al., "Mind Over Milkshakes: Mindsets, Not Just Nutrients, Determine Ghrelin Response," Health Psychology 30, no. 4 (2011): 424–29, https://psycnet.apa.org/record/2011–09907–001; Alix Spiegel, "Mind Over Milkshake: How Your Thoughts Fool Your Stomach," NPR, April 14, 2014, https://www.npr.org/sections/health-shots/2014/04/14/299179468/mind -over-milkshake-how-your-thoughts-fool-your-stomach.
34. "Rethinking Stress," Indiana Psychological Association, accessed August 15, 2023, https://indianapsychology.org/news_manager.php?page=12187.
35. Frankl, Man's Search for Meaning, 69.
36. Aharon E. Wexler, "Just a Thought on Radical Amazement," Jerusalem Post, May 7, 2020, https://www.jpost.com/opinion/just-a-thought-on-radical -amazement-627262.

ABOUT THE AUTHOR

Dr. Josh Axe is a leadership expert, entrepreneur, and physician. He earned his doctorate from Palmer College and master of science in organizational leadership from Johns Hopkins University. Josh is the cofounder of Ancient Nutrition and founder of DrAxe.com. His company ranked on the Inc. 5000 fastest-growing companies list two years in a row. He is the bestselling author of *Eat Dirt, Keto Diet,* and *Ancient Remedies.*

Josh is the founder of Leaders.com, an online platform that provides the latest on news, leadership, business, and wealth. He regularly teaches lectures and trains entrepreneurs on leadership, mindset, and self-development.

Josh and his wife, Chelsea, have two daughters: Arwyn and Aylin. They divide their time between Nashville, Tennessee, and Dorado, Puerto Rico, and enjoy cooking, staying active swimming and cycling, and prioritizing time for their faith and family.